D1609437

Location Strategies for Retail and Service Firms

Avijit Ghosh
New York University

Sara L. McLafferty
Columbia University

Lexington Books
D.C. Heath and Company/Lexington, Massachusetts/Toronto

To Smita

Library of Congress Cataloging-in-Publication Data

Ghosh, Avijit.
  Location strategies for retail and service firms.

  Includes bibliographies and index.
  1. Stores, Retail—Location. 2. Service industries—
Location. I. McLafferty, Sara L. II. Title.
HF5429.275.G47   1987   658.1'1   85–45583
ISBN 0–669–12032–4 (alk. paper)

Published simultaneously in Canada
Printed in the United States of America
Casebound International Standard Book Number: 0–669–12032–4
Library of Congress Catalog Card Number: 85–45583

The paper used in this publication meets the minimum requirements of
American National Standard for Information Sciences—Permanence of
Paper for Printed Library Materials, ANSI Z39.48–1984. ∞™

87 88 89 90 91 8 7 6 5 4 3 2 1

Contents

Tables

Figures

Preface and Acknowledgments

Ten years ago, as graduate students, we were introduced to retail-site–selection procedures and location-allocation models. The two literatures, we found, addressed similar issues. Both focused on location analysis. They dealt with methods for assessing the desirability of alternative location plans and developing optimal spatial configurations for serving a geographically dispersed population. Yet, although they have shared focuses, the two literatures, until recently, have developed quite independently of each other. This book brings together the strengths of each of these literatures and develops location-analysis procedures that fuse the empirical traditions of store-location research with the analytical sophistication of location-allocation models. The procedures are uniquely suited to take advantage of computerized geographic information systems that provide ready access to demographic and location data for small areas.

For retail and service-oriented firms, the importance of developing a well-formulated location strategy can hardly be overemphasized. The location strategy gives spatial expression to the firm's corporate goals. It equilibrates among the firm's marketing program, the geographic pattern of demand, consumer patronage behavior, demographic characteristics, and the availability and desirability of individual sites. Crucial to the development of location strategy is the understanding of the relationship between corporate and location policy — a topic often neglected in the literature. We fill this void with a detailed analysis of the role of location in setting retail corporate strategy and in creating competitive leverage.

This book provides a detailed discussion of location policy and the procedures and analytical techniques for developing location strategy. The presentation focuses on the appropriate use of consumer information and geographic data bases and methods for analyzing such data. We illustrate these with various case studies and examples from a variety of retail situations. In total, the book provides a comprehensive overview of location policy and approaches to developing location strategy.

We owe considerable gratitude to a number of people. Gerard Rushton, at the University of Iowa, introduced us to the literature. Sam Craig, at New York University, coauthored a number of our previous publications, helped us refine our thoughts, and provided numerous ideas. We would also like to thank our parents and our colleagues at Columbia and New York Universities for their support and encouragement; and the people at Lexington Books for their patience. Finally, this book is dedicated to Smita for bringing us such joy and happiness.

1
Introduction

A well-designed location strategy is an integral and important part of corporate strategy for retail firms. Whether selling goods or services, the choice of outlet locations is perhaps the most important decision a retailer has to make. It is through the location that goods and services are made available to potential customers. Good locations allow ready access, attract large numbers of customers, and increase the potential sales of retail outlets. In the extremely competitive retail environment, even slight differences in location can have a significant impact on market share and profitability. Most importantly, since store location is a long-term fixed investment, the disadvantages of a poor location are difficult to overcome. As Jain and Mahajan note: "In the development of competitive strategies, prices can be matched, services can be extended and improved, merchandise may be duplicated, and promotion can be imitated, but a retailer's locational advantages are difficult to assail or neutralize" (1979, p. 219).

The objective of store-location strategy is to determine the spatial pattern of outlets that best meets corporate goals and objectives. It develops guidelines for selecting optimal sites for store openings and estimates the expected sales and profits of the outlets. In selecting optimal locations, a balance is achieved between the requirements of corporate marketing objectives and the needs of the marketplace with the availability and desirability of individual sites. The store-location decision is not merely the question of choosing sites. It also involves the juxtaposition of the spatial characteristics of a market with the overall corporate and marketing goals of the firm.

Opening new stores is inherently risky. There are significant monetary costs associated with opening a new outlet. Rising costs of real estate and construction have heightened the risk of developing new sites. In addition to such monetary risks, the failure of retail stores due to poorly chosen locations can have a significant negative impact on the firm's image. Perhaps the most important element of risk in opening a new outlet is the possibility that the outlet will never achieve its sales potential or be profitable.

Location analysis is vital for any organization that provides goods and services to a spatially dispersed population through retail outlets. In addition to aiding traditional retail firms (such as department stores, discount outlets, specialty stores, and supermarkets), location analysis is also an important part of the planning process for such diverse organizations as shopping centers, retail banks and other providers of financial services, hospitals, HMOs, emergency medical centers, restaurants and fast-food outlets, drug stores and convenience merchandisers, automobile dealers and repair centers, and movie halls and theaters, to name only a few.

Given the importance of the location decision, a number of analytical procedures have been developed for location analysis and site selection. These constitute a distinct body of knowledge from both theoretical and practical perspectives. The origin of store-location research can be traced to the practices of numerous entrepreneurs and managers who, based on their judgments and intuitions, made location decisions for their firms. The wisdom underlying these decisions eventually were codified into rules of thumb and checklists which others could follow. These checklists included information necessary to evaluate the relative attractiveness of a site compared with other potential sites in the area. It listed various factors that are likely to impact on sales and costs at a site. The checklists were the first attempt to develop a systematic basis for site selection.

In the United States, the post–World War II years witnessed major changes in retail location patterns. A growing population, rising income levels, and the emergence of suburbs presented retailers with new challenges. Department stores, mass merchandisers, and supermarkets expanded rapidly, spreading from the central cities into shopping centers and free-standing locations in the suburbs. The rapid increase of outlets raised new concerns and gave rise to the need for a more systematic approach to location analysis. Checklists that were mostly oriented toward evaluating characteristics of urban sites were no longer adequate. Many retail firms sought the assistance of store-location analysts and a large number of them opened in-house location analysis departments around this time. In Britain, during this same period, local governments, which played a much more active role in retail trade than their U.S. counterparts, were instrumental in making formal location analysis studies an integral part of store location plans. A number of major studies on the inter- and intrametropolitan spatial structure of retailing were initiated by the local agencies entrusted with overseeing the expansion of retail centers.

While subjective judgments and managerial experience in site selection continued to be important, these developments led to a much greater reliance on systematic and objective bases for location decision making. The result was an array of techniques that focused both on finding optimal sites for retail stores and forecasting sales and profits for the outlets based on objective criteria. Methods for forecasting sales of retail outlets are distinctly different from other sales forecasting techniques and this difference lies at the heart of all store location analysis methods. The sales potential of a retail outlet depends on the quality and price of the merchandise it carries, its physical characteristics, the characteristics of customers, the level of competition, and the relative accessibility of competing stores. The relative location of the outlet is a critical determinant of store patronage since it affects accessibility to consumers and ultimately the level of expected sales. Modeling the variability of sales potential at different locations is a central concern in location analysis.

Sales forecasts are important for new as well as existing stores. For existing stores, the sales forecast provides targets for the individual store managers. The targets are based on historical performance as well as a consideration of the outlet's trade area characteristics and the level of competition in the area. These provide yardsticks against which the actual performance of individual outlets can be compared. Sales forecasting for existing stores is especially useful to managers of retail chains, who, based on a comparison of actual and predicted performance levels, can identify the strong and weak performers in the firm's network of outlets. The manager can ask questions such as: What factors affect the sales of individual outlets? Why do sales of two outlets vary? In comparing the sales of individual outlets, the manager can differentiate between variations due to structural differences in potential and those due to ineffective marketing. In addition, retail sales forecasting models allow management to predict the likely consequences of contemplated changes in marketing strategies as well as shifts in the competitive structure and economic base of the trade area. Simulating the impact of potential changes provides the firm with a hedge against the uncertainties of the marketplace.

Evolution of Store Location Strategy

An important component of any retail sales forecasting method is to define the trade area of outlets. To forecast retail sales, the geographic area from which the outlet is likely to draw most of its customers must first be delineated. The sales potential of an outlet is limited by the size of the store's trade area. Information on trade area size and composition is also useful for obtaining a profile of potential customers, determining the spatial pattern of patronage, and planning advertising and sales-promotion strategies. An early approach to trade area delineation was provided by Reilly (1931) in his "law of retail gravitation." Based on an analogy to the Newtonian law of gravity, Reilly's formula predicts the retail trade area of competing towns, cities, and shopping centers using information on population size and distance. Reilly's formula was one of the first attempts at developing a formal method for demarcating retail trade areas. The formula was extensively investigated and further extended by a number of researchers. (See, for example, Converse 1949.)

More recent approaches to retail sales forecasting rely on surveys of consumer shopping patterns. The foundations of contemporary approaches to delineating trade areas were laid by William Applebaum. Based on his experience in the supermarket industry, Applebaum established the method of trade area delineation known as "customer spotting." The customer-spotting technique is used to estimate sales at alternative sites. Based on these estimates, the retail analyst can choose optimal locations for new outlets. The "analog" method of site selection proposed by Applebaum was the first attempt at a formal procedure for retail site selection and sales forecasting. (See, for example, Applebaum 1966, 1968.) The work of Applebaum and his coworkers has been very influential in establishing a system of data collection including information on consumer travel patterns, expenditure potentials, competitive conditions, and site characteristics. The analog procedure, now refined and extended by many researchers (see, for example, Rogers and Green 1978), is used extensively by many retail firms.

Moving beyond the primarily descriptive focus of the analog method are *spatial-interaction models*. Spatial-interaction models analyze the factors affecting consumer choice of retail outlets and predict the pattern of shopping trips in an area. The development of spatial-interaction models for retail sales forecasting owes its origin to the work of David Huff. Huff's model provided, for the first time, an approach that made it possible to look at the complex interactions within the total system of retail trade areas in a market. Huff was the first to suggest that trade areas should be viewed as continuous and probabilistic rather than the simple nonoverlapping areas proposed by the earlier "gravity" formulations (Reilly 1931) and the "nearest center hypothesis" of central place theory (Christaller 1935).

Like Applebaum, Huff stressed the importance of surveying consumer travel patterns in estimating trade areas and forecasting sales of outlets. Huff's work has played an important part in the development of store choice and retail forecasting models. (See Huff 1964, 1966). His probabilistic "revealed preference" approach to modeling store choice has been extended further by the multiplicative competitive interactive (MCI) model of Nakanishi and Cooper (1974) and by the application of multinomial logit (MNL) techniques (Arnold, Roth, and Tigert 1980). Like the analog model, spatial-interaction models (often somewhat erroneously called "gravity models") are extensively used by retail firms to provide sales estimates for new and existing outlets in a market area and to simulate the effect of changes in market conditions on store performance. These models constitute a major element of contemporary store-location research.

Recent Advances in Location Modeling

The works of Applebaum, Huff, and their coworkers represented for many years the state of the art in store-location theory and practice. In recent years, however, store-location and sales forecasting models have entered a new phase of sophistication and refinement. This has been initiated, in part, by the increasing use of computers and the availability of machine-readable geographic data bases with information on trade area demographics and expenditure patterns. Geocoded data bases have reduced significantly the time and effort needed to collect information on small-areal units for forecasting retail sales. Computers have also improved significantly the state of the art in formal methods of selecting optimal or near-optimal patterns of retail outlets. Computers allow efficient evaluation of large numbers of possible location strategies in order to choose the one that best meets corporate objectives.

The availability of computers and machine-readable data bases has prompted the search for site-selection methods that take advantage of these new tools. Concurrent with these developments during the past decade, the field of location-allocation modeling has now grown into a well-established discipline. (For a review of the development of the literature on location-allocation modeling, see Ghosh and Rushton 1987.) Location-allocation models provide an efficient, powerful technique for creating decision support systems for developing location strategies. Using the power of the computer, these models systematically evaluate a large number of potential store locations in order to find sites that maximize corporate goals such as market share or profits. In addition to determining optimal locations, the models simultaneously determine the allocation of consumers to the outlets, thus providing a basis for forecasting sales of individual outlets. While most early applications of location-allocation models dealt with public services, their use in retail site selection is increasing rapidly. These techniques, we believe, present new opportunities for retail location analysis and will have a significant impact on both the theory and practice of store location.

Another major advantage of location-allocation models is their ability to systematically evaluate the impact of each store on the entire network of outlets in a market area. They are, therefore, ideally suited for analyzing the location decisions of retail firms operating multiple outlets in the same market. Until recently, most retail siting methods considered only the selection of single sites. In practice, however, one increasingly faces the situation where retail chains locate several outlets in a market area either simultaneously or in sequence to achieve scale economies and market presence. The problem then is one of selecting store locations that optimize the performance of the firm's entire network of outlets. In developing multiunit networks, it is important to coordinate the location of the entire network and not just evaluate outlets individually. Single-store location procedures ignore the impact that an individual store may have on other outlets of the firm located in the same market area. Multiple-outlet location-allocation models allow the analyst to focus on the systemwide interactions and total network profitability. This, too, we feel, will bring location-allocation models to the forefront of retail siting techniques.

While sales and profits are important in making location decisions, sole reliance on current profitability may be limiting. First, one must distinguish between immediate and long-term returns. Since store locations are long-term investments, the criteria for evaluating alternative location plans must include performance over the entire planning horizon. Immediate returns may be sacrificed in order to preempt desirable sites from competitors and protect long-term profitability. One of the most complex problems in location planning is to identify location strategies that are responsive to the uncertainties of the future environment. The firm's marketing environment may change due to a number of reasons. A new environment may result from new consumer buying preferences, shifts in residential patterns, or actions of other firms attempting to achieve their own objectives. The addition of a new store by a competitor, for example, can radically alter the competitive environment and negatively impact on the performance of a store whose location was chosen without knowledge of the coming competition. Rarely does a firm possess precise knowledge of its competitors' future plans. Most decisions are made under uncertainty about the future. For locational models to be useful in practice, they must be able to consider possible changes in the market environment.

Organization of the Book

This book presents a concise yet comprehensive guide to developing a retail location strategy. It develops a systematic framework for formulating a well-designed strategy that balances corporate needs with the spatial dimensions of the marketplace. Each of the currently used methods for sales forecasting and site selection are discussed in detail. The book also brings together for the first time a number of more recent approaches to retail site selection. Since there is no one method that can be used in all situations, the focus is on delineating the applications, strengths, and limitations of each method. The book bridges the gap between theory and practice for retail location analysis by the use of illustrative case studies, placing special emphasis on issues of implementation.

The rest of the book is divided into six chapters, each of which is organized around a major element of the retail location process. The premise underlying the book's organization is that the retail location decision involves a series of steps ranging from an analysis of the firm's marketing strategy to determining optimal sites, sizes, and characteristics of outlets and forecasting their sales. These are shown in table 1–1 as a sequence of steps, though in practice, the issues are dealt with somewhat simultaneously. While for clarity we discuss them separately, the individual components are quite interrelated and there is constant feedback of information from one component to another. Coordination of the different steps is essential in developing a well-balanced location strategy.

The starting point for formulating a location strategy is an assessment of the firm's marketing program. A store-location decision always raises such issues as: What is the firm's value platform? Who are its customers? Who are its competitors? What are its future plans and goals? It is only by first answering these questions that the location analyst can create a strategy that reflects the company's needs. The link between a firm's strategy and its location policies is the focus of chapter 2. In that chapter, we develop the concepts of "value platform" and "strategic group" and discuss their implication for retail competition and locational analysis.

Once the corporate and marketing goals are understood, the spatial aspects of markets must be analyzed. Spatial analysis may be viewed as comprising three steps, each aimed at a different geographic scale. First, the *market selection* component focuses on the desirability of different cities, towns, or SMSAs in which to locate new stores. Of concern here are regional variations in such factors as population growth, migration trends, and economic potential along with regional variations in the level of overall retail competition. Demographic characteristics such as income, age, and occupation are

Table 1–1
The Retail Location Process

Purpose	Factors to Consider	Chapter
Corporate strategy analysis	Value platform and competitive structure	2
Market selection	Regional variations in economic potential and level of competition	3
Areal analysis	Variation within the region	3
Site analysis	Traffic flow, accessibility, land use, and real estate costs	3
Sales forecasting	Trade area size and composition, and travel patterns	4 and 5
Network development	Optimal number of outlets, locations, and store characteristics	6
Scenario planning	Changes in market environment and competitive reactions	7

also studied. Even within a city or town, demand and supply of retail activities vary considerably over space. The second component, *areal analysis,* focuses on these intramarket variations and ranks areas within the region on their suitability for retail development. The third step, *site analysis,* consists of a detailed analysis of the characteristics of individual sites. The quality of the real estate, the cost of developing the site, traffic flow patterns, and the ingress and egress qualities of alternative sites are studied along with local competition. Systematic approaches to regional analysis, areal analysis, and site analysis are discussed in chapter 3.

The focus in chapters 4 and 5 is on retail sales forecasting methods and procedures for defining and analyzing trade areas. The entire range of procedures is covered, from rudimentary rules of thumb to the state-of-the-art spatial-interaction approaches. In each case, we discuss the assumptions underlying the approach and provide detailed guidelines for applying them in practice. A number of case studies from a variety of retail contexts are used as illustrations.

In chapter 6, we consider location-allocation models for retail site selection and developing the spatial organization of multioutlet networks. Central to any location-allocation model is the technique used to estimate overall demand and to allocate that demand to individual outlets. We present a number of alternative approaches based on different assumptions regarding consumer spatial behavior and store choice. The appropriateness and usefulness of each model is discussed in detail. As in the previous chapters, the application of these models is illustrated through case studies. In an appendix to that chapter, guidelines for developing computer algorithms for solving location-allocation problems are provided.

Chapter 7 deals with the impact of uncertainty on location choice and describes procedures for dealing with uncertainty. To be useful in practice, location models and site-selection procedures must consider the uncertainties inherent in the retail environment. By doing so, the location analyst can create a meaningful decision support system for retail managers. To conclude the book, chapter 8 summarizes the previous chapters.

References

Applebaum, W. (1966). "Methods for Determining Store Trade Areas, Marketing Penetration and Potential Sales." *Journal of Marketing Research* 3: 127–141.

Applebaum, W. (1968). "The Analog Method for Estimating Potential Store Sales" in C. Kornblau (ed.), *Guide to Store Location Research*. Reading, Mass.: Addison-Wesley.

Arnold, S.J.; Roth, V.; and Tigert, D. (1980). "Conditional Logit versus MDA in the Prediction of Store Choice." *Advances in Consumer Research* 8: 665–670.

Christaller, W. (1935). *Die zentralen Orte in Süddeutschland*. Jena, East Germany: G. Fischer.

Converse, P.D. (1949). "New Laws of Retail Gravitation." *Journal of Marketing* 14: 379–384.

Ghosh, A., and Rushton, G. (1987). "Progress in "Location-Allocation Models" in A. Ghosh and G. Rushton (eds.), *Spatial Analysis and Location Allocation Models.* New York: Van Nostrand Reinhold.

Huff, D.L. (1964). "Defining and Estimating a Trade Area." *Journal of Marketing* 28: 34–38.

Huff, D.L. (1966). "A Programmed Solution for Approximating an Optimum Retail Location." *Land Economics* 42: 294–295.

Jain, A.K., and Mahajan, V. (1979). "Evaluating the Competitive Environment in Retailing Using Multiplicative Competitive Interactive Models" in J. Sheth (ed.), *Research in Marketing.* Greenwich, Conn.: JAI Press.

Nakanishi, M., and Cooper, L.G. (1974). "Parameter Estimate for Multiplicative Interactive Choice Model: Least Squares Approach." *Journal of Marketing Research* 11: 303–311.

Reilly, W.J. (1931). *The Law of Retail Gravitation.* New York: Knickerbocker Press.

Rogers, D.S., and Green, H.L. (1978). "A New Perspective on Forecasting Store Sales: Applying Statistical Models and Techniques in the Analog Approach." *Geographical Review* 69: 449–458.

2
Corporate Strategy and Location Policy

Like all business organizations, retailers seek growth and expansion in order to increase sales and profits. In deciding how to achieve growth, they face an endless array of possible strategies such as opening new outlets, increasing advertising and marketing efforts, adopting new merchandising practices, and diversification. Retail strategies have an important spatial element, since the retailer must decide both where future investments will be allocated and which strategies will be most effective at particular stores or locations.

Regardless of what type of strategy is considered, the final choice depends greatly on the firm's goals and objectives and the nature of its business. Before developing a corporate strategy, the firm must have a clear understanding of the kind of business it is involved in and the market it intends to serve. Identifying the firm's value platform, competitors, and target market are of fundamental importance in establishing corporate marketing strategies.

The marketing strategy describes how the firm will compete, integrates the different activities of the firm, and underlies the actions of the firm's management. Without a coherent marketing strategy, whether explicitly stated or implicitly practiced, the firm is likely to lose sight of its marketing goals and decrease its ability to compete in a rapidly changing environment. As retail environments have become more competitive and the pace of change has accelerated, a well-defined, formally stated strategic plan has become essential for success.

This chapter explores the link between a firm's corporate and marketing strategies and its location policies. We first discuss the various types of growth strategies and the geographic limits to growth for retail and service firms. We then present the concepts of *value platform* and *strategic groups* as key elements in understanding the structure of retail competition and as the foundations for developing retail marketing strategy. The role of location in creating differential advantage and influencing retail competition is stressed. Examples are provided to illustrate how firms create competitive leverage through their location policies.

Strategies for Growth

The need to grow forces retail firms to continually innovate and adopt new strategies to generate increased sales and profits. There are many avenues through which retailers can achieve growth, some of which are shown in figure 2–1. One can distinguish broadly between strategies that increase sales of existing stores and those that achieve growth through the opening of new retail outlets. Sales of existing outlets can be increased by intensified marketing of existing merchandise and through aggressive promotion and pricing policies. Another avenue for increasing sales and profitability of existing outlets is scrambled merchandising—diversifying the types of merchandise carried by the stores. Well-planned market share strategies and merchandise diversification can have a significant impact on sales. During the seventies, for example, supermarkets and drug stores implemented scrambled merchandising strategies and significantly diversified their merchandise to improve sales and margins. At the same time, these firms have been aggressive in maintaining and improving the market share of their outlets.

The scope for increasing the sales of existing outlets is limited by the size and economic potential of the geographic market served by the outlets. A distinguishing feature of retail outlets is the spatial orientation of their markets. Each outlet has a well-defined geographic trade area from which most of its customers originate. The geographic trade area for each outlet is a spatial expression of the limits to its market potential. The trade area of a typical supermarket, for example, is the geographic area defined by a radius of one–and–one-half miles from the outlet—the area from which it draws most

		Existing Merchandise	New Merchandise
New outlets	New market areas	Increase market coverage	Geographical expansion and store diversification
	Existing market areas	Expand network of outlets	Store diversification
Existing outlets		Increase market share	Scrambled merchandising

Figure 2-1. Retail Growth Strategies

of its customers. Market potential, therefore, is limited by the expenditure pattern of these residents. While department stores and shopping centers have larger trade areas, their potential, too, is determined by the spending pattern of the residents within their trade areas.

These limits to sales potential are not static, but change through time in response to changes in population size, composition, and socioeconomic characteristics. The forces of population growth and decline, gentrification, and neighborhood abandonment make up the social landscape to which retailers must respond and which determines in part the viability of retail institutions. Any change in that landscape translates into changes in sales potential, which, in turn, are reflected in the changing pattern of retail growth and decline. It is increasingly common to see established stores in changing neighborhoods threatened by increased rents or by their inability to meet the needs of a completely new clientele. Given the potential of these sites, they are likely to be upgraded or replaced by newer, often different, stores. Outlets in declining areas, on the other hand, are faced with decreasing demand and are unable to retain their profitability. In these areas, disinvestments and store closures are most likely to occur.

The relationship between trade area characteristics and disinvestments for one type of service activity—hospitals—is shown in figure 2–2. Based on a study of hospital closures in New York City (McLafferty 1986), the figure

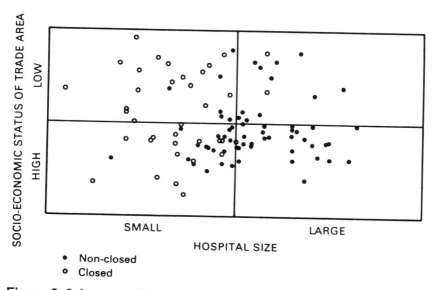

• Non-closed
○ Closed

Figure 2–2. Impact of Trade Area Characteristics and Facility Size on Hospital Closure

plots the hospitals in the city according to their size (measured by the number of beds) and the socioeconomic status of the trade area. It also differentiates between hospitals that closed and those that remained open between 1966 and 1984 (a period when more than one-third of all hospitals in the city closed). As is evident from the figure, closures were concentrated among smaller institutions located in neighborhoods of population decline and low socioeconomic status. The majority of these institutions closed for financial reasons—their population base or "payer mix" was simply unprofitable. Many also were established originally to serve particular ethnic or immigrant groups that subsequently moved from the area during the period of suburbanization. The hospitals were unwilling or unable to meet the needs of the new population groups that moved in. This example shows how dependent the profitability of service and retail outlets is on location and how the prospects at a location shift through time as a result of population change.

Given the geographic limits to increasing sales of individual outlets and the uncertainty surrounding future-location viability, significant increases in sales volume can only be achieved by expanding the geographic coverage of outlets. It is for this reason that retailers expand their network of outlets. Retail chains continually add new stores in existing markets or open outlets in new geographic markets. The addition of new outlets, whether in existing markets or in new ones, expands the area served by the firm. Increased geographic coverage creates the potential for increased sales and provides a hedge against the uncertainty of the effects of population change on sales of any one store. A coordinated strategy of outlet expansion also provides opportunities for managerial and operating efficiencies through scale economies in advertising, promotion, and distribution. In the sixties and the seventies, supermarket, discount store, and department store chains expanded rapidly through network expansion. Later, many fast-food chains followed a similar strategy to expand their geographic coverage.

Yet another avenue for retail growth is diversification of the types of stores operated by the firm. Large retail firms often follow pluralist strategies and create a portfolio of retail operations. Even when located in the same geographic market, the stores, because of their different marketing strategies, appeal to different target markets or are patronized by customers with different purchase motives. In addition to providing an avenue for growth, it is often argued that portfolio diversification reduces the firm's vulnerability to the economic environment. One example of a company following this strategy is Dayton Hudson, which operates a portfolio of stores including department stores (Dayton's and Hudson's), discount stores (Target), specialty book stores (B. Dalton Booksellers), promotional soft goods stores (Mervyn's), and hard goods stores (Lechmere). A number of other retail corporations have adopted similar pluralist strategies. On a more limited scale, the Gap clothing company initiated a similar diversification strategy when it acquired the Banana Republic chain. While both stores sell casual clothing, the target consumers of the two stores are different. Thus, outlets of both chains can be located in the same geographic market without fear of extensive cannibalization of sales.

Retail growth—whether through the expansion of local networks, increase in market coverage, or portfolio diversification—requires the location of new retail outlets. Selecting the right sites for these outlets and developing a good location strategy is probably the single most important factor in overall retail profitability (*Convenience Store Merchandiser* 1986). The starting point for developing a firm's location strategy is an understanding of its corporate objectives and goals and the nature of the firm's business. The type of merchandise sold by the firm or the service it provides determines in a major way the location strategy that the firm must follow. A location well suited for a supermarket, drug store, or branch bank, for example, is not likely to be appropriate for a department store or specialty high-fashion apparel outlet. The requirements of a good location are different for each type of store.

Value Platforms and Location Policy

Even stores selling similar types of merchandise differ in their location objectives because of differences in their marketing strategy. Discount stores as well as many specialty boutiques sell clothing. The specific market segments and target consumers that these two types of stores pursue are, however, quite different. This difference in market segments is reflected in the contrasting location strategies followed by these firms. A similar difference is evident when the location policies of traditional department stores and "off-price" retailers are compared. Traditional department stores and specialty fashion clothing stores tend to locate in well-known urban shopping districts or in large shopping centers. Discount stores and off-price retail outlets, on the other hand, are often freestanding or located in small shopping centers along urban corridors.

The location policies of service retailers, too, differ because of their contrasting marketing strategies. Many local banks—in an attempt to create a differential advantage over larger, regional banks—target their services predominantly to senior citizens. Their location policies favor older urban neighborhoods with concentrations of elderly populations. In the field of health care, the recent growth of freestanding emergency medical centers has, in a large part, been fostered by their unique location strategy. Initially, many of these emergency facilities were located near existing full-service hospitals in an effort to attract some of the hospitals' traditional patrons. The competitive advantages of the emergency centers were significantly enhanced, however, when the centers were located in suburban areas—locations convenient to suburban residents who often do not have easy access to full-service hospitals.

As these examples illustrate, the location program is an integral part of a retailer's marketing strategy. The location choice must be consistent with the firm's market orientation and the expectations of its target consumers. To design the firm's location policy, therefore, one must first understand the firm's corporate objectives and the marketing strategy that it plans to pursue. The location program must be consistent with the firm's overall marketing goals.

The Value Platform

The foundation of retail marketing strategy is the firm's *value platform*. The value platform specifies the manner in which the firm differentiates itself from its competitors in the minds of the consumers it intends to serve. A well-established value platform is the reason why consumers patronize the firm's outlets rather than its competitors'. The aim of retail marketing strategy, therefore, is to create and maintain a unique value platform that allows the firm to most effectively achieve a sustainable differential advantage over its competitors. The various functional policies followed by the firm—such as merchandising, pricing, advertising, promotion, store atmosphere, service, and location—must all be consistent with the value platform.

Creating a successful value platform requires an understanding of customer needs and wants as well as the nature of competition faced by the firm. Customers vary in their needs, wants, and ways in which they perceive the value of a shopping experience. These differences create the potential for segmenting the market based on different customer expectations. The firm must select the segment it can serve best and orient its activities to meet the needs of this group. In choosing the target market, the firm must also consider the strengths and weaknesses of potential competitors as well as its own resources. It must have the ability to compete against them and create a differential advantage for itself. As Davidson, Sweeney, and Stampfl note: "The continual striving for differential advantage is characteristic of competition in retailing" (1984, p. 82). In today's maturing retail markets, growth in overall demand for retail goods and services is unlikely to occur. For most retailers, growth can come only from winning customers from other firms. An assessment of the competitive environment, therefore, is essential in selecting a target segment. A high level of potential competition may make an otherwise attractive segment less desirable.

Value Position and Segmentation. Creating a value platform implies a choice by the firm of the target market it aims to serve. The value platform must be consistent with the needs of that target market. Not all consumers respond to a marketing strategy in the same manner. Consumers differ not only in needs, but also in income, location, and ability to use retail services. These differences—caused by variations in socioeconomic status, age, education, psychological characteristics, lifestyle, and so on—give rise to varying expectations about the shopping experience and differences in the willingness and ability to use retail stores. Such differences form the basis for segmenting the market into groups of customers with similar needs and expectations about their shopping experience. The groups differ in the way they perceive the benefit of retail offerings, the manner in which they evaluate the stores, and, therefore, the likelihood of their patronizing the retail offering. The retailer's target market, then, is the customer segment that perceives more benefit in its value platform than those of its competitors—the group whose expectations are best fulfilled by the firm's offering.

Although consumers evaluate retail outlets on a wide variety of factors, these factors may generally be grouped into five categories:

1. *Merchandise assortment and quality.* The merchandise offering is the core benefit provided by a retail store. Retail outlets produce utility for customers by creating assortments of desirable goods and making them easily available to a spatially dispersed population. Consumers form expectations about the variety and relative quality of the merchandise and services offered by the firm.

2. *Atmosphere.* The ambiance of the store, its merchandise display, and its decorations form its atmosphere. In addition to the tangible goods and services, the store's atmosphere is an important part of the retailer's offering. Customers have expectations about the appropriate ambiance for a store.

3. *Service.* Service includes the level of sales assistance and information provided by the retailer and the level of ancillary services such as acceptance of credit cards, gift wrapping, and delivery.

4. *Location and convenience.* Accessibility and the time taken to reach the store are two of the most important determinants of store patronage. Consumers evaluate location and convenience in relation to their own "time-space constraints," which define the limits (in both time and space) to daily travel. Locations such as the home and workplace serve as major nodes around which consumer travel patterns are oriented. Stores accessible to these nodes are most convenient to consumers and, therefore, most likely to be patronized. Travel patterns are also affected by the consumer's daily routine, which determines the specific times at which shopping trips are made. The convenience of the shopping hours is, therefore, another important determinant of patronage.

5. *Price.* Based on their perceptions of the store's merchandise, atmosphere, service, and location, consumers form an expectation about the price of goods and services sold by the store and assess their willingness to pay. The consumer's income is an important limiting factor determining the price the consumer is able and willing to pay for specific goods and services.

Retail stores differ in the manner in which they fulfill consumer expectations. Consider, for example, the different types of retail outlets that sell clothing. In any market area, these may include high-fashion specialty stores, traditional department stores, mass merchandisers, discount stores, and off-price retailers. While all of these stores sell clothing, their marketing strategies and operational policies are distinctly different. Each of these stores caters to different customer needs. The customer segments differ in their expectations and the relative importance they give to the various store characteristics of merchandise, atmosphere, service, location, and price.

In analyzing a retail market, therefore, it is necessary to first distinguish among the potential customers based on the manner in which they evaluate a store's offerings. Although the process by which consumers choose among alternative retail outlets is complex, the first step involves selecting the desired quality of shopping. The attributes of merchandise quality, service level, and atmosphere, put together, may be viewed holistically as the quality of shopping experience offered at an outlet. The quality of the shopping experience at an outlet, however, is usually correlated with the price. The higher the quality of shopping experience, the higher the price. (See also Hirschman 1978.)

Figure 2–3 shows the typical relationship between the quality of a shopping experience and willingness to pay. The "value" a customer receives from shopping at a particular store is determined jointly by the quality of the shopping experience and price. The "value line" portrays the different combinations of price and quality available to customers at different retail outlets. In effect, it shows the total set of shopping opportunities. Since high quality is associated with higher prices, the value line is upward-sloping.

Customers seek to maximize value. Depending on their ability and willingness to pay, they choose the quality of shopping experience that best meets their expectations. The result is the evolution of customer segments based on the manner in which customers trade off their expectation about the quality of shopping experience with the price they are willing to pay for it. Some desire a high-quality experience and are willing to pay higher prices, while others seek a lower price at the expense of shopping quality. The former may frequent fashionable specialty stores, while the latter may patronize discount stores.

An understanding of the value orientation of customers—the way in

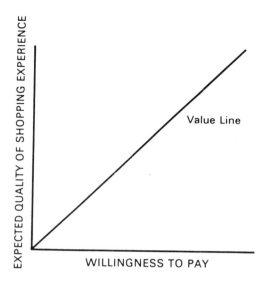

Figure 2–3. Customer Value Orientations along a Value Line

which they trade off shopping experience with price—is the basis on which firms make target market decisions. The difference in value orientation of customer groups is the underlying rationale for segmentation of the retail market. Retailers adopt a particular strategy to create a value platform appropriate for the customer segment it desires to serve. Target market selection is then a question of selecting the customer segment whose value orientation best matches the value platform of the firm. Retail marketing is the process of matching the store's offerings in terms of merchandise, atmosphere, service, location, and price with the expectation of that target group. (See figure 2–4.)

Value Platforms and Strategic Groups. The concept of value platforms also provides the key to understanding the competitive structure of retailing. In any market area, there are probably a large variety of retail stores selling similar products and services. Analyzing the value platforms of the different stores allows one to determine the nature and extent of competition. The more similar the value platforms of two outlets, the greater the overlap in their target markets and, therefore, the higher the level of competition between them. Retail firms can thus be grouped into competitive clusters based on the similarity of their value platforms. These competitive clusters represent strategic groupings within that retail category. Firms belonging to the same strategic group follow similar marketing strategies and compete directly with each other. A strategic grouping of department and discount stores is

Figure 2-4. Developing a Retail Marketing Strategy

shown in figure 2–5. Low-end discount stores, for example, represent the combination of low price and quality and so fall near the origin on the value line. The other extreme of the value line—high quality and high price—is represented by upscale prestige department stores. Other types of stores represent different combinations of price and quality of shopping.[1]

The intensity of rivalry among firms depends on the degree of similarity in their value platforms. The level of competition among the firms in a strategic group is likely to be intense because they compete for the same set of customers. The opening of new outlets will be strongly resisted by other firms in the market area that have similar value platforms. Existing firms will compete aggressively to protect their market shares and the new firm can succeed only if it has the resources to create a differential advantage for its outlets. The more different are the value platforms of two firms, on the other hand, the less the overlap in their target markets and, therefore, the less intense the competition between them.

The concept of value platform is important in understanding retail markets and in creating successful retail marketing strategies. It helps the

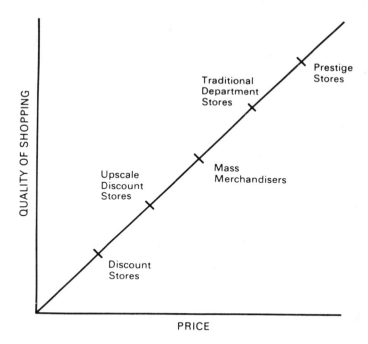

Figure 2-5. Strategic Grouping of Department and Discount Stores

retailer identify potential target segments of customers as well as its potential competitors. The target market is the customer segment whose expectations are best fulfilled by the firm's offerings. In choosing the target market, the firm must also ascertain its likely competitors. By simultaneously considering both consumer and competitive structures, the value platform plays a critical role in creating a differential advantage for the firm.

Value Platforms and Marketing Programs

Once the value platform is determined, the retail firm is in a position to plan its marketing program. The different elements of the marketing program must be consistent with the value platform the firm is trying to create. As suggested earlier, the needs and expectations as well as the demographic, social, economic, and life-style characteristics of a store's customers influence its value platform. Knowledge of the target customers' value orientation is a bridge between the firm's overall marketing strategy and its retailing program. The relative importance the firm places on the different components of the retail mix must reflect directly the importance given to these components by the target customers. For example, as one moves to the right along the value line, consumers exhibit a greater willingness to pay for higher levels of shopping experience. To cater to the consumers in the extreme upper-right segment, therefore, stores must provide high levels of service, create a pleasant shopping atmosphere, and carry unique, high-quality merchandise. Customers in the lower-left segment, on the other hand, are likely to pay more attention to price in making their shopping decision. To meet the expectations of these consumers, firms must focus especially on costs. Firms usually cut costs by emphasizing self-service, having minimum expenditures on store interiors and decoration, and locating at low-rent sites.

The firm's value platform is thus critical in determining its operating policies in terms of the merchandise it carries, the depth and breadth of selection, the level of service, store design and size, and the overall ambiance of the outlets. The firm's policies on location, advertising, promotion, and pricing are also determined by the value platform. The different components of the firm's marketing program must all reflect the value platform that the firm is trying to create. All components must be consistent with each other. Consistency with the firm's overall value platform is the yardstick by which the marketing program must be judged.

The influence of a firm's value orientation on location strategy is apparent in the case of Wal-Mart. This highly successful discount chain has created a value platform that meets the needs and expectations of low- and middle-income families in rural areas and small towns. Its location policy, therefore, has been to concentrate on sites in rural and small-town markets. The typical Wal-Mart outlet is smaller than the outlets of many other discount stores, which are predominantly targeted toward middle-income suburban households. Wal-Mart stresses basic merchandise in a simple setting which is valued by its target market. The location, store size, decor, and merchandising policies are all consistent with the marketing strategy adopted by the firm. The success of the strategy is reflected in one of the highest levels of profitability per square foot among discount store operators.

A comparison of the location strategies of two toy retailers, Toys R Us and F.A.O. Schwarz, further illustrates the link between a firm's value platform and its location strategy. While both stores sell toys, their value platforms are very different. Toys R Us is a large chain which has expanded rapidly in the past few years. Central to this firm's strategy is the policy of marketing wide and deep assortments of popular toys in outlets typically of around forty-thousand square feet. Another important element is its pricing policy. The Toys R Us price, on an average, is about a third less than that charged by department stores carrying comparable merchandise. The low-price policy is followed year-round and no special seasonal price promotions are used.

The first F.A.O. Schwarz outlet was opened in 1862 in Baltimore. The firm, which describes itself as the world's most unique toy store, offers new, trendy, and prestigious children's toys of high quality at full price to high-income customers. The target market is characterized by people who are status- and prestige-conscious, are concerned with quality, and have a willingness to pay for what they perceive as unique and special merchandise and high levels of service. The merchandise ranges from such basic items as stuffed animals to customized model cars and doll houses priced at several thousand dollars. Consistent with its value platform, the firm offers high levels of service to its customers. At its flagship store, there are nearly one-hundred sales people.

The locational strategies followed by the two retailers reflect their differing value platforms. To cater to its high-income target market, F.A.O. Schwarz outlets are located at prime retail sites in urban areas. Its flagship store is located on Manhattan's Fifth Avenue, one of the world's premier retail districts. The location attracts not only local residents but also shoppers from the suburbs who are willing to travel great distances to visit the store. In addition, the location is a popular shopping area for tourists. Due to lack of space for expansion, the firm recently announced the relocation of the flagship store to a new site just two blocks away, with forty-thousand square feet across two floors containing one-hundred boutiques organized around such themes as trains and clowns.

Toys R Us outlets, while approximately the same size, are organized like supermarkets with regimented aisles and high stacks. The over four hundred Toys R Us outlets are usually freestanding or located in small shopping complexes. Most are on sites along major traffic arteries in the vicinity of regional shopping malls in suburban areas.

Value Platforms and Retail Competition

The array of value platforms created by different retail stores is an indication of the competitive structure of the retail industry. Retail strategy can be viewed as attempts to adjust the value platform in response to changing market conditions and competitive activities. There are three levels at which retail competition occurs. First, competition exists among groups of stores offering different types of products and services. An example is the competition among bowling alleys, game arcades, and amusement parks for consumers' expenditures on leisure activities. This is the most general type of competition and, to some extent, the most unpredictable, since it occurs between firms offering products or services that are substitutes in the broadest sense of the word. We will not address this type of competition here. Second, there is competition among strategic groups that offer similar types of merchandise. For example, off-price clothing outlets compete with both traditional department stores and upscale discount stores. Although each type of store forms a different strategic group serving a particular target market, each group can attempt to attract customers from others and new groups may emerge to cater to unserved market segments. The third type of competition occurs among stores within a particular strategic group. These are stores offering similar kinds of merchandise at similar levels of price and quality. Competition among these stores is usually intense since they aim at the same target group and each tries aggressively to gain market share.

In each type of competition, location plays an important role. It determines not only how effectively stores serve their target market, but also the level and intensity of retail competition. In this section, we discuss the role of location in determining competition among and within strategic groups.

Competition among Strategic Groups

The competitive structure of the retail industry is made up of the various strategic groups offering similar types of merchandise but at different positions in the price–quality continuum. For a firm in any given strategic group, the essence of competitive strategy is to differentiate itself from firms in other strategic groups and thus establish itself in relation to a particular market segment. Competition is fiercest among groups located near each other on the value line. For example, whereas prestige department stores face strong competition from traditional department stores, they face little competition from discount stores that serve a very distinct and different customer group. Strategic groups located in the middle of the value line experience competitive pressures from both sides. The competitive positions of traditional department stores, for example, have been affected both by the emergence of prestige department stores and specialty stores and by the growth of mass merchandisers and upscale discount stores. Competitive strategy thus consists of successful positioning or repositioning of the firm's value platform.

The Evolution of Competitive Structures

Competitive structures are not static. They change when existing firms revise their value platforms and when new retail firms enter the market with a different value platform in order to serve an unsatisfied market niche. The emergence of discount toy chains such as Toys R Us is an example of how firms create new value platforms. Prior to the growth of discount toy specialty stores, toys were mainly sold by department stores and some specialty stores. Department stores, however, did not offer much variety and selection. The selling space devoted to toys was limited. Chains such as Toys R Us and Child's World have created a value platform that has fulfilled the unmet needs of the typical toy buyer. Their large assortment and everyday low prices produce a significant differential advantage over toy departments of traditional department stores.

Retail competitive structures are also affected when existing firms change their strategy. While there are significant mobility barriers that impede shifts across strategic groups (Porter 1980), retail firms often change their value position in order to target consumers with a different value orientation. The strategic changes implemented by the J.C. Penney Company in recent years are an example of this type of shift in value orientation. Penney's changes may be viewed as an attempt to reposition the firm on the value line and move more to the upper-right direction as shown in figure 2–6. This repositioning, it is argued, would make J.C. Penney more competitive with regional department store chains such as Davison's and Rich's and specialty clothing stores that are often located in the same shopping center as Penney outlets. Such a change in value position also differentiates J.C. Penney from Sears, its traditional competitor. It should be noted that Sears, too, attempted, although in a more modest way, to reposition itself in order to create a more fashion-oriented image.

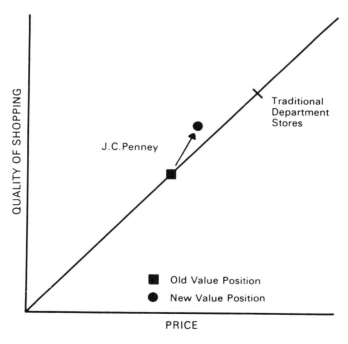

Figure 2-6. Change in Relative Value Position of J.C. Penney

To shift its value platform, J.C. Penney implemented numerous changes in its retail program in order to meet the expectations of its new target consumer. The new emphasis was on working women who are major purchasers of women's clothing. To appeal to this new target market, the firm emphasized soft goods rather than consumer durables and automotive repairs and supplies: Special emphasis was placed on women's, men's, and children's apparel and home furnishings. To appeal to the more fashion-oriented target market, in 1982, the J.C. Penney Company signed a design and licensing contract with Halston Enterprises, a well-known marketer of designer merchandise in the fragrance and cosmetics and women's and men's clothing categories.

Repositioning to emphasize fashion and style also necessitated upgrading store atmosphere. New stores were opened with contemporary looks creating an ambiance that customers associated with fashion-oriented stores. A number of existing stores were closed or extensively remodeled to reflect the changed positioning emphasis. The outlet-development program stressed locations in fashionable shopping malls rather than the downtown sites where many of Penney's old stores were located. While implementing these changes, the company aimed at maintaining a price advantage over similar department and specialty stores in order to create a differential advantage over other stores. (See figure 2–6).

A unique value platform is also the reason behind the recent success of off-price retailers. These retailers offer merchandise similar to that of many department stores at a price reflecting considerable savings for consumers. This establishes a value platform that many consumers find superior to department stores'. Off-price retailers lower costs by cutting expenditures on store interiors and advertising. Further, because of more lenient purchase conditions, off-price retailers are able to negotiate better purchase prices with manufacturers. To control costs, off-price outlets are usually located at low-rent sites. Although these sites are not as convenient as the large shopping malls and shopping districts where traditional department store outlets are located, consumers are willing to travel to these locations because of lower prices. In total, the off-price retailers have created a value platform highly attractive to many consumers.

The value position of department stores has traditionally stressed the quality and selectivity of their merchandise, location convenience, and service. With the popularity of nationally advertised designer-label clothing, department stores have lost much of their advantage as superior merchandisers. The manufacturers—in a desire to expand their sales—have made their labels widely available to different types of retail outlets, reducing the differential advantage of traditional department stores. National advertising has also presold these labels to consumers, thus eroding the value of the department store sales personnel. The decline in the quality of the service provided by department stores in the meantime has further increased their vulnerability to off-price retailers. To regain their competitive advantage, department stores must enhance their value position. A key necessity is a stronger merchandising policy that reflects current fashion trends and exclusivity. Thus, many department stores are giving greater emphasis to private labels and exclusive licensing of designer labels. A second necessity is improvement in the level of service and sales help. Through these improvements, traditional department stores will regain their competitive advantage.

Competition within Strategic Groups

Thus far, our discussion has focused on the differences in marketing strategies of firms with different value platforms. But how do firms with similar value platforms compete with each other? How do they create differential advantages? Firms within the same strategic group follow similar merchandising strategies and compete for the same customers. The more similar the value platforms of two firms, the greater their homogeneity in the minds of the consumers. How do consumers choose among these similar shopping alternatives?

The competitive advantage of firms offering similar merchandise and shopping experiences is largely determined by the price they charge and the location of their outlets. A firm can enhance its competitive position by lowering its price without a commensurate drop in the quality of the shopping experience. Competitive advantage can also be created by selecting good locations. In choosing among similar retail alternatives, a consumer is likely to select the one that is most conveniently located, ceteris paribus. Price and location are, therefore, the most important factors at this stage of the consumer's choice process.

Consider, as an example, the case of gasoline retailing. Most consumers do not perceive any difference in the quality of the gasoline or in the services offered by different gasoline outlets. Because of this lack of differentiation in product or service, price and location are the most important competitive tools in gasoline retailing. Gasoline retailers strive to find sites on high-traffic routes that are accessible to the largest number of motorists. Firms attempt to create spatial monopolies in order to reduce competition within their trade areas. The focus on key locations, however, often leads to a clustering of competitive gasoline stations at or near prime sites. Such spatial clustering makes gasoline stations even more homogenous and increases the importance of price as a competitive tool. The result is price wars that recurrently affect the gasoline industry. Only gasoline stations with some form of location advantage can protect themselves from this intense price competition.

A similar emphasis on price and location is evident for supermarkets. Most supermarket outlets rely on lower prices and convenient locations to attract customers, resulting, once again, in intense price competition among neighboring outlets. Only those outlets that are able to differentiate themselves through the quality of their merchandise and their service can escape this intense competition.

Location and price are critical determinants of the relative competitive position of outlets that offer similar merchandise and shopping quality. Location is a major factor in differentiating a retail outlet from similar retailers in the market area. By choosing locations accessible to consumers but distant from competitors, the firm improves its competitive position. In determining these sites, the location analyst must anticipate shifts in residential patterns of the target consumers and take into account the extent of present and anticipated competition. Preempting prime locations and foreclosing the entry of competitors from these sites are vital in creating the competitive advantage of a spatial monopoly.

Market-Coverage Objectives

Another avenue by which firms create competitive advantage is by establishing a high level of market presence. Many firms have explicit or implicit goals regarding the desired level of market coverage. Chains, for example, often attempt to fully saturate an existing market prior to expanding into new ones. High coverage (the establishment of a number of outlets in the same market) creates managerial efficiencies as well as efficiencies in physical distribution and transportation. Greater market coverage also increases the impact of advertising and promotional campaigns in local markets. Moreover, such a strategy creates a market presence for the chain. Concentrated presence in a market may create a synergy causing improved performance by individual outlets since they are a part of a larger local network.

A number of empirical studies have shown that a firm's share of sales in a market area is related to its share of outlets in the area in a nonlinear fashion (Lillien and Rao 1976). The relationship between outlet share and market share is often S-shaped as shown in figure 2–7. This is especially true for convenience-oriented retailing, where the format and size of outlets are very similar. The nonlinear relationship implies that after a threshold level is crossed, the addition of new outlets benefits both new and existing outlets and there is a disproportionately higher increase in the total market share of the firm, although, beyond a second threshold level, the growth in market share gets smaller. The possibility of such synergy as well as operational and managerial efficiencies have prompted a number of retail chains to adopt a policy of saturating local markets prior to expanding to other geographic areas. Examples of such policies can be seen in the location strategies of gasoline stations, supermarkets, convenience stores, discount stores, drug retailers, and fast-food outlets, among others.

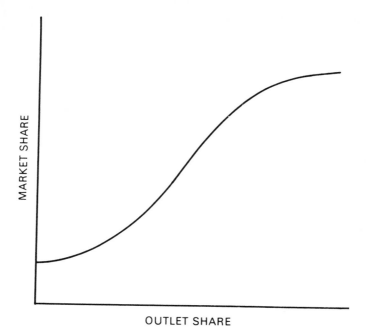

Figure 2–7. Relationship between Outlet Share and Market Share

While market coverage has its advantages, creating a network of outlets in an area requires a well-designed location strategy. As Davidson, Sweeney, and Stampfl note, "In the case of multi-unit retailers, the concept of managing a market rather than managing a single store becomes important" (1984, p. 192). The implication is that sites that may be optimal when considered individually may not be so when the location of the entire network is considered. Due to the possibility of cannibalization of sales of one outlet by another one belonging to the same chain, considerable attention must be given to the relative location of the individual outlets in the network. At the same time, the outlets must be well located with respect to the distribution of potential customers and competitive outlets. Methods and procedures for developing multiunit retail networks are discussed in considerable detail in chapter 6.

Conclusion

In the competitive retail environment, a firm's success depends greatly on its ability to establish a well-defined image, a distinct target market, and an overall strategy for differentiating itself from its competitors. We have argued that the key component in retail strategy is the value platform — an overall strategy that differentiates the firm from its competitors in the minds of the customers it intends to serve. In retailing, the two major dimensions of a store's value platform are price and the quality of the shopping experience. These two attributes define broad groups of stores which make up the overall competitive structure of the industry. Within this framework, the growth and decline of firms and groups of firms as well as the emergence of new retail activities can be viewed as attempts at positioning and repositioning value platforms to achieve competitive advantage.

Retail competition can be viewed at three levels. First, in a broad sense, competition exists among different categories of retail firms. Second, there is competition among firms selling similar goods and services but having different value platforms. Finally, competition is most intense among similar firms pursuing the same value platform. Through a series of examples we have shown the role of location in determining the competitive environment. Since firms can create competitive leverage through their location policies, it is a crucial determinant of the success of retail corporate strategy. Location affects a store's market area, costs, image, and competitive position — a broad segment of the range of corporate activities. In subsequent chapters, we focus in detail on the questions of location and methods for defining retail location strategies.

Note

1. The term *strategic group* is used here somewhat differently than in the industrial organization literature. There, strategic groups are determined based on the similarities among the technological, financial, and marketing strategies of firms. Here, we define strategic groups based on only the marketing strategy.

References

Convenience Store Merchandiser (1986). "It's Your Move: Retail Site Selection." 13(1): 57–62.

Davidson, W.R.; Sweeney, D.J.; and Stampfl, R.W. (1984). *Retailing Management*. New York: John Wiley & Sons.

Hirschman, E. (1978). "A Descriptive Theory of Retail Market Structures." *Journal of Retailing* 54(4): 29–48.

Lillien, G.L., and Rao, A. (1979). "Emerging Approaches to Retail Outlet Management." *Sloan Management Review* 12 (Winter): 27–36.

McLafferty, S. (1986). "Geographical Restructuring of Urban Hospitals: Spatial Dimensions of Corporate Strategy." *Social Science and Medicine* 23: 1079–1086.

Porter, M. (1980). *Competitive Strategy.* New York: Free Press.

3
Spatial Analysis of Markets

After the firm's value platform and overall marketing strategy have been determined, the stage is set to plan its location strategy. The location strategy is the blueprint for the company's growth objectives and expansion plans. It fixes those objectives in geographic space by targeting the firm's investments toward specific locations and market areas. In so doing, it translates the marketing strategy into a concrete policy that is sensitive to the spatial pattern of demand and the availability of desirable sites.

Formulating a location plan involves an in-depth analysis of the geographic market for the merchandise or services offered by the firm. Such analysis needs to be performed at a number of spatial scales, ranging from the regional scale, in which the firm chooses the regions or metro areas that offer the greatest market potential, to the local scale in which the firm evaluates specific sites for locating new outlets. At each stage, the firm narrows down the range of geographic alternatives and the scope of the analysis as it moves closer to the final site-selection decision. (See figure 3–1.)

This chapter considers three stages of the market analysis process. The first, which we call *market selection,* involves the choice of region(s) or metropolitan area(s) for locating new stores. The regions are compared in terms of their economic base and the relative retail potential based on the firm's value platform and marketing objectives. Important factors in the market selection process include population size and growth characteristics, income potential, level of competition, and regional economic base.

Even within regions or cities, there is considerable spatial variation in retail potential due to diversity in land use and housing patterns. The second stage of market analysis, which we refer to as *areal analysis,* evaluates the spatial structure of different subareas of the city in terms of their market potential and level of competition. The final stage of market analysis is *site evaluation.* The focus here is on specific characteristics of individual sites. The quality of real estate, cost of development, traffic flow patterns, and ingress and egress qualities are some of the factors considered in evaluating a site.

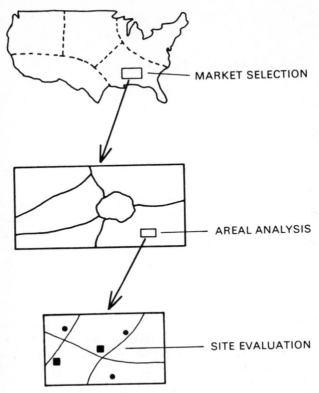

MARKET SELECTION

AREAL ANALYSIS

SITE EVALUATION

Figure 3–1. Three Levels of Spatial Analysis

Market Selection

The market selection decision (or the selection of geographic markets—metropolitan regions, cities, or towns—in which to open new outlets) is a vital one for retailers. It is the potential of the market that ultimately determines the profitability of the outlets. The market must have adequate population and income to provide a sufficient economic base and potential for the new outlets. In addition, the demographic and socioeconomic characteristics of the population must be consistent with the firm's target market. A final and important consideration is the existing level of competition in the area which, when compared with the total size of the market, provides an indication of the level of market saturation.

Retail analysts have traditionally relied on different secondary data sources to ascertain the attractiveness of geographic markets. Commonly used sources include Bureau of the Census publications on population and housing characteristics, the *Census of Retailing,* "Survey of Buying Power" published annually by the *Sales and Marketing Management* magazine, and the *Editor & Publisher Market Guide.* Recently, a number of commercial firms have made census data available to individual users through on-line computerized data bases and microcomputer diskettes. These machine-readable data bases have greatly enhanced access to market information for individual retailers.

The "Survey of Buying Power" provides a ready source of information about geographic market areas that is especially useful to retailers. The survey reports the buying power index (BPI) of different metropolitan areas, cities, states, and television-viewing areas (ADIs). The BPI rates the overall retail sales potential for an area, expressed as a percentage of the total retail sales potential in the United States. The index is a quantitative measure of the relative purchasing power or demand in an area based on a weighted average of its population, income, and total retail sales in the preceding year. It is calculated as follows:

$$\text{BPI} = 0.5(\text{percentage of U.S. effective buying income})$$
$$+ 0.3(\text{percentage of U.S. retail sales})$$
$$+ 0.2(\text{percentage of U.S. population}) \quad (3.1)$$

Effective buying income is personal income adjusted for taxes.

In addition to the overall index, the survey also provides graduated buying power indices for each area. The graduated BPIs reflect the buying power in households with different income levels. Three graduated BPIs (corresponding to low-, middle-, and high-income groups) are published by the survey. The premium-priced product (PPP) index, for example, considers only families with more than $35,000 annual income. For retail stores with a high-income target market, the PPP index provides a more accurate assessment of potential than the overall BPI.

Purchasing power indices such as the BPI provide a measure of total retail potential in a market area. The attractiveness of a market area, however, cannot be assessed by examining potential demand alone. It is the interplay of demand and supply that creates market opportunities. Although an area may have high purchasing power and residents that match the retailer's target market, the existing level of competition may make it a poor choice for new outlets. Similarly, areas with low aggregate demand may be attractive if the level of existing competition is low.

Several factors need to be considered in assessing the level of competition in an area: the number of stores, their sizes, and the strengths and weaknesses of the competing firms. The overall level of competition must be judged relative to the level of demand. Different types of ratios have been proposed to measure the relative level of retail saturation in an area or in different areas. These include the number of retail stores per capita, per capita retail sales, average sales per establishment, and average sales per square foot.

Index of Retail Saturation

A commonly used general measure of the attractiveness of a market area for new stores is the index of retail saturation (Lalonde 1961). The index compares the level of retail expenditures in an area with the level of supply of retail selling space. The index of retail saturation (IRS) is computed as follows:

$$IRS_i = \frac{POP_i \times EXP_i}{RSS_i} \qquad (3.2)$$

where IRS_i = index of retail saturation in area i

POP_i = population in area i

EXP_i = per capita retail expenditure in area i

RSS_i = retail selling space (in total square feet) in area i

The data necessary for calculating IRS can be obtained from a variety of sources. Population information is available from census data and various other publications. Information on per capita retail expenditure for different retail categories can be obtained from the Bureau of Labor Statistics or computed from data published in the *Census of Retailing*. The number of retail facilities in an area can be determined by first-hand observation as well as from publications such as the *Census of Retailing* and the *Editor & Publisher Market Guide*. Various trade organizations and data service firms provide similar information.

Since the IRS measures the level of demand relative to supply, a low value indicates saturation of the area. The higher the value of the index, the greater the attractiveness of the area for new store openings. As is the case with all indices, the IRS is meaningful only if compared against some norm. The norm may be a standard set by the retailer based on past experience. Alternatively, the relative attractiveness of different market areas can be ranked using the index.

The Assumption of Fixed Demand

Implicit in the construction of indices such as the IRS is the assumption of fixed *in situ* demand. The assumption of fixed demand is that the level of retail sales in a geographic market is determined "by such environmental variables as population, income and other factors essentially beyond the control of the industry" (Ingene and Lusch 1980, p. 23). This implies that total retail sales in an area and sales within particular retail categories are not influenced by the actions of retail managers. Demand in an area, then, is essentially fixed by population characteristics.

The assumption of fixed demand is implicit in many studies of retail potential. Hoyt (1969) argued that total sales in an area are a function of income and that the growth of retail sales depends on the growth of population in the area. An empirical study by Ferber (1958) showed that about 95 percent of the variation in total retail sales of Illinois communities with population above ten thousand could be statistically accounted for by their size and distance from neighboring communities. Both population and distance had a positive relationship with sales. The greater the distance of a community from its neighbors, the less the opportunity for outshopping (purchasing in other communities). The significant positive relationship between population and sales provides presumptive support of the fixed-demand assumption. Studies by Liu (1970), Ingene and Lusch (1980), Ingene and Yu (1981), and Ingene (1984) have also shown that variations in per capita income consistently account for a significant portion of the variation in total retail sales within different geographic areas.

The positive impact of population and income on sales is also evident when sales are analyzed for specific retail categories. Ingene and Lusch (1980), for example, found that most of the variation in total department store sales at the SMSA level could be accounted for by total SMSA income and total SMSA population. Using data from 213 of the 258 SMSAs in the continental United States, the authors regressed total department store sales in each SMSA for 1972 against the SMSA's population and income. They obtained the following results:

$$TED = 4.74 + 0.29(POP) + 0.71(INC) \qquad (3.3)$$

where TED = total department store sales in SMSA

POP = total SMSA population

INC = per capita income

Both population and income were significantly related to total department store sales at the $p = .05$ level. Together, they accounted for 95.7 percent of the variation in sales across the 213 SMSAs. The authors found virtually similar results when the total population size was replaced by the number of households.

Although these results support the argument that market potential is determined by the size and characteristics of the population in a market area, some researchers have argued that the index of retail saturation does not provide a true assessment of the attractiveness of different markets (Ingene and Lusch 1980; Ingene 1984). According to these authors, if the demand is indeed determined by population characteristics, it should be possible to account for total sales as well as per capita or per household sales in an area with a set of socioeconomic and demographic variables. If variations in per capita sales cannot be explained by population characteristics alone, the assumption of fixed demand cannot be supported. The implication is that a market with a low value on the index of retail saturation may under some circumstances be attractive to enter because the low value may result from the inability of existing retailers to satisfy consumer demand.

The inability of existing retailers to satisfy consumer demand may lead to high levels of outshopping and sales leakage from the area. Outshopping occurs when stores outside the area offer better merchandise, prices, service, or convenience. Consumers are then willing to travel extra distances to patronize stores located in nearby cities or shopping centers. Outshopping affects the level of sales in stores in the area and thus affects the calculated IRS value. It makes the market unattractive in terms of its retail potential. However, when outshopping is high, an effective retailer may enter a low-IRS market and attract customers who engage in outshopping; in effect the retailer may be able to generate "new" demand by presenting customers with an attractive and accessible shopping alternative.

A Test of the Fixed-Demand Assumption

The observed relationship between total sales, population, and income does not establish the validity of the fixed-demand assumption. The critical test of the validity of the fixed-demand assumption is that sales per household or per capita be largely explainable in terms of population characteristics. Ingene and Lusch (1980) provided a test of this assumption for department store sales. They regressed average household expenditures in department stores for 213 SMSAs against various measures of population characteristics. (Table 3–1 provides a list of variables and their definitions.) The result of their analysis was as follows:

$$HED = .245 + .868HI - .336SD - .071SK + .608HS$$
$$+ .510M + .027DEN$$

$$R^2 = .221 \hspace{4cm} (3.4)$$

The regression results do not support the fixed-demand assumption. Although all the variables have the predicted sign and nearly all are signif-

Table 3–1
Socioeconomic Variables Used to Analyze Department Store Sales

Symbol	Definition	Predicted Sign
HED	Average household expenditures at department stores	Dependent variable
HI	Average household's effective buying income	+
SD	Standard deviation of HI	−
SK	Skewness of HI	−
HS	Average household size	+
M	Mobility (autos per 1,000 households)	+
DEN	Density (population per square mile)	+

Source: Adapted from C.A. Ingene and R.F. Lusch, "Market Selection Decisions for Department Stores," *Journal of Retailing* 56, no. 3 (1980): 21–40. Reprinted with permission.

icantly related to average household expenditure (the only exception being *SK*), they explain little of the variation in per household expenditures across the SMSAs. Statistically, the six explanatory variables together account for only about 22 percent of the variation in expenditures per household. (Recall that for the same set of SMSAs, more than 95 percent of the variation in *total* department store sales was accounted for by population and income.) The lack of explanatory power of this model implies that demand at the household level is not strongly determined by population characteristics alone and raises serious questions about the validity of the fixed-demand assumption.

Based on this evidence, Ingene and Lusch presented an alternative viewpoint that demand at the household level is not fixed, but rather is influenced by the nature of the retail industry in the area. They argued that in addition to socioeconomic characteristics, demand is affected by the marketing policies of existing stores. Factors such as the assortment of merchandise offered by the outlets, the quality and level of service, and store atmosphere all affect the total sales in an area. To test this hypothesis, they proposed an expanded regression model which included both population characteristics and variables measuring the overall marketing environment in the area as explanatory variables. An empirical test of the expanded model was performed by the authors using the department store sales data. The marketing variables used in the model are defined in table 3–2. The authors obtained the following results:

$$HED = .139 + .332HI - .096SD + .090SK + .908HS + .203M$$
$$+ .008DEN + .028G + .776W + .827DSS + .706LF$$
$$R^2 = .890$$

$$(3.5)$$

Table 3–2
Marketing Variables Used to Analyze Department Store Sales

Symbol	Definition	Predicted Sign
W	Annual wage rate	+
G	Growth rate of population, 1970–72	+
DSS	Thousands of square feet of department store space per person	+
LF	Employees per thousand square feet of deparment store space	+

Source: Adapted from C.A. Ingene and R.F. Lusch, "Market Selection Decisions for Department Stores," *Journal of Retailing* 56, no. 3 (1980): 21–40. Reprinted with permission.

The addition of the new variables significantly increases the explanatory power of the model. The adjusted R^2 rises to 0.890. The large growth in explanatory power over that obtained with only the socioeconomic variables demonstrates "that retail expenditures per household are in a large part determined by the managerial decisions of department store executives" (Ingene and Lusch 1980, p. 35). The variables with the largest and most significant effects on sales per household are the per capita department store selling space in the area and the number of employees per thousand square feet of department store selling space. Both variables have positive effects on sales which indicate that, even after controlling for the effects of income and other demographic factors, retail sales increase as the supply of selling space and the level of service increases. Analysis of 1977 sales of eight separate retail categories (apparel, department, drug, furniture, general merchandise, grocery, hardware, and variety) by Ingene (1984) led to a similar conclusion. The empirical results, therefore, do not seem to support the assumption of fixed demand. Retail managers can significantly affect market potential by their own actions.

The implication of these studies is that the index of retail saturation by itself does not provide a complete measure of market potential. It is important to also consider the potential for increasing per capita sales in the area. If per capita sales can be increased, the total market potential of the area will also expand. If the potential for market expansion exists, an area with a low value on the index of retail saturation may still be attractive for new outlets.

Market Expansion Potential

The potential for market expansion can be computed by comparing the actual per capita or per household sales in an area with the expected sales given the characteristics of the population and the existing retail environment in the area. The expected level of sales can be calculated based on a regression model with per capita or per household sales as the dependent variable and population and marketing characteristics as explanatory variables. An index of market expansion potential (MEP) can then be defined as follows:

$$MEP_i = \hat{S}_i - S_i \qquad (3.6)$$

where $\hat{S}_i$ and S_i are the expected and actual expenditures per household (or per capita) for the ith geographic area. The higher the value of MEP for an area, the greater the potential for market expansion. Areas with negative MEP values have little possibility of market expansion. Consequently, these markets will be attractive only to firms that can wrest market share away from existing outlets (Ingene 1984).

Classification of Market Attractiveness

Examining the indices of both retail saturation and market expansion potential provides a more accurate picture of market attractiveness than that obtained by looking only at the saturation level. The IRS and MEP indices can be used jointly to design a market-classification scheme as shown in figure 3–2. The most attractive markets are those that are high on both IRS and MEP (quadrant 1). The sales potential of these markets can be expanded by the retailer and the existing level of market saturation is also low (as indicated by a high IRS). Markets in quadrant 4, on the other hand, are low on both IRS and MEP and, thus, not attractive for locating new outlets. The attrac-

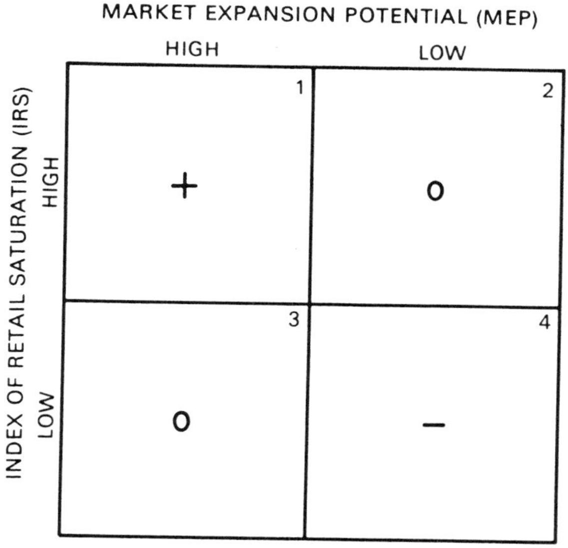

Figure 3–2. Classification of Market Areas

tiveness of the market areas falling in the other two categories depends critically on the entering firm's competitive strength. Markets in quadrant 2 have a low level of saturation (high IRS), but their MEP is also low. Although the level of existing competition is low, the lack of growth potential reduces the attractiveness of these markets. The growth potentials of markets in quadrant 3 are high. Because of the intensity of the competition, however, new outlets can benefit from this growth only by aggressively fighting for and winning market share.

Both IRS and MEP focus on the market potential of different geographic areas. IRS looks at existing conditions, while MEP is more future-oriented. In making market selection decisions, however, factors besides market potential need also to be considered. In assessing geographic areas for possible store expansion, it is important to consider the characteristics of the area's overall economic base. A retailer may find a local economy based on a single industry unattractive in comparison to an area with a diversified base. The potential for future growth in the region is closely linked to its economic base. For example, the market potential of areas dominated by "smoke-stack" industries has changed significantly in the past few years as a result of shifting employment structures and loss of industrial jobs. Similarly, retail outlets in regions dominated by oil-related industries have been hurt by the recent decline in oil prices.

Another important factor to be considered in selecting market regions for new stores is the accessibility of the market area to the distribution system used by the firm. Outlets of chain stores are often served by one or a few strategically located warehouses. Proximity to the firm's network of warehouses is a major consideration in making market selection decisions for these firms. Such proximity is especially important for regional chain stores whose distribution system is geared toward serving a particular region of the country.

In addition to economic base and proximity to supply points, some other important factors are: the availability and cost of media for advertising, availability and cost of labor, responsiveness of local government to new business, availability of credit, and the access to credit-investigation and collection services. The regulatory and legal environment, zoning regulations, and local tax laws must also be taken into consideration in making market selection decisions.

Prior to concluding this section, a cautionary note is necessary regarding the use of indices such as IRS and MEP for making market selection decisions. The greater the attractiveness of a region based on these indices, the more likely it is that other retailers will also target their store expansions in that area. Consequently, an attractive market can quickly become glutted with stores. Such was the case in the past decade in many cities in the Southwest. Attracted by the rapid population growth in the Sunbelt, many retailers, especially department stores, targeted their expansion in cities in this area. In the seven-year period 1974–81, the number of department stores in Phoenix, for example, increased from 21 to 46 (Davidson, Sweeney, and Stampfl 1984, p. 183). The opening of so many new stores in such a short time span greatly increased the level of competition in the city. This fact, if anticipated, may have altered the decisions of some of the entrants.

Areal Analysis

The market selection decision concerns the potential of different geographic regions for store expansion. The broad geographic scope of the analysis, however, often masks spatial variations in market potential within a city or metropolitan region. Because of spatial variations in land use and residential patterns, there are significant intracity differences in market attractiveness. In large metropolitan areas, especially, retail potentials vary considerably over space in relation to differences in population characteristics and growth potential. Market analysis, therefore, must also focus on the characteristics of local areas within a city. Information on demographic characteristics of the local areas, types of land use, and the level and quality of competition must be evaluated for this purpose. We refer to this evaluation process as areal analysis.

The Physical Environment

After a market has been selected for consideration, one of the first tasks is to evaluate its physical environment. The physical environment of an area determines, in a major way, the travel and shopping patterns in the region. Land-use patterns, physical barriers such as rivers and lakes, road systems, and transportation networks all influence the residential patterns and the location of shopping opportunities. The patterns of travel and spatial interaction within the city reflect its physical structure and spatial organization.

By studying the physical structure of the city, it is often possible to subdivide the region into smaller areas. Information on population characteristics and projected growth patterns of these subareas must be obtained to determine the potential for new outlets. Figure 3–3 provides an example of a map of a city divided into six subareas based on land-use patterns, physical features, and road networks.

Data on population characteristics of local areas within a city are obtained directly from the *Census of Population* or from independent suppliers of census information. Typically, these data are organized by census tract or zip code area. To obtain information on the subareas, the first step is to identify the census tracts or zip codes within each subarea. Data for these small areas are then aggregated to provide a profile of each subarea. As an

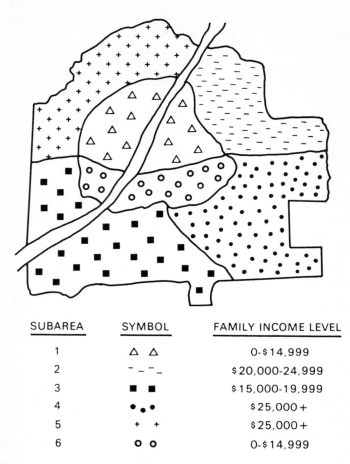

SUBAREA	SYMBOL	FAMILY INCOME LEVEL
1	△ △	0-$14,999
2	- _ -_	$20,000-24,999
3	■ ■	$15,000-19,999
4	•₀•	$25,000+
5	+ +	$25,000+
6	○ ○	0-$14,999

Figure 3–3. Subareas in an Urban Market

illustration, the past and projected population size of each subarea in figure 3–3 was computed by identifying the census tracts within each subarea. These figures are shown in table 3–3. It is apparent that there are significant differences among the sectors in population size and growth potential. While the southwestern area (subarea 3) has the highest level of population, future growth is expected most in the eastern parts of the city. Subareas 2 and 4 have comparatively newer housing developments and continue to experience substantial real estate activity. One reason for this growth is the establishment of a number of new commercial firms near those areas but just outside the city limit.

An alternative to using census tracts and zip code areas as the basis for

Table 3–3
Population Trend by Subareas, 1980–90
(thousands)

Subarea	1980	1985	1990	Net Change 1980–90
1	62	56	54	– 15%
2	144	172	196	+ 36
3	215	236	248	+ 15
4	130	165	172	+ 32
5	92	97	103	+ 12
6	85	70	68	– 20
Total market	728	796	841	+ 15

aggregating subarea data is to define subareas with regular geometric properties. A number of commercial firms supply population data for different
user-defined areas. For example, the area may be a circle of two-mile radius
surrounding a particular point. The center point may be defined by its longi-
tude and latitude or as the intersection of two streets. An example is shown in
appendix 3–1.

Information on population size provides only a partial picture of the suitability of an area for locating new outlets. The demographic and socioeconomic characteristics of the population must also be appraised to gain a
better insight. The key criterion is the extent to which the population characteristics match the target market of the store. The target market of a department store, for example, may predominantly consist of families in the middle-
and upper-income groups holding white collar jobs. These stores, therefore,
will be more concerned with the number of families with annual income of,
say, more than $25,000. Supermarkets, on the other hand, may be more con-
cerned with total population size because they have a wider target market.
Information on other socioeconomic characteristics is also very relevant. For
hardware and DIY stores, data on home ownership is critical, since home-
owners account for a significant portion of their sales. Stores selling infant
clothing and toys, similarly, will be interested in the number of families with
children residing in each subarea and the growth of this demographic group.

The Competitive Environment

Just as market analysis requires consideration of demand and supply, both
population and competitive factors must be considered in areal analysis too.
The firm's location strategy must reflect the spatial structure of existing and
future outlets. Only by comparing the retail potential in the subarea with the

competitive environment can the suitability of opening new outlets be determined. Failure to consider the existing retail structure and the nature of local competition has been a major pitfall in numerous site-location decisions.

Measuring Competition. There are many ways in which the level of competition can be measured. Indices such as number of stores, stores per capita, and per capita selling space are often used for this purpose. Prior to constructing such indices, it is important that the relevant competitors be identified. While this may seem a simple task, in practice it is often difficult. The sales of an outlet are affected by other outlets competing directly with it, as well as by intertype competitors. A department store, for example, not only competes with other department stores in the area but also with specialty stores selling merchandise similar to that carried by the department store. In recent years, specialty clothing stores, toy stores, audio and video retailers, and off-price clothing stores have all had significant impacts on the sales of department and discount stores. Although department stores are especially vulnerable to intertype competition, other retailers are not immune from it. For example, there is a high level of competition between supermarkets and drug stores because of the considerable overlap in their merchandise. In general, the level of intertype competition has increased considerably in the past decade and brought about major changes in retail competition.

Another issue in defining competitors concerns the specification of the geographic area in which competition occurs. Because people freely move across urban subarea boundaries, it makes little sense to view only those stores located within a subarea as relevant competitors. At the same time, not all stores in the city compete with each other. Thus, it is necessary to identify all stores competing to serve residents of a subarea, or, more specifically, all stores patronized by the residents of that subarea. Some of these stores may be located outside the boundaries of the area, either near the area or at major shopping centers serving a large regional market. The best way to gather information on competitors is to first conduct a small survey of consumers residing in the area to determine the stores patronized by them. An easier but perhaps less accurate alternative is to include all large stores located within a predefined distance of the subarea and other prominent stores at major shopping centers.

The Competitive Inventory. A complete inventory of all competitive outlets is essential for assessing the retail environment. The location analyst must rely on personal observation, surveys, and publications of local government agencies and trade organizations. The competitive inventory should include information on the number, sizes, and physical designs of competitive outlets; site characteristics; types of services provided; merchandizing and pricing policies; and the target market served by existing outlets. Both quantita-

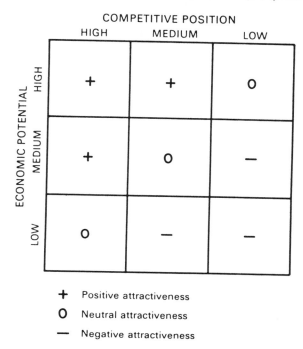

Figure 3–4. **Attractiveness of Subareas**

tive factors (such as sales area) and qualitative factors (such as the quality of management and customer satisfaction) must be assessed in order to determine the level of competition.

Ranking of Areas

Based on the population characteristics and competitive environment in each subarea, the suitability for store expansion can be judged. To facilitate comparison of different subareas, it is helpful to create an attractiveness matrix (or portfolio matrix) as shown in figure 3–4. The matrix portrays the attractiveness of a subarea using the two factors discussed earlier. The vertical dimension of the matrix represents economic potential; the horizontal one represents competitive position. Economic potential is measured as a composite index of such factors as population size, growth rate, income and spending patterns, and the degree of match between population characteristics and characteristics of the firm's target market. Competitive position is based on information from the competitive inventory. Note, however, that the competitive position of a subarea is inversely related to the level of competitive activity. A subarea with high level of competitive activity will be low on competitive position and vice versa. The two axes are demarcated into three regions representing high, medium, and low scores.

The position of a subarea in the nine-cell matrix reflects its overall attractiveness for opening new outlets. An area falling in the upper-left corner is highly attractive for both economic potential and competitive position. An area in the lower-right cell, on the other hand, is unattractive in terms of both dimensions. In the figure, cells with high overall attractiveness are designated by a positive sign, while those with low attractiveness are shown with a negative sign. The areas in the remaining diagonal cells are either highly attractive in one dimension and poor in the other or are only moderately attractive in terms of both dimensions. Overall, subareas falling in these diagonal cells represent areas of moderate attractiveness. The attractiveness matrix is a useful tool for screening different subareas and eliminating those that are not suitable for new outlets. This type of matrix is used extensively in marketing to assess product market opportunities. (For a general discussion of portfolio matrices, see Wind and Mahajan 1981. For an application to site selection, see Mahajan, Sharma, and Srinivas 1985.)

Site Evaluation

The matrix in figure 3–4 helps to identify the subareas for locating new outlets. At this point, the focus of market analysis shifts to evaluation of individual sites in these subareas. At this site-evaluation stage, the objective is to prepare a list of feasible sites from which a final choice can be made. The available sites in these areas must be identified and studied in depth in order to determine their feasibility for locating new outlets.

It is often said that the essence of site evaluation is to find a "100 percent" location—one that has all the desirable characteristics of a good site. It is the one that is located in a good shopping area, has high accessibility and traffic flow, and represents a good real estate investment. Unfortunately, finding a site that has all the desirable characteristics may not be an easy task. Moreover, the ideal characteristics of a site differ for different types of retail outlets. The site that is good for one type of store may not be suitable for another. A 100 percent location for a discount store is not necessarily good for a fast-food or convenience outlet.

A common approach to site evaluation is to first develop a checklist to ensure that all relevant factors are considered. The checklist procedure was one of the first attempts to systematically appraise the relative value of a site (Applebaum 1965). Essentially, it involves an evaluation of various factors that are likely to impact upon sales and costs at a site. A judgment about the desirability of the site is made based on this evaluation. Several standard

Table 3–4
Checklist for Site Evaluation

Local Demographics
Population base of the local area
Income potential in local area

Traffic Flow and Accessibility
Number of vehicles
Type of vehicles
Number of pedestrians
Type of pedestrians
Availability of mass transit
Access to major highway
Level of street congestion
Quality of access streets

Retail Structure
Number of competitors in area
Number and types of stores in area
Complementarity of neighboring stores
Proximity to commercial areas
Joint promotion by local merchants

Site Characteristics
Number of parking spots available
Distance of parking areas
Visibility of site from street
Size and shape of the lot
Condition of existing building (if any)
Ingress and egress quality

Legal and Cost Factors
Type of zoning
Length of lease
Local taxes
Operations and maintenance costs
Restrictive clauses in lease
Voluntary regulations by local merchants

checklists have been published to aid the evaluation process. (See, for example, Nelson 1958; Kane 1966; Applebaum 1966; Gruen and Smith 1960.) These checklists commonly include information on the socioeconomic and demographic composition of the neighborhood, level of competition, and existing retail outlets in the area. Site-specific factors such as traffic count, parking facilities, ease of ingress and egress, and visibility are also considered.

The checklist in table 3–4 provides a systematic procedure for evaluating information about a potential site. While some of the data may be quite subjective, the use of checklists allows standardization of the data-collection procedure and some comparing of information on different potential sites. Moreover, as Goldstucker et al. (1978) note, the relative ease with which the checklist procedure can be implemented and its reliance on expert opinion are seen as advantages by many.

The site-evaluation process is important in identifying feasible locations for new outlets. While ultimately the selection of the optimal site or sites must depend on forecasts of sales and profitability, the site-evaluation process is extremely helpful in defining the set of sites to be considered in the final selection process. We now briefly discuss the factors to be considered in the site-evaluation process.

Relative Location

A major factor determining the suitability of a site is its physical setting and its location relative to the existing retail structure in the region. One must, therefore, ask such questions as: Is the site located at a planned shopping center or in the downtown shopping district? What types of stores are located nearby? Is the site near a commercial area or recreation center? Where is the site located relative to major residential areas?

Conceptually, the spatial organization of retail outlets in a metropolitan region may be viewed as a hierarchical structure, with each level of the hierarchy containing different numbers and types of retail outlets (Berry 1963). The highest level of this retail hierarchy is represented by regional shopping malls and the central business district (CBD), which have the greatest concentration of retail opportunities in terms of both numbers and types of outlets. Regional shopping malls serve a large population and range in size from 300,000 to more than 1,000,000 square feet. Both regional malls and the CBD are anchored by traditional department stores and mass merchandisers. The majority of the tenants are specialty stores providing a variety of merchandise. Progressing down the hierarchy, one encounters community shopping centers and smaller malls. These centers may range from 100,000 to 200,000 square feet of gross selling area providing a variety of merchandise. Finally, at the lowest level are neighborhood centers and freestanding sites offering limited, convenience-oriented shopping. Neighborhood centers typically range from 20,000 to 50,000 square feet and often have a supermarket as an anchor.

A major trend in the retail organization of North American cities is the decentralization of trade from the CBD to regional shopping malls. The post–World War II period witnessed a rapid growth of suburban populations and the consequent decline in the importance of the CBD. These trends, which were often accentuated by traditional downtown merchants locating branch outlets in the regional malls, are well documented. (See, for example, Hartshorn 1980.) In an effort to reverse this trend, cities such as Boston, Baltimore, Minneapolis, Vancouver, and St. Louis have engaged in innovative programs of downtown revitalization. The more successful programs have tended to create downtown shopping malls or shopping streets to attract retail customers back to the CBD. Although it has not necessarily reduced the relative attraction of suburban shopping malls, downtown revitalization has in many cases brought retail customers back to the city center.

Locations in shopping centers have a number of advantages. The clustering of different shopping opportunities facilitates multipurpose shopping by the customers who can purchase different items on a single shopping trip. This creates a synergy and increases the volume of traffic in the center. In evaluating a site in a shopping center, it is important to consider the compatibility of neighboring stores. A paint store, a lumber yard, and a hardware store, for example, benefit each other when located in a cluster. Similarly, almost all kinds of shopping goods stores seem to have a strong affinity for department stores because of the complementarity of their merchandise offerings (Davidson, Sweeney, and Stampfl 1984).

Because of multipurpose shopping, small specialty stores benefit when they are located close to large department stores due to the greater drawing power of the larger store (McLafferty and Ghosh 1986; Ghosh 1986). Since the large anchor store has a beneficial impact on the smaller stores located in the shopping center, anchor stores usually pay a lower rent per square foot than do smaller specialty stores. The freestanding store, on the other hand, may develop a loyal local clientele who provide a steady sales volume. The store in the mall will usually be competing with other stores in the center for clientele.

Shopping clusters also result when similar stores locate next to each other. Stores selling comparable merchandise often cluster to facilitate comparison shopping and maintain close links with competitors. The shopping districts found in many urban areas, where similar outlets locate in the same neighborhood, provide vivid evidence of such clustering. This type of clustering, too, creates synergy and increases the volume of traffic. However, comparison shopping increases the level of competition among the stores located together. To gain competitive advantage, each store in the cluster tries to differentiate its merchandise, price, or service level in order to create a unique value platform.

Accessibility and Traffic Flow

Because retail outlets serve a spatially dispersed population, access to retail outlets is critical in determining their ultimate success. Accessibility is affected by several factors such as road conditions, the ease of ingress and egress from the site, and travel barriers. Accessibility ultimately determines the level of vehicular and pedestrian traffic flow around a site. For convenience stores and outlets selling impulse items, such as ice cream, adequate traffic flow is crucial in achieving the projected sales potential.

The nature of the road system and the quality of the road network are basic aspects in evaluating accessibility. The questions to be asked are: Can potential customers easily reach the site? Are there major traffic arteries that connect the site to the neighboring area? Interrelated with these questions are the level of congestion, physical conditions of the roads, and the presence of natural or artificial travel barriers. Another consideration is the availability of parking space.

A quantitative enumeration of the level and composition of traffic flow is always important in site evaluation. In general, the higher the level of traffic flow, the greater the level of potential sales. However, the composition of the total traffic is also important. A large volume of truck traffic or pedestrians not shopping in that neighborhood is not desirable. Moreover, every person passing by a store may not be a prospective customer. Selective counting procedures such as counting only adults or only those carrying shopping bags may be used to obtain a more refined traffic count. In addition, selective interviews should be undertaken to verify the proportion of passersby who are prospective shoppers.

The level and quality of traffic flow, in addition to providing a basis for comparing alternative locations, can help in projecting the sales of new outlets. This approach is often used by convenience store chains whose sales result from intercepting pedestrian and vehicular traffic. Many chains have gathered extensive information on the relationship between traffic flow and sales. This information is used to project sales of new outlets based on a measurement of traffic count at the new site.

Site Characteristics

The final factor in site evaluation is the physical characteristics of the site and the quality of the real estate. A vacant piece of flat land with good visibility and access is considered ideal. At the same time, a vacant piece of land may be costly to develop. In practice, especially in urban areas, many available sites are locations of earlier stores. A decision must be made in such cases as to whether the present structure can be remodeled or if the structure or any part of it needs to be demolished to make room for new construction. Whether a parcel of real estate is vacant land or a vacant store, the expense of developing the land and constructing the desired store format and the cost of real estate must be weighed against the projected sales volume at that site.

Experience and subjective judgments are essential in evaluating the physical characteristics of a site. With the exception of real estate costs, most of the factors are not easily quantifiable. It is common to develop a checklist of factors such as the one shown in table 3–4. The potential sites should be rated on each factor on the checklist. An overall rating for each site is then obtained by summing the ratings across the individual items. Sites with high overall ratings are therefore logical choices for store locations.

Conclusion

This chapter has presented different analytical steps in selecting the metro-politan region or city in which to open new outlets and identifying feasible sites for those outlets. Although we have discussed this as a series of discrete steps, it is important to note that not all firms follow the three stages of market selection, areal analysis, and site evaluation described here. In fact, many firms omit the market selection stage and simply limit their location planning to the particular geographic region in which the firm is already located. Moreover, small firms often restrict their search to a specific neigh-borhood or local area, thus avoiding the first two stages of the analysis com-pletely. Only the largest national retailers have the research staff and access to information necessary for performing a complete comparison of retail potential across a large number of regions and cities. This situation is chang-ing, however, as computerized data sets describing market characteristics become widely available and firms have access to geocoded data bases and computer software needed to analyze such data.

Although the three-stage scheme is intuitively appealing, widely dis-cussed, and often followed (albeit incompletely, in practice), it may not always be the best strategy overall to follow in planning the spatial organiza-tion of outlets. The reason is as follows: Decisions made at each stage of the analysis may limit or constrain those made in the subsequent stages. As a result, important options may be excluded prematurely from consideration. For example, at the second stage, the firm specifies the particular area of a town in which stores will be located, thereby eliminating sites outside those areas from consideration. While the area chosen may be superior in overall potential, it may be that a combination of sites from both inside and outside the area would provide a better coverage of the target market as a whole. Good quality sites need not be located in the areas of highest potential. Thus, in successively narrowing the scale of analysis, the firm may prevent itself from making the "best" location decision. (For a similar argument in another context, see Rushton and Mahadev, 1982). In chapter 6, we present a set of methods for location analysis that overcomes this problem by finding the optimal network of store locations within any large geographic market area. These methods determine the set of sites that maximize the expected levels of sales or profits for the firm, thus enabling the development of a coherent spa-tial network for serving the target market.

References

Applebaum, W. (1965). "Can Store Location Research Be a Science?" *Economic Geography* 41: 234–237.

Applebaum, W. (1966). "Methods for Determining Store Trade Areas, Market Pene-tration and Potential Sales." *Journal of Marketing Research* 3: 127–141.

Berry, B.J.L. (1963). *Commercial Structure and Commercial Blight,* Research Paper No. 85. Department of Geography, University of Chicago, Chicago.

Davidson, W.R.; Sweeney, D.J.; and Stampfl, R.W. (1984). *Retailing Management.* New York: John Wiley & Sons.

Ferber, R. (1958). "Variation in Retail Sales between Cities." *Journal of Marketing* 22: 295–303.

Ghosh, A. (1986). "The Value of a Mall and Other Insights from a Revised Central Place Model." *Journal of Retailing* 62(1): 79–97.

Goldstucker, Jac L.; Bellenger, D.N.; Stanley, T.J.; and Otte, R. (1978). *New Developments in Retail Trade Area Analysis and Site Selection.* Research Monograph No. 78. Atlanta: Georgia State University.

Gruen, V., and Smith, L. (1960). *Shopping Town USA: The Planning of Shopping Centers.* New York: Rheinhold.

Hartshorn, T. (1980). *Interpreting the City: An Urban Geography.* New York: John Wiley & Sons.

Hoyt, H. (1969). *The Location of Additional Retail Stores in the United States in the Last One-Third of the Twentieth Century: A Research Monograph.* New York: National Retail Merchants Association.

Ingene, C.A. (1984). "Structural Determinants of Retail Potential." *Journal of Retailing* 60(1): 37–64.

Ingene, C.A. and Lusch, R.F. (1980). "Market Selection Decisions for Department Stores." *Journal of Retailing* 56(3): 21–40.

Ingene, C.A., and Yu, E. (1981). "Determinants of Retail Sales in SMSAs." *Regional Science and Urban Economics* 11: 529–547.

Kane, B.J. (1966). *A Systematic Guide to Supermarket Location Analysis.* New York: Fairchild.

Lalonde, B. (1961). "The Logistics of Retail Location." *Proceedings, American Marketing Association.* Chicago: American Marketing Association.

Liu, B.C. (1970). "Determinants of Retail Sales in Large Metropolitan Areas: 1954 and 1963." *Journal of the American Statistical Association* 65: 1460–1473.

Mahajan, V.; Sharma, S.; and Srinivas, D. (1985). "An Application of Portfolio Analysis for Identifying Attractive Retail Locations." *Journal of Retailing* 61(4): 19–34.

McLafferty, S., and Ghosh, A. (1986). "Multipurpose Shopping and the Location of Retail Firms." *Geographical Analysis* 18: 215–226.

Nelson, R. (1958). *The Selection of Retail Locations.* New York: F.W. Dodge.

Rushton, G., and Mahadev, T. (1982). "Locational Efficiency of Rural Health Services in an Indian District." Paper presented at the Annual Meeting of the Association of American Geographers, San Antonio, Texas.

Wind, Y., and Mahajan, V. (1981). "Designing Product and Business Portfolios." *Harvard Business Review* 59(January–February): 155–165.

Appendix 3A
An Example of Demographic and Socioeconomic Data for Trade Areas

Acct #   0   02/02/84

1980 Census
National Decision Systems
Pop-Facts—Full Data Report
619-942-7000

Prepared for ABC Company

Westheimer Road and West Loop 610   Site #   1
Houston, Texas   Cord. 29.444 95.275

Description	1.0-mile radius	2.0-mile radius	3.0-mile radius
Population			
1988 projection	13,272	56,968	147,569
1987 estimate	12,418	53,254	137,830
1980 Census	11,903	51,016	131,966
1970 Census	10,229	43,662	112,177
1970–80 growth	16.37%	16.84%	17.64%
Households			
1988 projection	7,998	33,040	81,985
1987 estimate	7,465	30,447	75,092
1980 Census	7,069	28,582	70,207
1970 Census	4,795	19,147	46,356
1970–80 growth	47.41%	49.27%	51.45%
Population by race and Spanish origin	11,903	51,016	131,966
White	92.48%	90.37%	87.72%
Black	1.90%	3.85%	5.68%
American Indian	0.16%	0.19%	0.21%
Asian and Pacific islander	1.28%	1.72%	2.38%
Other races	4.18%	3.88%	4.01%
Spanish origin—new category	10.17%	8.65%	10.15%
Occupied Units	7,069	28,582	70,207
Owner-occupied	32.16%	36.81%	35.38%
Renter-occupied	67.84%	63.19%	64.62%
1980 persons per household	1.68	1.78	1.87
Year-round units at address	8,169	32,934	79,753
Single units	40.79%	46.98%	48.38%
2–9 units	7.07%	7.13%	6.66%
10 + units	52.04%	45.78%	44.84%
Mobile home or trailer	0.10%	0.11%	0.12%
Single/multiple-unit ratio	0.69	0.89	0.94
1987 estimated households by income	7,465	30,447	75,092
$50,000 or more	25.43%	23.39%	21.25%
$35,000–$49,999	15.43%	15.41%	14.52%
$25,000–$34,999	19.63%	18.71%	17.93%
$15,000–$24,999	20.54%	20.77%	21.48%
$7,500–$14,999	12.24%	13.32%	15.17%
Under $7,500	6.73%	8.41%	9.64%
1987 estimated average hh income	$49,630	$45,831	$42,582
1987 estimated median hh income	$31,674	$32,476	$31,145
1987 estimated per capita income	$29,838	$26,211	$23,242

Description	1.0-mile radius	2.0-mile radius	3.0-mile radius
Population by sex	11,903	51,016	131,966
Male	48.36%	48.59%	49.44%
Female	51.64%	51.41%	50.56%
Population by age	11,903	51,016	131,966
Under 5 years	2.48%	3.54%	4.30%
5–9 years	2.49%	3.10%	3.64%
10–14 years	2.50%	3.21%	3.60%
15–19 years	3.84%	4.51%	5.12%
20–24 years	12.23%	14.09%	14.85%
25–29 years	16.22%	17.11%	17.04%
30–34 years	11.14%	11.21%	10.94%
35–44 years	12.24%	12.09%	11.57%
45–54 years	10.62%	10.00%	9.20%
55–59 years	5.85%	5.35%	4.90%
60–64 years	5.39%	4.42%	4.02%
65–74 years	8.41%	7.05%	6.67%
75 + years	6.61%	4.33%	4.15%
Median age	35.66	33.71	32.54
Average age	40.32	37.22	35.97
Female population by age under 5 years	6,147	26,229	66,727
Under 5 years	2.47%	3.36%	4.18%
5–9 years	2.34%	2.96%	3.54%
10–14 years	2.21%	3.01%	3.45%
15–19 years	3.56%	4.41%	5.12%
20–24 years	11.95%	14.17%	14.78%
25–29 years	14.82%	15.94%	15.58%
30–34 years	10.30%	10.49%	9.92%
35–44 years	10.66%	10.82%	10.57%
45–54 years	10.39%	10.02%	9.35%
55–59 years	6.44%	5.82%	5.36%
60–64 years	6.06%	4.90%	4.51%
65–74 years	9.82%	8.28%	7.97%
75 + years	8.98%	5.81%	5.68%
Female median age	34.02	32.88	31.85
Female average age	42.44	38.78	37.59
Population by household type	11,903	51,016	131,966
Family households	55.65%	60.02%	62.92%
Nonfamily households	44.33%	39.87%	36.39%
Group quarters	0.02%	0.11%	0.70%
Hispanic population by race	1,210	4,414	13,391
White	61.65%	61.79%	67.10%
Black	0.59%	0.83%	0.88%
American Indian and Asian	0.51%	1.01%	1.07%
Other race	37.25%	36.37%	30.95%
Hispanic population by type	11,903	51,016	131,966
Not of Hispanic origin	89.83%	91.35%	89.85%
Mexican	7.62%	6.09%	7.51%
Puerto Rican	0.14%	0.19%	0.19%
Cuban	0.43%	0.35%	0.41%
Other Spanish	1.97%	2.03%	2.04%

Description	1.0-mile radius	2.0-mile radius	3.0-mile radius
Marital status of males 15 +	5,300	22,207	57,465
Single	40.00%	39.07%	39.25%
Married	43.28%	44.66%	45.23%
Separated	2.39%	2.40%	2.46%
Widowed	1.85%	1.52%	1.56%
Divorced	12.47%	12.35%	11.51%
Marital status of females 15 +	5,715	23,783	59,275
Single	29.93%	30.36%	29.16%
Married	38.03%	40.41%	42.60%
Separated	2.01%	2.11%	2.27%
Widowed	14.41%	11.28%	11.14%
Divorced	15.62%	15.84%	14.84%
Persons in unit	7,069	28,582	70,207
1-person units	54.16%	49.77%	46.68%
2-person units	32.38%	33.66%	34.29%
3-person units	7.58%	9.18%	10.11%
4-person units	3.88%	4.82%	5.57%
5-person units	1.26%	1.62%	2.08%
Over-6–person units	0.73%	0.96%	1.27%
Persons in renter units	4,795	18,060	45,367
1-person units	63.24%	58.49%	55.33%
2-person units	28.12%	29.93%	30.85%
3-person units	5.43%	7.36%	8.32%
4-person units	2.15%	2.70%	3.25%
5-person units	0.56%	0.81%	1.21%
Over-6–person units	0.50%	0.72%	1.03%
Households by type	7,069	28,582	70,207
Single male	23.63%	22.58%	22.37%
Single female	30.53%	27.19%	24.30%
Married couple	29.83%	32.59%	34.80%
Other family—male head	2.13%	2.26%	2.37%
Other family—female head	4.48%	5.52%	6.14%
Nonfamily—male head	5.79%	5.96%	6.23%
Nonfamily—female head	3.60%	3.91%	3.78%
Households with children 0–18	692	3,858	11,221
Married-couple family	70.48%	70.70%	72.07%
Other family—male head	7.16%	5.93%	5.07%
Other family—female head	19.00%	21.07%	20.82%
Nonfamily	3.36%	2.29%	2.04%
1980 owner-occupied property values	1,341	6,158	16,924
Under $25,000	0.70%	1.32%	2.17%
$25,000–$39,999	1.23%	2.73%	4.03%
$40,000–$49,999	2.57%	4.07%	5.30%
$50,000–$79,999	12.82%	20.76%	26.06%
$80,000–$99,999	10.94%	11.59%	13.13%
$100,000–$149,000	29.08%	19.90%	19.05%
$150,000–$199,999	16.46%	12.70%	9.65%
$200,000 +	26.20%	26.92%	20.61%
1980 median property value	$143,913	$134,301	$117,344

Description	1.0-mile radius	2.0-mile radius	3.0-mile radius
Population by urban vs. rural	11,903	51,016	131,966
Urban	100.00%	100.00%	100.00%
Rural	0.00%	0.00%	0.00%
Population enrolled in school	1,673	8,518	23,977
Nursery school	4.50%	5.93%	5.63%
Kindergarten and elementary (1–8)	30.90%	34.15%	36.30%
High school (9–12)	15.74%	16.77%	16.76%
College	48.86%	43.14%	41.30%
Population 25 + by education level	9,145	36,576	90,438
Elementary (0–8)	4.90%	4.35%	5.49%
Some high school (9–11)	5.10%	5.80%	7.17%
High school graduate (12)	17.45%	17.68%	19.84%
Some college (13–15)	26.99%	25.70%	24.26%
College graduate (16 +)	45.57%	46.47%	43.24%
Population 16 + by occupation	8,178	34,283	85,700
Executive and managerial	20.54%	21.17%	18.71%
Professional specialty	21.81%	20.87%	19.88%
Technical support	3.45%	4.50%	4.71%
Sales	17.19%	15.25%	14.46%
Administrative support	18.18%	20.05%	20.14%
Service: private household	0.46%	0.48%	0.53%
Service: protective	0.40%	0.66%	0.85%
Service: other	8.86%	5.97%	6.34%
Farming, forestry, and fishing	0.61%	0.54%	0.60%
Precision production and craft	4.42%	5.84%	7.55%
Machine operator	1.37%	1.77%	2.79%
Transportation and material moving	1.53%	1.62%	1.89%
Laborers	1.18%	1.28%	1.56%
Males 16 + with children 0–18	606	3,537	10,359
Working with child under 6	18.11%	20.40%	22.73%
Not working with child under 6	27.41%	25.92%	25.88%
Working with child 6–18 only	28.02%	31.05%	31.94%
Not working with child 6–18 only	26.46%	22.63%	19.45%
Households by number of vehicles	7,072	28,589	70,159
No vehicles	5.27%	4.64%	5.50%
1 vehicle	57.50%	54.50%	53.40%
2 vehicles	28.26%	31.03%	30.61%
3 + vehicles	8.97%	9.82%	10.48%
Population by travel time to work	7,919	33,588	83,348
Under 5 minutes	4.61%	3.52%	3.07%
5–9 minutes	13.94%	11.56%	10.44%
10–14 minutes	18.89%	16.35%	15.51%
15–19 minutes	17.84%	19.74%	20.20%
20–29 minutes	25.60%	24.60%	24.96%
30–44 minutes	14.22%	18.11%	18.77%
45–59 minutes	3.16%	3.72%	4.34%
60 + minutes	1.73%	2.40%	2.71%
Average travel time in minutes	18.37	19.89	20.55

Description	1.0-mile radius	2.0-mile radius	3.0-mile radius
Population by transportation to work	8,104	33,835	84,342
Drive alone	70.94%	74.64%	73.18%
Car pool	15.63%	14.73%	15.80%
Public transportation	2.08%	3.24%	3.89%
Walk only	8.17%	4.45%	4.18%
Other means	0.80%	1.15%	1.23%
Work at home	2.38%	1.78%	1.71%
Housing units by year built	8,170	32,937	79,705
Built 1979–March 1980	1.46%	6.15%	3.98%
Built 1975–78	4.65%	9.70%	11.90%
Built 1970–74	13.78%	19.67%	20.20%
Built 1960–69	43.98%	34.19%	31.43%
Built 1950–59	26.85%	19.91%	17.31%
Built 1940–49	8.82%	7.84%	9.46%
Built 1939 or earlier	0.47%	2.54%	5.72%
1980 households by 1979 incomes	7,107	28,662	70,270
$75,000 +	8.99%	7.59%	6.27%
$50,000–$74,999	7.00%	6.65%	6.09%
$40,000–$49,999	5.83%	6.04%	5.62%
$35,000–$39,999	3.16%	4.00%	4.18%
$30,000–$34,999	5.24%	6.33%	6.39%
$25,000–$29,999	9.88%	9.16%	8.57%
$20,000–$24,999	13.29%	12.47%	12.00%
$15,000–$19,999	15.79%	15.39%	15.06%
$10,000–$14,999	15.93%	15.47%	16.64%
$7,500–$9,999	5.43%	5.75%	6.57%
$5,000–$7,499	4.50%	4.38%	5.27%
Under $5,000	4.96%	6.78%	7.35%
1979 average household income	$35,043	$32,841	$30,383
1979 median household income	$21,477	$22,606	$21,735
1980 families by 1979 incomes	2,599	11,681	30,624
$75,000 +	19.18%	15.30%	12.08%
$50,000–$74,999	11.70%	11.46%	10.21%
$40,000–$49,999	7.79%	9.06%	8.80%
$35,000–$39,999	4.73%	5.44%	5.95%
$30,000–$34,999	5.29%	8.30%	8.68%
$25,000–$29,999	11.59%	9.63%	9.36%
$20,000–$24,999	13.08%	11.75%	12.01%
$15,000–$19,999	8.99%	9.39%	11.08%
$10,000–$14,999	9.37%	9.19%	9.90%
$7,500–$9,999	2.73%	3.21%	3.94%
$5,000–$7,499	3.22%	2.92%	3.30%
Under $5,000	2.33%	4.35%	4.69%
1979 average family income	$55,215	$48,788	$43,630
1979 median family income	$33,315	$34,713	$32,142

Source: National Decision Systems. Reprinted with permission.

4
Sales Forecasting and Store-Assessment Methods

Forecasting the sales and profitability of retail outlets is an essential part of store-location research. Sales forecasts are necessary for assessing the potential and performance of existing stores, projecting the future performance of these stores, and predicting the viability of new outlets. Sales forecasts are also useful in evaluating the impact of store closure or relocation. In the previous chapter, we examined techniques of market analysis to assess the relative attractiveness of market areas for retail expansion. This chapter and the next one focus on methods for forecasting sales of individual outlets in a market area. A variety of procedures—ranging from simple rules of thumb to computerized simulation models—have been proposed for this purpose. The intent of these two chapters is to discuss and evaluate these methods and illustrate their application in a variety of situations.

The discussion of sales forecasting methods is organized into four sections. First, we describe three simple methods: the *space-sales ratio method,* the *proximal area method,* and *Reilly's law of retail gravitation.* To forecast sales, these methods use simple normative rules or subjective judgments to estimate the geographic area from which the outlets draw their customers and the served population. Although more sophisticated methods are now available, in certain situations these relatively simple methods are quite appropriate. They are often used in practice.

The next section focuses on the *analog* procedure popularized by Applebaum. (See, for example, Applebaum 1966, 1968.) The major difference between the analog method and the procedures discussed in the previous section is its use of customer surveys to determine the geographic pattern of trade areas. Rather than relying on a priori assumptions regarding consumer travel patterns, actual travel patterns are analyzed using "customer spotting." The analog procedure, now refined and extended by many researchers (see, for example, Rogers and Green 1979), is used extensively by retail firms.

The third type of forecasting systems are those that use *multiple regression techniques.* Regression-based forecasting systems develop a statistical relationship between store performance and various site and trade area characteristics that are expected to influence sales. Regression analysis identifies the factors that are significantly related to sales and provides a quantitative estimate of the relative impact of each factor. Based on this quantitative relationship, the expected performance of existing and new outlets can be forecast. Regression analysis does, however, require access to computers and the creation of a relatively large data base of information on existing stores. The method is widely used by chain stores.

The final type of forecasting methods is the *spatial-interaction model.* In general, spatial-interaction models attempt to predict the spatial pattern of consumer travel by analyzing past store choices of consumers. An understanding of the determinants of consumer travel patterns allows the location analyst to forecast the market shares of competing stores and simulate the impact of changes in the retail environment on outlet performance. The use of empirical spatial-interaction models for forecasting retail market shares was first suggested by Huff (1964). The method has since been refined and improved and is widely used by a variety of retail firms.

The first three types of forecasting procedures are discussed in this chapter. In the next chapter, we describe in depth the use of spatial-interaction models. In each case, we discuss the principles underlying the method, the steps necessary to implement it, the relative strengths and weaknesses of the approach, and the questions that typically arise in implementation. Examples of their application in a number of different retailing contexts are also presented.

The Concept of Trade Areas

The accuracy of retail sales forecasts depends to a large extent on the accuracy with which the trade area of the outlet can be estimated. The trade area is the geographic area from which the store draws most of its customers and within which market penetration is highest. In forecasting the sales of a retail outlet, it is necessary to first define the spatial extent of the trade area and then to determine the store's likely level of market penetration within that area. Since the concept of trade areas is critical to retail-sales–forecasting models, we discuss some general features of trade areas prior to describing the different forecasting methods.

The trade area, as noted earlier, is a geographic concept defining the area from which a store's sales originate. The size of a store's trade area depends on a variety of factors. These include a facility's type, size, and attractiveness; the varieties and prices of merchandise and services offered; the characteristics of customers in the area; and the location of competitive outlets. Even for a particular type of store, trade areas may vary greatly in size depending on the geographic environment in which the store is located. The trade area size of a supermarket, for example, depends on whether the outlet is located in a rural or urban area. In highly urbanized areas, where consumers often walk to grocery stores and the level of competition is very high, supermarket trade areas may be less than a half-mile in radius. In rural areas, on the other hand, supermarket trade areas usually extend much farther, because of the lower density of population and the lower level of competition.

Trade areas of shopping centers, of course, are much larger in size than supermarket trade areas. Consumers are willing to travel farther to visit shopping centers and there are fewer alternatives to choose from. In general, the less frequently a good or service is purchased, the greater the distance consumers are willing to travel to procure it. Economic geographers refer to this distance as the "range" of a good or service. The range is a theoretical construct defining the maximum distance consumers are willing to travel to purchase a good or service. In addition to the frequency of purchase, the range also depends on consumers' incomes and their access to transportation. In general, the higher the level of consumer mobility, the greater is the range.

The range of a good defines the maximum extent of the geographic trade area of a store selling that type of good. The distance that consumers actually travel may be much less due to the availability of alternative sources of supply. The higher the density of alternative sources of supply, the greater is the accessibility to retail outlets. Consequently, the distance consumers actually travel to procure a good decreases as the number of stores in the area offering that good increases. The number of alternative outlets that can profitably offer the same good or service in an area, on the other hand, depends on the density of population and purchasing power. Thus, the density of outlets in an area increases as the density of population and purchasing power rises. The geographic extent of the actual trade area of an outlet will tend to be smaller in highly populated areas, since consumers usually have more alternatives to choose from.

While the range and the density of alternatives determine the size of the trade area on the average, the trade area of a particular store in an area depends on the relative attractiveness of that store compared to other stores in its vicinity. The attractiveness of a store results from a number of factors, including its size (which is often a surrogate for the breadth and assortment of goods carried), its relative prices, and consumer perceptions of quality of merchandise and service. The greater the attractiveness of the store, the farther consumers are willing to travel to patronize it and, hence, the greater the size of its trade area.

Trade areas are not static, but change through time in response to changes in marketing strategy, prices, store size, and competition. A price reduction, for example, extends the scope of the trade area by attracting customers from a greater distance. Consumers are willing to travel farther to purchase goods at a lower price. Increases in the size of the store, level of service, and variety of assortments offered may have similar effects on the size of the trade area. Trade area size may also expand with advertising and promotion. Since expanding trade areas is one way for a retailer to increase the store's customer base and, thus, increase its revenues, it is important to understand how trade areas evolve and how and why they change.

Trade-area estimation is central to retail sales forecasting. A variety of retail forecasting methods have been proposed in the literature. Each method uses a different approach to estimate the trade area of the store. Some rely solely on the analyst's judgment, while others survey consumer travel patterns to determine the size of the trade area. The application of retail forecasting procedures is now discussed.

Subjective and Normative Approaches

Space-Sales Ratio Method

The space-sales ratio method is perhaps the simplest approach to forecasting the sales of retail outlets. It works from the assumption that a store's share of retail sales in an area will be directly proportional to its share of the total selling space. There are three steps in implementing this method.

In the first step, the size of the trade area is estimated by the analyst based on past experience and subjective judgment. Typically, the trade area is visualized as a circular area around the store. The radius of the circle is equal to the distance consumers are expected to travel to patronize the outlet. Concentric circles of different radii are often used to examine the sensitivity of forecasts to different travel patterns.

In the second step, data on the total population residing in the trade area must be combined with information on per capita sales to gauge potential sales for that retail category. The necessary data are available from secondary sources. As illustrated in appendix 3–1, a number of commercial firms maintain geocoded data bases allowing useful tabulations of census data around a location defined by the analyst. Per capita sales data are also available from these same sources or from the U.S. Dept. of Labor's Bureau of Labor Statistics.

In the final step, which involves estimating the potential for a particular outlet, the size of the outlet relative to total retail space in the area is first measured. The analyst then forecasts the sales of the new outlet based on the assumption that the outlet's market share will equal its share of total retail space in the area. For example, if a department store has 20 percent of the total department store selling space in the area, one-fifth of the potential department store sales in the area will be allocated to that outlet.

Because of the ease with which it can be implemented, the space-sales ratio method is one of the simplest ways to forecast sales of new outlets. The method, however, relies critically on the analyst's ability to define the trade area radius correctly. The trade area sizes of similar stores may vary considerably from one geographic area to another and may be difficult to predict without conducting a study of consumer travel patterns. For this reason, the method is typically used to predict sales of outlets in small and intermediate-sized towns, where the trade area boundary often corresponds with the boundary of the town and is therefore easy to predict.

Another drawback of this method is the assumption that market share equals the share of space. This ignores the variations in abilities of store managers, merchandising techniques, and store image among retail outlets. As a result, the forecasts should be adjusted to reflect the store's expected competitive position. If, for example, a particular chain consistently achieves a greater than average sales per square foot, the projections for outlets belonging to that chain should be adjusted upward.

Proximal Area Method

The proximal area method is another relatively simple procedure for forecasting sales of retail outlets. The assumption underlying the proximal area method is that when consumers are faced with making a choice among similar outlets, they select the one nearest to them. This is the *nearest-center hypothesis* of classical central-place theory (Christaller 1935; Losch 1954). Thus, in this method, the trade area of an outlet is found simply by demarcating the geographic area that is closer to this outlet than any other. Called the "proximal area," it represents the geographic area within which the outlet has a spatial advantage over its competitors. Consumers residing within an outlet's proximal area are closer to that store than any other. After determining the proximal area, the analyst can forecast sales by analyzing the characteristics of the population residing within the proximal area and surveying their buying habits—procedure similar to that discussed earlier.

The first step in demarcating proximal areas is to construct Thiessen or Dirichlet polygons (Dirichlet 1850; Thiessen and Alter 1911). The polygon corresponding to each store defines the area closer to that store than any other neighboring store. Thiessen polygons can be drawn by following some simple geometric steps. (See figure 4–1). First, the location of each existing facility is designated on a map of the region (figure 4–1a). Second, lines are drawn joining each facility to the ones neighboring it. Next, the perpendicular bisector of each of these lines is drawn by finding the midpoint of each line (figure 4–1b) and then drawing a line perpendicular to the original one at that point. The final step is to join each perpendicular bisector to its adjacent bisectors to complete the Thiessen polygons. (See figure 4–1c.) The

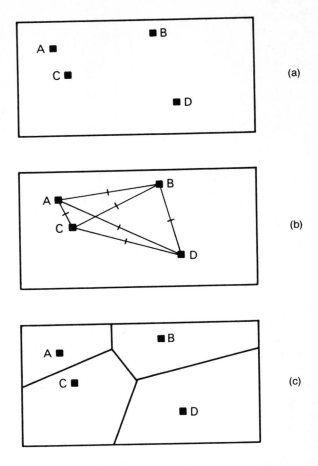

Figure 4-1. Steps in Determining Proximal Areas

area enclosed by each Thiessen polygon represents the trade area of the facility enclosed in the polygon.

The proximal area maps in figure 4–1c can be used in a number of different ways. First of all, Thiessen polygons provide a simple, straightforward way to forecast revenues of facilities at different sites. As in the space-sales ratio method, this is done by subdividing the proximal area into smaller subareas and calculating the retail potential of each subarea. The potential sales of the outlet is determined by summing the retail potentials of the subareas contained within the proximal area. The entire system of creating Thiessen polygons and calculating retail potentials can easily be computerized. Computerized systems are helpful when there are a large number of outlets in the area.

Proximal area maps are also useful for identifying sites for new outlets. The geometric pattern of the proximal areas highlights understored areas and indicates regions for future expansion. In general, the size of the Thiessen polygon is inversely related to the level of competition—the greater the number of stores in an area, the smaller the sizes of the polygons. In contrast, large-sized polygons reflect low levels of competition and are indicative of areas attractive for locating new outlets. A scrutiny of the proximal area map can also help identify sites that are maximally distant from existing outlets. Any site on the shared edge of two polygons is maximally distant from two existing outlets, while one at a vertex of a polygon is maximally separated from the three closest neighbors. Locations near these interstitial areas have a spatial advantage because they are far away from competing outlets, which makes the sites good candidates for locating new stores.

Proximal areas also can be used to predict the sales of stores at new locations in order to determine the viability of a new outlet. To forecast sales, the location of the proposed site of the new store is designated on the map and its proximal area is found by drawing the Thiessen polygon for the new site. The sales potential of the new site can be calculated by aggregating the retail potential within the proximal area in a manner similar to that described for the space-sales ratio method. The expected sales at the site are equal to this potential. The sales forecast can then be compared to the expected costs of opening and operating the store to provide an estimate of expected profits. Site-selection procedures based on proximal areas are described in chapter 6.

Because of its reliance on the assumption of nearest-center patronage, the proximal area method is best suited for forecasting sales for retail categories in which outlets are similar in size and attractiveness and sell undifferentiated products, and when geographic accessibility is an important determinant of store choice. Convenience stores, emergency medical centers, branch banks, automatic teller machines, liquor stores, dry cleaning services, copy centers, and drug stores are examples of services whose trade areas can be estimated quite accurately by this procedure.

Even in situations where consumers do not always patronize the closest outlet, constructing proximal areas is a useful exercise. The map of proximal areas gives a quick birds-eye view of the network of existing facilities and their trade areas within the entire market region. In this way, the degree of market coverage, as well as areas of saturation or opportunity, can be easily ascertained. With most other methods of trade area estimation, it is difficult to obtain an integrated pictorial representation of the trade areas of all stores in the region. Although the estimated trade areas may only be approximate, the proximal area map provides a broad view of the spatial pattern of outlet locations and trade areas in the region.

Reilly's Law of Retail Gravitation

Although distance has an important influence on consumer travel patterns, the assumption that consumers always visit the nearest outlet may not be reasonable in many situations. When the characteristics of stores providing the same kinds of goods and services vary, as they most often do in practice, consumers are likely to bypass the closest facility if the extra effort of travel is compensated by better shopping opportunities. One reason for travelling further may simply be to obtain a better price. If the price of a good varies across alternative outlets, it is logical for the consumer to visit the store that offers the lowest real price—that is, the price at the store plus transportation costs. Even when prices are similar, consumers may bypass the closest store to patronize outlets with better goods, larger assortments, or a better image. Moreover, due to opportunities for multipurpose and comparison shopping, a store in proximity to other shopping opportunities may be more attractive than a similar store in an isolated site.

The notion that agglomeration tends to increase the attractiveness of stores is key to Reilly's "law" of retail gravitation (Reilly 1931). The focus of Reilly's law is the intermetropolitan trading area boundaries between neighboring cities in a region, rather than the trade area boundaries of individual stores. Based on an analogy to the Newtonian law of planetary attraction, the law argues that the proportion of retail trade attracted from intermediate towns by two competing urban areas is in direct proportion to their populations and in inverse proportion to the square of the distances from those cities to the intermediate towns. This can be expressed mathematically as:

$$\frac{R(A)}{R(B)} = \frac{P(A)}{P(B)} \left[\frac{D(B)}{D(A)} \right]^2 \tag{4.1}$$

where $R(A)$ and $R(B)$ are the proportions of retail trade from the intermediate town attracted by cities A and B, respectively; $P(A)$ and $P(B)$ are the populations of the two cities; and $D(A)$ and $D(B)$ are the distances from the intermediate town to the two cities. Equation 4.1 expresses the relative powers of the two cities to attract shoppers from the neighboring rural areas. It can, therefore, be used to estimate the relative retail potentials of the two cities.

To demarcate trade area boundaries, Reilly's law is often expressed as the "breaking-point" formula popularized by Converse (1949). As illustrated in figure 4–2 the breaking point is the point between two cities A and B such that all consumers to the left of the point patronize retail facilities in one city and all consumers to the right patronize facilities in the other. If the nearest-center principle was being used, the breaking point would simply be halfway between the two cities. However, according to Reilly's law, the breaking

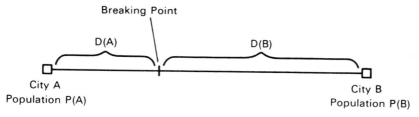

$D(A)$ = distance from city A to breaking point.
$D(B)$ = distance from city B to breaking point.

Figure 4-2. Illustration of Breaking-Point Formula

point is where the relative attractiveness of the two cities are equal. Starting from equation 4.1, the breaking point can be defined as follows (see figure 4–2):

$$\frac{\text{distance from breaking point}}{\text{to city } B} = \frac{\text{distance between cities } A \text{ and } B}{1 + \sqrt{\dfrac{P(A)}{P(B)}}} \quad (4.2)$$

Equation 4.2 thus defines the boundary between the two towns' trade areas according to Reilly's law. In delineating the entire trading zone of a city, the breaking point between the city and its neighbors in all directions must be found as illustrated in figure 4–3. Once the trading area has been demarcated, the retail potential within the area can be easily calculated.

A number of empirical studies have used Reilly's law to define the trade areas of urban centers. Reilly himself conducted extensive field studies of intermetropolitan trade areas (Reilly 1931). The results generally supported his hypothesis that customers between two cities gravitate toward the larger one in a manner similar to that postulated by his law. Reilly did find, however, that the exponent on distance was not the same for each pair of cities. He chose the squared exponent since it represented an average value and because of its similarity to the Newtonian gravitational formula. Converse (1949) conducted detailed studies to verify Reilly's law for a number of urban centers in Illinois. He validated the theoretical predictions of Reilly's law with information collected from shopper surveys. Converse's results, too, generally supported Reilly's predictions—especially when estimating the trade area boundary between a large urban center and its intermediate-sized neighbors. The predictive power of the formula seemed to decline when the competing centers were approximately of equal size. A similar study by Douglas (1949) applied Reilly's formula and four alternative methods to define the trading area of Charlotte, North Carolina. The study concluded that Reilly's formula was quite accurate in defining the city's trade area.

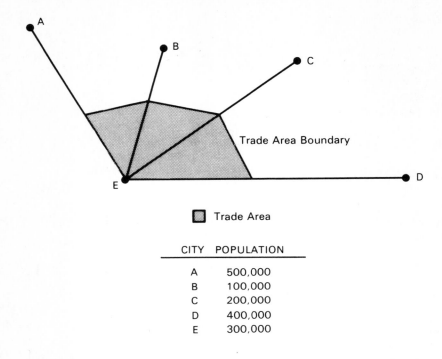

CITY	POPULATION
A	500,000
B	100,000
C	200,000
D	400,000
E	300,000

Figure 4-3. Estimating a Trade Area by the Breaking-Point Method

The three forecasting methods described in this section—space-sales ratio, proximal area, and Reilly's formula—are all easy to implement and provide forecasts of reasonable, but usually unknown, accuracy. They are particularly useful when detailed customer-patronage data and data on past performance of existing outlets are not available or when collecting the data is deemed to be too costly or time-consuming. The fact that such information is not used, however, is at the same time a major drawback of these methods and makes them inappropriate in many situations. Information on consumer patronage and past performance of existing stores should be incorporated in sales forecasting methods whenever possible because it is essential for judging the accuracy and validity of model predictions. This is the point of departure for the analog and regression procedures discussed later in this chapter and spatial-interaction models discussed in the next chapter. These methods use surveys of consumer travel patterns or data on past performance of stores as inputs for the forecasting system.

Analog Method

Popularized by William Applebaum, the analog method is one of the most common procedures for retail sales forecasting. To forecast sales, the analog approach uses an existing store or a sample of stores to serve as analogs. The sales performance of these analog stores is assessed from customer surveys usually referred to as "customer spotting." The level of market penetration or per capita sales achieved by these stores is used as the basis for forecasting sales at the new site. The analog procedure was the first systematic retail forecasting system based on empirical data. It is useful not only for determining market penetration and trade area boundaries, but also for forecasting sales at new sites and planning advertising and promotion strategies for existing stores.

The most important step in applying the analog forecasting system is to identify retail outlets that are similar or analogous to the proposed facility. The facilities should be similar in terms of store characteristics, customer shopping patterns, socioeconomic and demographic characteristics of the customers, and the level of competition within their trade areas. Once the analog stores have been chosen, a sample of customers from each analog store is surveyed to determine their geographic origin, demographic characteristics, and spending habits. Customer spotting usually involves in-store intercept interviews with randomly chosen customers. In some applications, the information is obtained from customer checks and store credit card applications. Although the latter procedure reduces the cost of data collection, the data should be used with considerable caution since the resulting sample may not be representative of the store's overall customer base.

To determine the size of each analog store's trade area, the geographic origin of each sampled customer is plotted on a map. This is often done manually by locating on a detailed map the street address of each such customer. A computerized digitizing system can speed up this rather tedious process by creating a data base of the coordinates corresponding to each address. The coordinates can then be used as inputs to mapping software. The greater availability of address-matching software and data bases such as the US Census BGF/DIME files (U.S. Department of Commerce 1980)—which is now available for most metropolitan areas in the United States—and the TIGER system (Marx 1983) reduces the time needed to create customer-origin maps and makes them more accurate.

After constructing the map of customer origins, the trade area of the store can be determined by inspecting the map. Concentric circles representing different distances from the store are drawn on the map using the location of the analog store as the center. (See figure 4–4.) The pattern of customer

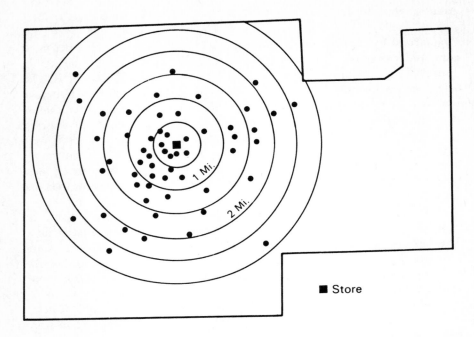

Figure 4-4. Example of a Customer-Spotting Map

origins and the relationship between the level of market penetration and distance can be seen from the map. Market penetration patterns usually demonstrate a distinct geographic pattern in which the inner circles (the areas closest to the outlet) account for the largest proportion of customers, with the density of customers decreasing as one moves away from the outlet. Called the "distance-decay effect," this reflects the impact of geographic accessibility on store patronage. To define the trade area of the outlet, the cumulative proportion of customers in each zone is calculated starting from the innermost zone. The circle containing 75 to 80 percent of the customers is used to demarcate the spatial extent of the trade area of the outlet. In figure 4–4, the radii of the circles are incremented by one-half mile and the circle with radius of two miles is used to demarcate the trade area since it contains about 80 percent of the consumers. The actual size of the trade area will, of course, vary from one situation to another depending on the type of store being studied. The sharper the distance-decay effect, the smaller the trade area.

Based on the map of customer origins and information on customer spending patterns, the market share and per capita sales of the analog store in each distance zone can be calculated as shown in table 4–1. The spatial pat-

Table 4–1
Market Penetration of Stores Using Analog Forecasting System

Radius (miles)	Percentage of Customers	Cumulative Drawing Power	Weekly Sales	Population	Per Capita Sales
0–0.5	38%	38%	$15,200	3,800	$4.00
0.5–1.0	24	62	19,440	8,100	2.40
1.0–1.5	14	76	29,312	22,900	1.28
1.5–2.0	6	82	25,116	32,200	.78
2.0 +	18	100			

tern of actual sales is obtained from the survey and the potential in each circular zone is calculated from secondary sources. To forecast sales at a new site, the analog procedure assumes that the market penetration level of the new store will follow the same general pattern as that of the analog stores. The different steps used to arrive at the forecast are shown in table 4–2. First, concentric circles are drawn around the new site, as done for the analog store. Next, the population residing within each distance zone is found from secondary sources. Then, the expected sales from each zone are calculated by multiplying the population size of each zone by the corresponding per capita sales achieved by the analog store. Total sales at the site are then estimated by aggregating the expected sales from each distance zone. For the illustration in table 4–2, this results in projected weekly sales of $120,174. As shown, however, this forecast is adjusted because of the greater level of competition at this site compared to the site of the analog store.

The basic procedure for analog forecasting illustrated in table 4–2 can be extended in a number of ways. First, instead of relying on only one analog store, patronage patterns from a number of similar stores can be obtained and an average sales-performance level calculated for each distance zone.

Table 4–2
Weekly Sales Projection for Location X Using Analog Forecasting System

Radius (miles)	Population	Per Capita Sales	Total Sales
0–0.5	4,900	$4.00	$19,600
0.5–1.0	11,800	2.40	28,320
1.0–1.5	24,000	1.28	30,720
1.5–2.0	35,300	0.78	27,534
2.0 +			14,000
Total weekly sales			120,174
Adjusted weekly sales			110,000

This reduces the possibility of bias in the forecasts due to the idiosyncratic characteristics of a single store. Second, to forecast the relationship between distance and per capita sales, the circular zones can be subdivided into smaller areas to account for differences in drawing power within the zone. The drawing power within the zone may vary due to topography, population density, and the location of competing outlets. Subdividing the zone into smaller areas helps to account for such directional biases.

In addition to its use in forecasting sales, customer spotting also helps in determining advertising and promotional strategies of existing stores. The customer origin map exhibits the spatial pattern of customer patronage. This pattern is a reflection of local market conditions, topography, and, most importantly, the relative competitive strength of the outlet. The spatial variation in per capita sales reflects the differential drawing power of the outlet in different areas. An understanding of this pattern provides valuable insights into promotional strategies. Areas with low market penetration, for example, could be specifically targeted for free-trial coupons and special promotional campaigns. Areas with high market penetration, on the other hand, may require different kinds of promotion to reinforce patronage or increase usage rates. The effectiveness of promotional campaigns is increased significantly by analyzing the spatial pattern of patronage.

Although the analog procedures is easy to implement and is based on information on actual shopping patterns, the forecasts often need to be adjusted to reflect any unique condition in the area surrounding the new store. As Applebaum notes, the analog procedure "depends partly on quantified experience and partly on subjective judgment" (1966, p. 134). Considerable judgment is required in selecting the appropriate analog stores. Even when the analog store is chosen with care, the sales forecasts should be adjusted to reflect any difference between the analog store and the new outlet. The new store, for example, may have more aggressive competitors or may differ in store characteristics, image, or managerial expertise. Although the subjective judgments of the analyst are important and should not be ignored, the analytical base of the analog procedure can be strengthened by developing a quantitative relationship between a store's market share and situational and site characteristics and market factors.

Regression Models of Retail Performance

The forecasting systems discussed so far are all relatively easy to implement. They do, however, ignore the complex array of factors that might affect the performance of retail outlets. A more rigorous approach is the use of regression models to determine the factors that influence the performance of retail outlets at particular sites. The advantage of regression models is that they allow the systematic consideration of trade area characteristics, site variables, store characteristics, and measures of competition in a single framework. Further, regression models provide a quantitative measure of the relative impact of these variables on store performance. Because the application of regression models requires information from a large number of existing stores, the method is most popular with retail chains that operate many outlets.

The development of regression models is based on two assumptions: (1) that the performance of a store is significantly affected by the location characteristics of the site, socioeconomic composition of the trade area, level of competition, and store characteristics and (2) that these underlying factors can be isolated by systematic analysis. In general, the regression model can be written as follows:

$$Y = b_0 + b_1 x_1 + b_2 x_2 + \ldots + b_n x_n$$

where Y (the dependent variable) is some measure of the performance of a store (usually sales or profitability), and the xs (independent variables) are measures of factors hypothesized to influence store performance. The parameter b_0 is the intercept term and $b_1, b_2 \ldots b_n$ are the regression coefficients corresponding to each independent variable. The regression coefficients measure the relative impact of each variable on performance.

There are two alternative approaches to implementing regression-based forecasting systems. A common procedure is to start with a large number of potential explanatory variables and then to use "stepwise" regression to identify the variables most highly related to performance. The stepwise regression procedure introduces the variables into the regression model based on a ranking of their ability to explain variations in the dependent variable. The alternative approach is to first select a small number of variables likely to be important in assessing retail performance. These variables are directly entered into the multiple regression model to measure their relative impact on store performance. The set of variables to be included can be ascertained from past studies or represent the analyst's judgment and management considerations. Principal component or factor analysis techniques can also be used to select the variables to be included in the regression model. These techniques identify the latent factors in a large set of possible explanatory variables. The reduced set of factors are then included in the regression analysis. These approaches are illustrated in the following sections.

A Branch Bank Example

A typical illustration of the use of regression models for analyzing retail outlet performance is the retail bank study reported by Olsen and Lord (1979).

The study analyzed the performance of branch offices of a retail bank in Charlotte, North Carolina. Two measures of performance were used in this study: daily checking deposits and daily savings account deposits made by individual account holders in each branch. To explain the variation in daily deposit levels among different branches, the authors initially chose the seven variables shown in table 4–3. The seven variables can be broadly viewed as representing trade area demographic characteristics, competitive conditions at each site, and the characteristics of each branch bank.

Purchasing power and median household income, which measure the potential for deposits and the attractiveness of the trade area, were expected to have a positive impact on deposit levels. To calculate purchasing power, the size of the trade area was first defined by surveying customer origins. The trade area of each branch was defined as the area within a 1.5-mile radius of the branch since most customers were found to reside within this distance of the branch they patronized. Purchasing power was calculated by multiplying the number of households in the area by the mean household income. Another trade area characteristic included in the analysis was the percentage of housing units that were renter-occupied. The authors hypothesized that a large number of renters in the area would have a negative effect on savings account deposits since this "might indicate a population whose age and stage in the family life cycle would not lead to large savings account deposits" (Olsen and Lord 1979, p. 105).

Two measures of site attractiveness were used in the model. The variable "employment level in area" measured the potential for attracting deposits from people who worked at establishments located near the branch office. Previous research had shown that many individuals opened bank accounts at branches near their place of employment. The second site variable was the

Table 4–3
Explanatory Variables Used in Branch-Bank Performance Model

Variables measuring trade area characteristics
  Purchasing power
  Median household income
  Percentage of housing units that are renter-occupied

Variables measuring site attractiveness
  Employment level in area
  Retail square footage

Variables measuring level of competition
  Number of competing banks' branches in area
  Trade area overlap with branch of same bank

Source: Adapted from L.M. Olsen and J.D. Lord, "Market Area Characteristics and Branch Bank Performance," *Journal of Bank Research* 10 (Summer 1979): 102–110. Reprinted with permission.

level of retailing activity in the vicinity of each branch, calculated as the square feet of retail space in the neighborhood. By measuring the accessibility of the site with respect to other retail activities, this variable served as a surrogate for the potential of multipurpose trips. Both the level of employment and retail activity in the area were expected to be positively correlated with checking and savings account deposit levels. A radius of 0.5 miles was used in measuring the levels of employment and retail space since it had been found that customers visiting a branch from their place of work or shopping usually travel short distances.

Two other independent variables were included to measure the level of competition and were, therefore, postulated to be negatively correlated with performance. The first was the number of competitor branches within a 1.0-mile radius of the site. The other measured competition from branches of the same bank. This was calculated as a binary variable which took the value of 1 if there was another branch of the same bank within a 1.5-mile radius of the branch. If there was no such branch within that radius, the variable was assigned a value of 0.

The authors then used a stepwise regression procedure to identify the variables that had the greatest impact on bank performance. Two of the seven variables were found to be significantly related to checking account deposits: the median household income of population within a 1.5-mile radius of a branch and the total retail square footage within a radius of 0.5 miles from the branch. These two variables together accounted for about 72 percent of the variation in the performance of individual branches. (See table 4–4.) The regression coefficients associated with these variables were statistically significant at the $p = .05$ level. As might be expected, median income and the size of retail floor space were both positively related to daily checking account deposits; that is, "the highest volume branches were located in areas where the population had above average incomes and where there was a lot of retailing activity nearby" (Olsen and Lord 1979, p. 107). The third variable shown in the table, the number of competing branches, had a negative impact on checking account deposits. Although the regression coefficient for this variable was not highly significant, the authors included it in the final model because of its intuitive appeal.

The regression coefficients show the numerical relationship between each variable and performance. They show the nature and the magnitude of the impact that each variable has on the performance measure. For example, the checking account model shows that a $100 increase in median income is estimated to raise daily deposits by about $1,271. Similarly, an increase of 1,000 square feet of retail space in the area is expected to increase deposits by $236. The presence of a competitive branch within a 1.0-mile radius of an existing branch, on the other hand, decreases daily deposits by about $8,689. Savings account deposits are affected by different factors. Each $100,000 increase in

Table 4–4
Results from Branch-Bank Performance Model

Variable	Regression Coefficient	t-Value	Cumulative R^2
Checking account deposits ($1,000):			
Median household income ($100)	1.2706*	3.26	.55
Retail square footage (1,000)	0.2365*	3.36	.72
Number of competing banks' branches	− 8.6889	1.37	.79
Savings account deposits ($1,000):			
Purchasing power ($1,000)	0.0021*	6.25	.57
Employment level	0.0375*	3.93	.77
Percentage of housing that is renter-occupied	− 1.2973*	2.00	.81

Source: L.M. Olsen and J.D. Lord, "Market Area Characteristics and Branch Bank Performance," *Journal of Bank Research* 10 (Summer 1979): 102–110. Reprinted with permission.
* Significant at $p = .05$.

purchasing power in the area increases deposits by $210; the creation of ten new jobs increases deposits by $37. On the other hand, a 1 percent increase in renter-occupied housing decreases deposits by $129.

The variables best explaining the variation in the level of savings account deposits were different from those related to checking accounts. As shown in table 4–4, purchasing power, employment level, and the percentage of housing that is renter-occupied were the three variables significantly related to savings account deposits. Purchasing power and employment level had positive impacts on savings account deposits. The level of renter-occupied housing in the vicinity of the branch, on the other hand, had the expected negative effect. The three variables together accounted for 81 percent of the variation in savings account deposits across the different branches of the bank.

The study demonstrates the typical steps in applying regression models for assessing retail outlet performance. The main objective of this type of analysis is to identify the salient characteristics that influence the performance of different outlets. As one might expect, performance of retail outlets is affected by trade area demographics, level of competition, and site attractiveness. The determinants of retail performance will vary from one type of outlet to another and also among outlets in different geographic regions. Moreover, various measures of sales performance often respond differently to key location factors, as evidenced by the variation between the checking account and savings account models in table 4–4. By isolating the key determinants of performance, regression models offer a valuable tool for analyzing the complex relationship between location factors and retail performance.

Uses of Regression Analysis

Regression analysis results can be used in a number of ways. First, they can be used to isolate the determinants of outlet performance. Since the performance of an individual outlet depends on a number of different factors, regression analysis helps the analyst to identify which factors have the greatest impact for a particular type of retail business as well as the nature and magnitude of each impact. Many empirical studies of retail performance using regression models have now been published. They encompass a variety of retail outlets including banks (e.g., Clawson 1974; Martin 1967; Lynge and Shin 1981; Olsen and Lord 1979), grocery stores (Cottrell 1973), clothing stores (Davies 1973), liquor stores (Lord and Lynds 1981), convenience stores (Hise et al. 1983; Jones and Mock 1984; Lee and Koutsopoulos 1977) and hospitals (Erickson and Finkler 1985). These provide valuable insights into the determinants of retail performance in a variety of contexts.

Although it is impossible to discuss here all the findings of these studies, certain general conclusions emerge from them. In almost all studies, performance is significantly affected by the size and demographic composition of an outlet's trade area population. This is very consistent with intuitive expectations and supports the basic premise of the trade area models discussed earlier. In addition, most studies show, as expected, a positive relationship between service factors (such as local promotion and advertising) and sales. Competition, on the other hand, seems to have a more complex influence on performance. While many of the regression studies confirm that the farther a store is from its competitor, the better its performance (Lord and Lynds 1981), other studies show higher performance levels among outlets with *more* competitors located nearby. A possible reason for this result is that the clustering of stores increases the potential for multipurpose and comparison shopping and, thus, attracts a larger number of customers. The implication is that stores in retail clusters perform better and have higher sales than stores in isolated sites. In general, the effect of competitive location on performance depends on the type of product, level of comparison and multipurpose shopping, and other factors affecting store patronage decisions.

In addition to providing insight into the effect of market factors on outlet performance, the estimated regression equations can also be used to forecast performance at new sites. This is done by determining the values of different explanatory variables in the model for the new site and substituting these values in the regression equation to predict the expected level of performance at the new site. The regression coefficients can also be used to simulate the likely impact on performance of existing stores, when any one or more of the variables are changed. Simulating the impact of potential changes in market factors or site characteristics on performance increases the firm's ability to deal with the uncertainties of the marketplace.

Yet another use of regression models is in calculating an expected level of performance for each existing outlet based on its size, trade area characteristics, and so forth. These values provide an indication of the level of performance each existing store ought to achieve given its location and market environment. Since the forecasts are based on historical performance as well the unique locational and market factors of each outlet, these predictions provide a yardstick against which actual performance can be compared. The difference between forecasted and actual performance shows the degree to which an outlet is performing better or worse than expected. This is especially useful to managers of chain stores, who can identify the strong and weak performers in the firm's network of outlets based on these differences.

Methodological Issues in the Application of Regression Analysis

Despite the useful insights regression models provide, many applications of regression analysis illustrate the difficulties in calibrating models of retail performance. Two types of problems are considered here: *Multicollinearity* and *heterogeneity in the types of stores* used to create the data base. Procedures for dealing with these problems are now discussed.

The Multicollinearity Problem. Multicollinearity arises when there are significant intercorrelations among the independent variables in the regression model. The statistical theory of regression analysis requires that the explanatory variables be independent of each other and uncorrelated. Many regression analyses of store performance, however, violate this assumption. The studies often use a large number of independent variables to determine store performance, and because many of these variables measure the same underlying phenomena, the variables tend to be intercorrelated. This means that multicollinearity is a significant problem in many studies. Multicollinearity leads to unreliable parameter estimates and severe problems of interpretation. This can undermine the entire purpose of the study by preventing the analyst from determining precisely how various factors affect performance.

Several factors can alert the researcher to the presence of multicollinearity. One signal is the statistical insignificance of the individual regression coefficients (b-values) despite a high degree of fit for the model as a whole (indicated by high R^2 or F statistics). A second sign of multicollinearity is when the values of the coefficients fluctuate widely depending on which independent variables are included in the model. In stepwise regression, for example, the sign or level of significance of a regression coefficient may change at different stages of the stepwise procedure. This, too, indicates the possibility of multicollinearity.

The situations just discussed are symptoms of multicollinearity, but they provide little guidance concerning the level and significance of the problem. Several diagnostic tests can be performed to check for the level of multicollinearity. A few simple procedures are described here. For further discussion, the reader should refer to statistics texts such as those by Johnston (1972) and Malinvaud (1980). Articles by Lord and Lynds (1981) and Alpert and Bibb (1974) discuss the problem of multicollinearity in retail models.

The simplest diagnostic test for multicollinearity is to examine the simple correlations between the independent variables. High correlation coefficients indicate the potential for multicollinearity. It is commonly suggested that correlations greater than .5 or .6 are high enough to reduce the validity of the regression results. Lower correlations, however, do not necessarily indicate the absence of multicollinearity. It is often the case that while no pair of independent variables is highly correlated, linear combinations of groups of variables are. One way to detect this is to examine the tolerance values. The tolerance of an independent variable equals 1 minus the multiple correlation between that variable and all other independent variables in the model. Thus, tolerance values close to zero indicate high levels of multicollinearity. Most computer packages for statistical analysis compute and print tolerance values in their regression subprograms.

Another way to test for multicollinearity is split-half analysis. The data set is randomly divided into two or more groups, and separate regression models are computed for each sample. If there is a significant multicollinearity problem, the results from the different samples will tend to be different in terms of their regression coefficients and goodness of fit. Similarity of results across the samples indicates that the analysis is not affected by multicollinearity.

If multicollinearity is detected, a number of steps can be taken to reduce its impact on the results. The most obvious step is to reduce the number of predictor variables by eliminating those that are the main sources of collinearity. This calls for careful screening of potential variables based on theoretical reasoning and judgment. When two independent variables are highly correlated with each other, eliminating one of them from the model often reduces the impact of multicollinearity. The simple correlations among the dependent variables can be studied to determine the variables to be eliminated. Another way of reducing the number of independent variables is to use factor analysis or principal component analysis, which allow the researcher to express the underlying structure of the data in a parsimonious manner. As Alpert and Bibb (1975) note, one can choose one or few highly loaded variables for each major factor and thus reduce the total number of predictor variables. While using a smaller set of dependent variables reduces the likelihood of multicollinearity, it does not eliminate the possibility altogether. Careful consideration must still be given to testing for multicollinearity and assessing its possible impact on the results.

A study by Erickson and Finkler (1985) demonstrates the use of factor analysis to reduce multicollinearity in retail forecasting models. The authors used a regression model to explain the variation in market shares among hospitals in southeastern Pennsylvania. On inspecting the simple correlations among the sixteen independent variables originally selected for the model, the authors found significantly high intercorrelations (correlations greater than 0.5). The authors then performed a factor analysis to investigate the pattern of these intercorrelations. Two of the independent variables (the number of physicians affiliated with the hospital and the proportion of affiliated physicians not affiliated with other hospitals) were not included in the factor analysis because theoretical reasons dictated their inclusion in the final model. The factor analysis revealed that eight of the remaining 14 variables had high loadings on a single factor. To mitigate the impact of multicollinearity, the authors combined these eight variables into a composite measure of the "profile" of each hospital. Thus, nine independent variables were used in the final regression model. Together, these nine variables explained more than 90 percent of the variation in market share among sixty-three hospitals included in the study.

Heterogeneity of Sample Stores. A second problem in applying regression analysis involves the heterogeneity of stores in the sample. Here, segmentation criteria are needed. When a large number of stores with significantly different market area characteristics are being considered in a regression study, the predictive ability of the model can be improved by classifying the outlets into homogeneous groups. Examples of such classification can be found, for example, in the works Jones and Mock (1984) and Davies (1973). In a study conducted for a convenience store chain, Jones and Mock classified the outlets into five groups based on their location: central-city locations, suburban locations, locations in old established strips, locations in the urban fringe, and nonmetropolitan locations. Separate regression models were calibrated for each group of stores to explain the weekly variation in sales. Because of the differences in the geographic environment, the factors related to sales performance of individual stores differed among the groups. Sales performance of outlets in the central city and nonmetropolitan sites, for example, was affected most by presence of apartments in the neighborhood and the level of pedestrian traffic. Sales of outlets in the remaining groups, on the other hand, were related most to the level of new housing developments.

The sales performance of stores can also be affected by the type of site in which the store is located. Davies (1973), for example, found significant differences in the variables affecting sales between clothing outlets located at corner sites and those located in the middle of a block. Results of the Davies study are shown in table 4–5. The table is divided into three sections. First, the regression result for the entire sample of seventy-two stores is shown. This is followed by the results for each subsample. As can be seen from the

Table 4–5
Impact of Store Classification on Regression Results

Variables	Cumulative R^2
All Stores	
Selling area	0.544
Rent	0.635
Distance to nearest car park	0.657
Number of branches	0.680
Store accessibility	0.712
Corner-site stores	
Floor area	0.650
Store accessibility	0.692
Number of branches	0.723
Urban growth rate	0.762
Distance to nearest car park	0.800
Intermediate-site stores	
Total urban retail expenditure	0.473
Store accessibility	0.649
Selling area	0.712
Floor area	0.738
Number of branches	0.761

Source: Adapted from R.L. Davies, "Evaluation of Retail Store Attributes and Sales Performance," *European Journal of Marketing* 7, no. 2 (1973): 89–102.

table, the factors related to sales at corner sites are quite different from those related to sales at outlets located in the middle of the block, although all the stores belong to the same retail firm. Only two of the top five explanatory variables in each model appear in the other model as well. Gross floor area is the most important predictor of sales at corner sites, but it has little impact on sales of stores not at corner sites. Similarly, the most important predictor of sales in midblock sites (total urban retail expenditure) is not significantly related to sales at corner sites. It is important to note that the results shift dramatically when the two subsamples are combined into one. Consequently, it would be inaccurate to rely on the results of this overall model to assess the performance of the individual outlets. The predictions of the site-specific models more accurately reflect the potential of the stores at particular sites.

Other Problems. In addition to multicollinearity and heterogenity of stores, another problem in many regression studies of retail performance is the definition and measurement of variables used in the model. In analyzing such factors as store image and service levels, it is important to examine consumer perceptions of those factors rather than use surrogate measures (Stanley and Sewall 1976). Nevertheless, regression studies rarely use such consumer-perception data. Another factor that is difficult to measure is competition.

Most studies use the distance to the nearest competitor or the number of competing outlets within a given distance as indices of competition. But these measures may be inadequate if the competitors differ in terms of size, price, image, or assortment. Finally, the trade areas of outlets included in the sample must be measured with precision to determine the population base and economic potential in the area. Unfortunately, many studies fail to define actual market areas and use arbitrarily defined distance cutoffs to measure market and customer characteristics. This assumes that the residents of the designated area are representative of the store's patrons, which may not always be the case.

Multiple regression models have been commonly used in location research to gauge factors in retail performance. The wide availability of computer software for regression analysis has led to their popularity. The problems discussed here, however, emphasize the need for more carefully conducted studies. Before implementing the results of regression analyses, the validity and predictive accuracy of the models must be thoroughly assessed. Few of the published studies report the predictive performance of forecasting models. In most cases, the validity of the model is judged only by the degree of fit (R^2 value). Predictive accuracy should be tested with hold-out samples or by using data from a different time period. Even for models that exhibit a high degree of predictive accuracy, considerable care should be taken in extrapolating the results from one city or region to project performance of outlets in another region. Such factors as company image and the quality of competition may vary considerably from one region to another and systematically impact on performance. Finally, as is true for all forecasting models, the results must be periodically updated to reflect changes in the marketing and competitive environments.

Analog Regression

While regression models have mostly been applied to predict the overall level of retail sales or market share of outlets, they are also appropriate for predicting the market share or per capita sales of an outlet within parts of the trade area. Rogers and Green (1978), for example, illustrate how regression techniques can be used to refine the analog method to provide disaggregated market share forecasts. In principle, analog regression is similar to any other regression forecasting system. The unit of analysis, however, is different. In analog regression, the dependent variable is the market share of an outlet in different subareas within the outlet's trade area. In the examples discussed earlier, the focus was on predicting total sales for different outlets. The trade areas of the analog stores are divided into zones based on census tracts or blocks. The market shares of the stores within each zone are calculated through customer spotting. A regression equation is then estimated with the market share in each zone as the dependent variable and the characteristics of each zone as explanatory variables.

Table 4–6 illustrates the implementation of the analog regression method. In the example shown in the table, the spatial variation in market share of analog stores is significantly related to four variables: the distance separating each zone from the store, the size of the store, the size of competitive stores, and the level of home ownership. As might be expected, market share is negatively affected by the distance to the store and the size of the competitive store. It is positively affected by the other factors. The four variables explain more than 65 percent of the variation in market share among the zones.

The regression coefficients can be used to forecast the market share of zones surrounding the location of a new outlet. To obtain these estimates, the values of the four variables are measured for each zone of the new outlet's trade area and input in the regression equation. The calculation of the market share for one zone is shown in the table. Forecasts of sales from each zone can then be obtained by multiplying the market share estimates by the potential for the zone. The total sales forecast for the store is the sum of the forecast for each zone. While this forecast provides an objective assessment of the store's potential, due to the aggregation of a large number of forecasts, it is difficult to obtain a measure of expected levels of error and tolerance of the forecasts.

Table 4–6
Forecasting Sales by Analog Regression Method

Step 1. *Regression model*

$$MS = b_0 - b_1 x_1 + b_2 x_2 - b_3 x_3 + b_4 x_4$$

- MS = Market share of analog store in zone
- x_1 = distance separating zone from store (miles)
- x_2 = size of store (100 square feet)
- x_3 = size of nearest competitor (100 square feet)
- x_4 = percentage of homes that are owner-occupied

Step 2. *Market share forecast for zone 23*

$$MS = b_0 - b_1(1.2) + b_2(650) - b_3(600) + b_4(68)$$
$$= .069$$

Step 3. *Weekly sales forecast for zone 23*

Weekly sales = MS × per capita sales potential × population in zone
$$= .069 \times 21.08 \times 1948$$
$$= \$2,833$$

Step 4. *Sum forecasts of all zones*

Step 5. *Adjust forecast for sales from outside trade area*

The combination of the analog procedure with the regression technique provides the retail analyst with "a more rigorous and reliable method of retail site evaluation" (Rogers and Green, 1978, p. 458). The procedure is especially suited for retail chains who perform customer-spotting studies for their individual stores. It is important, however, to ascertain the homogeneity of the types of stores included in the analog regression. Outlets located in downtown shopping streets, for example, tend to have markedly different trade area characteristics than outlets located in small neighborhood malls. Retail chains having outlets in different types of locations should develop separate models for each type of location classification rather than aggregating them. Moreover, the analyst should always guard against the problem of multicollinearity discussed in the previous section. Finally, the use of analog regression does not eliminate the need to adjust the forecast to reflect factors not included in the model such as local topography and physical features.

Conclusion

Sales forecasting systems are an integral part of retail location analysis. Sales forecasts are important in selecting sites for new outlets, assessing the performance of existing outlets, and deciding on store closures and relocations. The various forecasting systems described in this chapter are each based on a different method of estimating the size and shape of the trade area. Since there is no one system that can be used in all situations, the contexts in which the models should be applied have been emphasized throughout the chapter. We have illustrated the difficulties that usually arise in applying these techniques and the types of questions that can be answered by them.

In spite of the increasing sophistication of forecasting systems, the need for subjective judgments by the analyst cannot be eliminated. Some may view this as a weakness of current forecasting techniques. We, however, view it as a strength. Each store possesses certain unique characteristics or faces specific market conditions that cannot be fully captured by a quantitative model. The quantitative techniques do, however, provide the foundation on which the well-trained retail analyst can build the forecast.

References

Alpert, M., and Bibb, J.F. (1974). "Fitting Branch Locations, Performance Standards, and Marketing Strategies: A Clarification." *Journal of Marketing* 38: 72–74.

Applebaum, W. (1966). "Methods for Determining Store Trade Areas, Market Penetration and Potential Sales." *Journal of Marketing Research* 3: 127–141.

Applebaum, W. (1968). "The Analogue Method for Estimating Potential Store Sales" in C. Kornblau (ed.), *Guide to Store Location Research.* Reading, Mass.: Addision-Wesley.

Christaller, W. (1935). *Die Zentralen Orte in Süddeutschland.* Jena, East Germany: G. Fischer.

Clawson, J. (1974). "Fitting Branch Locations, Performance Standards and Marketing Strategies to Local Conditions." *Journal of Marketing* 38: 8–14.

Converse, P.D. (1949). "New Laws of Retail Gravitation." *Journal of Marketing* 14: 379–384.

Cottrell, J. (1973). "An Environmental Model of Performance Measurement in a Chain of Supermarkets." *Journal of Retailing* 49(3): 51–63.

Davies, R. (1973). "Evaluation of Retail Store Attributes and Sales Performance." *European Journal of Marketing* 7: 89–102.

Dirichlet, G.L. (1850). "Über die Reduktion der Positiven Quadratischen Formen mit Drei Unbestimmten Ganzen Zahlen." *Journal für die Reine und Angewandte Mathematik* 40: 216.

Douglas, E. (1949). "Measuring the General Retail Trading Area—A Case Study: I." *Journal of Marketing* 13: 481–497.

Erickson, G.F., and Finkler, S.A. (1985). "Determinants of Market Share for a Hospital's Services." *Medical Care* 23: 1003–1014.

Hise, R.T.; Kelly, J.P.; Gable, M.; and McDonald, J.B. (1983). "Factors Affecting the Performance of Individual Chain Store Units: An Empirical Analysis." *Journal of Retailing* 59: 1–18.

Huff, D.L. (1964). "Defining and Estimating a Trade Area." *Journal of Marketing* 28: 34–38.

Johnston, J. (1972). *Econometric Methods.* New York: McGraw-Hill.

Jones, K.G., and Mock, D.R. (1984). "Evaluating Retail Trading Performance" in R.L. Davies and D.S. Rogers (eds.), *Store Location and Store Assessment Research.* New York: John Wiley & Sons.

Lee, Y., and Koutsopolous, D. (1977). "A Locational Analysis of Convenience Food Stores in Metropolitan Denver." *Annals of Regional Science* 10: 104–117.

Lord, J., and Lynds, C. (1981). "The Use of Regression Models in Store Location Research: A Review and Case Study." *Akron Business and Economic Review* 10: 13–19.

Losch, A. (1954). *Economics of Location.* New Haven, Conn.: Yale University Press.

Lynge, M., and Shin, T. (1981). "Factors Affecting Rural Bank Market Share." *Akron Business and Economic Review* 10: 35–39.

Malinvaud, E. (1980). *Statistical Methods of Econometrics.* New York: North Holland.

Martin, P. (1967). "Savings and Loans in New Submarkets: Search for Predictive Factors." *Journal of Marketing Research* 4: 163–166.

Marx, R.W. (1983). "Automating Census Geography." *American Demographics* 5: 30–33.

Olsen, L.M., and Lord, J.D. (1979). "Market Area Characteristics and Branch Bank Performance." *Journal of Bank Research* (Summer) 10: 102–110.

Reilly, W.J. (1931). *The Law of Retail Gravitation.* New York: Knickerbocker.

Rogers, D.S., and Green, H. (1978). "A New Perspective in Forecasting Store Sales: Applying Statistical Models and Techniques in the Analog Approach." *Geographical Review* 69: 449–458.

Stanley, T.J., and Sewall, M.A. (1976). "Image Inputs to a Probabilistic Model: Predicting Retail Potential." *Journal of Marketing* 40: 48–53.

Thiessen, A.H., and Alter, J.C. (1911). "Precipitation Averages for Large Areas." *Monthly Weather Review* 39: 1082–1084.

U.S. Dept. of Commerce (1980). *The Census Bureau's BGF/DIME System: A Tool for Urban Management and Planning.* Washington, D.C.: U.S. Government Printing Office.

5
Spatial-Interaction Models

L
ike the previous chapter, this chapter is concerned with forecasting retail sales and analyzing trading areas of retail outlets, but the focus now is on spatial-interaction models. Spatial-interaction models (or gravity models, as they are often called) are widely used to forecast sales of new outlets and to assess the impact of changes in the retail environment on outlet performance.

Interaction models are based on empirical analysis of the spatial pattern of consumer shopping in the study area. As a result, the spatial pattern of consumer shopping trips and the pattern of expenditures at different outlets in the area are predicted in more detail and with more accuracy than in other forecasting models. Because of their mathematical flexibility, spatial-interaction models can be used to analyze trade areas and forecast sales of many different types of retail and service institutions. It is for this reason that interaction models form the basis of many computerized simulation systems used to assess and predict retail performance.

The chapter is organized into four major sections. The first section presents the central concepts underlying the use of interaction models and traces the development of these models for retail forecasting. In the second section, the steps in creating the data base and model calibration are described. The third section presents examples of applying spatial-interaction models for predicting retail patronage and travel patterns. Examples of supermarkets, hospitals, and shopping centers are used to illustrate the application of spatial-interaction models. The final section addresses the issue of parameter nonstationarity in interaction models. Nonstationarity is a major methodological problem in the application of spatial-interaction models for retail forecasting. In this section, we first present evidence of nonstationarity and then discuss some procedures for dealing with the problem.

The Principle of Spatial Interaction

Underlying spatial-interaction models is the observation that the share of customers that an outlet attracts from a market area is inversely proportional to distance and directly related to the attraction of the store. This, it may be recalled, is similar to the principle of retail gravitation proposed by Reilly. In this respect, Reilly's law is the precursor of the spatial-interaction models commonly used today. In contrast to Reilly's law, however, spatial-inter-action models develop an empirical basis to determine the manner in which consumers trade off accessibility with attractiveness in choosing among alternative retail outlets. In addition, these models have a stronger theoretical foundation than Reilly's law. Their roots lie not in an analogy to Newtonian physics, but in empirically observed tenets of consumer choice.

Although spatial-interaction models are calibrated at the aggregate level, the models are based on principles of individual consumer behavior. It is argued that individual shopping-patronage patterns depend on the consumer's evaluation of the relative "utility" of each store. The greater the perceived utility, the higher the likelihood of the outlet being patronized by the consumer. Thus, in order to predict consumer shopping patterns, it is first necessary to understand how consumers evaluate shopping outlets. A store's utility to a prospective customer depends mainly on its location and attractiveness. The consumer utility function for retail stores can thus be written generally as:

$$U_{ij} = A_j^\alpha D_{ij}^\beta \qquad (5.1)$$

where U_{ij} is the utility of store j to consumer i, A_j is a measure of the attractiveness of store j, D_{ij} is the distance separating store j from consumer i, and α and β are parameters that reflect the consumer's sensitivity to store attraction and distance, respectively. Since utility decreases as distance to the store increases, the parameter β is expected to have a negative sign. The negative impact of distance on utility is often referred to as the "distance-decay effect" and β is called the "distance-decay parameter." The negative impact of distance, however, can be compensated for by enhanced store attractiveness based on such factors as store image, the breadth and mix of assortments carried, store size, the price of the merchandise, and the quality of service.

In forming their overall evaluation of a store, consumers trade off the disutility of traveling to the store with the attractiveness of the store. The values of the parameters α and β reflect the relative importance given to store attractiveness and distance in forming this evaluation. As the value of β becomes more negative, more importance is given to distance relative to store attraction. When the absolute value of β is very large compared to α, consumers' evaluations depend almost entirely on distance, with little or no concern for attractiveness. In this case, consumers tend to patronize the closest store. Thus, the nearest-center hypothesis of the proximal area method is a special case of this general type of utility function. Reilly's formula, too, is a special case of equation 5.1. In Reilly's formula, the values of α and β are fixed at 1.0 and -2.0 respectively.

Thus, the difference between normative approaches to defining trade areas (such as the proximal area method and Reilly's formula) and spatial-interaction models is that in the latter, actual consumer choices are used to determine consumer utility functions. Rather than analysts choosing their values a priori, the parameters of the utility function are found by calibrating the model to best fit observed consumer shopping patterns. This means, however, that in order to use spatial-interaction models, it is necessary to obtain information on the actual spatial pattern of shopping trips made by consumers in the study area.

Huff (1962, 1964) was the first to propose a spatial-interaction model for estimating retail trade areas. He suggested that the utility of a store depends on its size (square footage) and distance:

$$U_{ij} = S_j^\alpha D_{ij}^\beta \tag{5.2}$$

where S_j is the size of outlet j. Huff further argued that when consumers have a number of alternative shopping opportunities, they may visit several different stores rather than restrict their patronage to only one outlet. Each store within the geographic area with which the consumer is familiar has some chance of being patronized. Thus, Huff conceived trade areas to be probabilistic rather than deterministic, with each store having some probability of being patronized. The probability of patronage is positively related to the size of the outlet and decreases with distance.

To determine the probability of a consumer visiting a particular outlet, Huff followed the choice axiom proposed by Luce (1959). Luce's axiom postulates that when faced with several choice alternatives, the probability with which an individual chooses a particular alternative is equal to the ratio of the utility of that alternative to the sum of the utilities of all alternatives considered by the individual. The probability of a consumer visiting a particular store, therefore, is equal to the ratio of the utility of that store to the sum of utilities of all the stores considered by the consumer:

$$P_{ij} = U_{ij} \Big/ \sum_{k \in N_i} U_{ik} \tag{5.3}$$

where P_{ij} is the probability of a consumer at i visiting store j and N_i is the set of competing stores in the region. The denominator in equation 5.3 is the sum of the utilities of all stores considered as possible travel destinations by the consumer. Thus, if the outlets under investigation are supermarkets, the set N_i should include all supermarkets at which the consumer is willing or able to shop. This is similar to the concept of "choice set" used in brand choice modeling and this term is used hereafter to refer to the set of shopping opportunities considered by a consumer. Simply stated, it is the set of stores that compete with each other to attract customers. Now, substituting equation 5.2 in equation 5.3, we obtain the Huff model:

$$P_{ij} = S_j^\alpha D_{ij}^\beta \Big/ \sum_{k \epsilon N_i} S_k^\alpha D_{ik}^\beta \qquad (5.4)$$

Huff's original formulation did not include an exponent associated with the attraction or size factor. Later versions of the model, however, included such an exponent "on the grounds that the larger shopping centers tend to have an extra level of attraction beyond their greater size because of the increase in choice of goods and benefits of scale economies" (Davies 1977, p. 243).

As an illustration of the model, consider an individual who has the opportunity to shop at three shopping centers. The sizes of these shopping centers and their distances from the consumer's home are as follows:

Store	Distance (miles)	Size (square feet)
A	4	50,000
B	6	70,000
C	3	40,000

If $\alpha = 1.0$ and $\beta = -2.0$, the utilities of the three stores to this individual are:

Utility of store A = 50,000/4^2 = 3125

Utility of store B = 70,000/6^2 = 1944

Utility of store C = 40,000/3^2 = 4444

Based on these utilities, the probability that the individual will shop at store A is:

3125/(3125 + 1944 + 4444) = .328

Similarly, the probabilities of shopping at stores B and C can easily be found to be .204 and .467, respectively.

The likelihood of the consumer patronizing a store depends on the values of α and β. Changes in these values shift the relative importance given to store size and distance. Consequently, the store choice probabilities change, as illustrated in table 5–1. For example, if the value of the distance parameter changed to -3.0, the shopping pattern would shift away from the farther stores to the closer ones due to the greater weight placed on the distance factor. In our example, the probability of shopping at store C, the nearest store, increases from 46 percent to 57 percent when β decreases to -3.0. This gain in patronage at store C is offset by losses at the more distant stores.

Table 5–1
Impact of Parameter Values on Shopping Probabilities Using Three Scenarios

	Scenario 1 $\alpha = 1.0, \beta = -2.0$	Scenario 2 $\alpha = 1.0, \beta = -3.0$	Scenario 3 $\alpha = 2.0, \beta = -2.0$
Store *A*	.33	.30	.33
Store *B*	.20	.13	.29
Store *C*	.47	.57	.38

Note: See text for description of stores.

The probability of the consumer patronizing store *B*, the store farthest from the consumer, decreases from 0.20 to only 0.13. Store *A* is less affected because of its greater accessibility.

A change in the value of α also affects choice probabilities by changing the relative importance given to store size or attractiveness. As illustrated in table 5–1, if α increases to 2.0 and β remains at -2.0, the share of the largest store, store *B*, increases from 20 percent to 29 percent, despite its more distant location. Store *C* is the greatest loser in this case because of its smaller size. A key issue in the application of any spatial-interaction model, therefore, is the determination of the parameter values that best fit actual consumer shopping patterns in the area.

Uses of the Model

Since their introduction to the retailing literature by Huff, spatial-interaction models have played an important role in the development of trade area estimation and sales forecasting procedures. Many empirical studies support the usefulness of the models in predicting with reasonable accuracy the market share of shopping outlets. (See, for example, Huff 1962, 1963; Huff and Blue 1966; Forbes 1968; Haines, Simon, and Alexis 1972). The models are also useful for predicting the impact of changes in the retail environment on the performance of existing individual stores. One can answer, for example, such questions as: What impact would the expansion of one store have on the sales of other stores in the area? How would the opening of a new store affect the performance of existing stores? Yet another use of the model is in selecting optimal sites for new stores. Retail-location analysts in Europe and North America often determine the viability of new stores and shopping centers based on predictions from interaction models. Because of their ability to answer such questions, interaction models provide the location analyst with a powerful research tool and decision aid for sales forecasting and strategy formulation.

According to David Rogers, spatial-interaction models have been less popular in Europe than in North America due to the "greater difficulty of simulating consumer interaction over distance as a result of lower levels of car ownership and the greater usage of public transport for shopping trips" (Rogers 1984, p. 321). In Britain, however, spatial-interaction models have found favor with planning authorities, who, because of significant government control on retail locations, have played a more active role in location planning than their North American counterparts.

Conceptually, two of the major contributions of the Huff model are the suggestions that individual shopping behavior is best explained probabilistically rather than in a deterministic fashion and that retail trade areas are continuous, complex, and overlapping, rather than the nonoverlapping geometric areas of central-place theory (Berry 1967). Further, as Haines, Simon, and Alexis note, Huff's formulation "demonstrates that consumer spatial behavior is explained by a theory also capable of explaining nonspatial aspects of behavior" (1972, p. 154). Due to its derivation from Luce's choice axiom, Huff's model is similar to the general class of "attraction" models used to study brand market shares and consumer brand choice.

Generalization of the Spatial-Interaction Model

Since its first appearance in the literature in the early 1960s, a number of modifications to the Huff model have been suggested. These have generally been concerned with the proper definition of store attractiveness and more accurate measurement of attractiveness. In Huff's formulation, only size is used to measure store attractiveness, which has long been a source of dissatisfaction among researchers (Davis 1977; Stanley and Sewall 1976). In order to deal with this problem, Stanley and Sewall, for example, used a multidimensional scaling procedure to incorporate the effect of differing store images. The addition of image in the model significantly improved its predictive performance. Commercial computer packages used to implement interaction-forecasting systems also include store image as a variable affecting shopping probabilities. Gautschi (1981) found that including additional measures of accessibility (such as availability of mass transit) besides image also improved the model's predictive performance.

The desire to include multiple measures of store attractiveness and accessibility led Nakanishi and Cooper (1974) to suggest a more general form of the spatial-interaction model which they called the *multiplicative competitive interaction* (MCI) model. The MCI formulation is not limited to considering only size and distance in measuring the utility of a store. Other store characteristics can be incorporated in the model to measure both the attractiveness or retail facilities and geographic accessibility. The probability, P_{ij}, of a consumer at residential zone i patronizing facility j can now be more generally written as:

$$P_{ij} = \left(\prod_{l=1}^{L}A_{lj}^{\alpha l}\right)D_{ij}^{\beta} \bigg/ \sum_{k\epsilon N_i}\left(\prod_{l=1}^{L}A_{lk}^{\alpha l}\right)D_{ik}^{\beta} \qquad (5.5)$$

where, A_{lj} is a measure of the *l*th ($l = 1, 2, \ldots L$) characteristic of retail alternative *j*, and N_i is the set of alternatives considered by individuals at origin *i*.

The set of attributes used to define equation 5.5 should include all relevant store and site characteristics hypothesized to influence consumer choice of retail outlets. Both objective measures and subjective measures of consumer perception may be used in the model. In their study of food retailing, Jain and Mahajan (1979), for example, used such factors as the availability of credit card services, the number of checkout counters, and whether the store was located at an intersection, in addition to store size and distance, to explain the market share obtained by individual outlets. Similarly, in studying retail banking centers in California, Hansen and Weinberg (1979) found that the availability of walk-up windows at a shopping center and the newness of a branch were important determinants of bank patronage. The advantage of the MCI formulation is that there is no restriction on the number of factors that can be included in the model. In addition, the factors need not be measured on a continuous scale—the researcher can construct dummy variables to identify the presence or absence of certain store characteristics.

Data Base and Model Calibration

The first step in developing a forecasting system based on the spatial-interaction model is to create the data base and the geographic information system. To create the data base, the location analyst must first delimit the geographic extent of the study area and decide on the stores to be included in the analysis. It is important to define carefully the boundaries of the study area since it affects the accuracy of the forecasts. The study area must at least be as large as the trade areas of the stores whose sales are to be forecasted. Also, it must include the locations of all competing stores in the area. However, since the model is usually used to simulate the impact of future changes in the retail environment, a larger study area is generally necessary.

Another concern in defining the study area is the likelihood of cross-shopping. Ideally, the spatial limit of the study area should be such that no shopping trips are made across the boundary. For example, in analyzing the competitive environment of supermarkets, the study area should be defined such that all grocery trips made by residents in the study area are to stores included in the analysis. Similarly, consumers outside the study area ideally should not patronize stores included in the study area. In practice, some amount of cross-shopping will always occur. Based on knowledge about the geography of the area and past experience, the analyst must compromise between the need to keep the size of the study area manageable and the need to reduce excessive amounts of cross-shopping. Other factors that need to be considered in defining study area boundaries are the location of competitive stores, transportation and road networks, and the effect of natural and man-made boundaries such as rivers, lakes, and railway crossings.

Once the study area is delineated, the next step is to divide the area into a number of smaller zones or subareas from which consumer shopping patterns will be observed. The zones should be small in size so that each is relatively homogenous in its demographic and socioeconomic characteristics. The total number of zones should be large in order to capture the diversity of individual shopping patterns. On the other hand, because travel-pattern and population data must be obtained from each zone, the cost of data collection increases rapidly as the number of zones increases. Thus, a compromise is again necessary to determine the actual number of subareas to be used in a study. To define the subareas, researchers often utilize predefined areas such as census tracts, census-enumeration districts, and zip code areas. The major advantage of using these spatial units is that information on social, economic, and demographic characteristics of the subarea are available from secondary sources, often in computer-readable form. The primary data collection effort is, therefore, limited to gathering information on consumer shopping patterns for each zone.

Since census tracts, enumeration districts, and zip code areas differ in size, the most appropriate definition of subareas depends on the type of retail outlets being studied. Zip code areas may be appropriate for analyzing the trading areas of shopping centers because of the great distances from which shopping centers draw their customers. On the other hand, zip code areas would be too large for supermarkets, which tend to have much smaller trade areas than shopping centers. Enumeration districts, which are smaller in size, are more appropriate for supermarkets. In general, the more compact the trade area, the smaller the subareas should be.

Once the study area and the zones have been defined, information on existing stores and consumer travel patterns can be incorporated into the data base. The data base must contain two types of location information: the coordinates of the centroid (the geographic center) of each zone and the coordinates of the location of each store included in the study. The next step is to calculate the travel times or distances from the centroid of each zone to each store to measure the relative accessibility of each store to the consumers throughout the area. The best measures of accessibility—actual travel times—are rarely used in practice because of the substantial time and effort needed to calculate them. As an alternative, the actual road distance between the centroids and store locations can be calculated. Using computerized digitizing equipment and software, this can be done efficiently from detailed road maps. An even simpler, but less accurate procedure is to calculate distances from the coordinates of the centroids and store locations using the "Euclidean" or "city block" metric. The Euclidean distance between two points (x_1, y_1) and (x_2, y_2) is simply:

$$\left[(x_1 - x_2)^2 + (y_1 - y_2)^2\right]^{1/2}$$

In many North American cities, with their gridlike road networks, the city block distance may more correctly reflect actual travel times. The city block distance between two points is the sum of the horizontal and vertical distances between the points:

$$|x_1 - x_2| + |y_1 - y_2|$$

Irrespective of how distance is calculated, adjustments are always necessary to reflect physical and social barriers to travel in the study area. Physical barriers (such as rivers, lakes, railway lines, and limited-access highways) may decrease accessibility in some cases. In addition, accessibility may be restricted by social barriers such as the reluctance to travel through high-crime areas or industrial zones. Another factor affecting accessibility is congestion. Consumers perceive the distance through a highly congested area to be higher than it actually is because of the relatively long time needed to travel through congested areas. Since the real concern is with measuring the perceived time or effort a consumer must spend in traveling to a store—distance is merely a surrogate of this—any factor that impacts on travel time should be included. Thus, information on one-way streets or driving conditions should be included whenever possible. This is especially true in urban areas where travel times depend considerably on traffic conditions.

In addition to information on travel time or distances, the data base must also cover characteristics of stores being studied. Any factor that may potentially influence consumer shopping decisions should be included. These could be objective measures (such as store size, type of site, and relative prices) or subjective measures (such as consumer perception of image and the quality of service). Frequently, researchers conduct pilot consumer surveys to determine which store and site characteristics to include in the final data base.

The final step in creating the data base is to conduct a consumer survey to obtain information on shopping patterns. Individuals are randomly selected from each zone and their shopping patterns are elicited through personal or telephone interviews or by observing actual shopping choices. The objective is to estimate for each zone the relative frequency with which its residents patronize the different stores. There are a number of ways in which this information can be collected. First, the shopping pattern of a sample of shoppers from each zone can be observed over time. Although the reliability of data collected by this procedure is relatively high, it is not commonly used because of the time involved in collecting longitudinal data. An alternative way to obtain the same information is to ask sample respondents the frequency with which they have visited each store. A third possibility, which is ideally suited for telephone interviews, is to ask respondents to simply name the store they visited on their most recent shopping trip. This information is aggregated across respondents from each zone to compute the relative frequency with which the different stores are patronized by residents of each subarea. The sample size, therefore, has to be large enough to provide a reliable estimate of the overall trip patterns.

Irrespective of the procedure used to collect the data, proper sampling techniques must be followed in all cases. The survey respondents must match the target market profile of the store. Another concern is spatial coverage. Each subarea in the study must be adequately represented in the sample. If a shopper-intercept technique is used, the interviews should be spread over different days of the week and different hours of the day to ensure representation of the total shopper universe.

Model Calibration

The accuracy of forecasts from spatial-interaction models depends, to a large extent, on how well the model fits the observed trip pattern. To determine the parameters that best represent actual travel patterns, the model is calibrated against the observed data on shopping choice. Calibration involves finding the values of the different parameters in the interaction model that provide the best fit between the observed spatial pattern of shopping trips in the area and the pattern of trips predicted from the model. Most early studies used iterative grid-search procedures to calibrate spatial-interaction models. Iterative procedures systematically try different values for the parameters (the early models were limited to considering size and distance only) to find the ones that give the best fit between actual and predicted trip patterns. The sum of the squared deviations between actual and predicted trip probabilities is generally used as a yardstick to measure the goodness of fit of the model.

Although conceptually simple, the iterative search algorithms do not guarantee optimal results. Moreover, they are quite tedious and time consuming when a large number of variables are considered in the interaction model. A further drawback is that because they are not based on any statistical estimation theory, iterative procedures do not provide any indication of the statistical properties of the estimate—such as the level of significance of the different parameters and the standard errors of estimation.

The problems inherent in the iterative procedure led a number of researchers to seek alternative methods for calibrating spatial-interaction models. In 1974, Nakanishi and Cooper demonstrated that the MCI model could be calibrated by the method of ordinary least squares (OLS) used in linear regression analysis. Since the OLS procedure is commonly used in statistical analysis and computer packages for OLS are widely available, this is a relatively simple way to calibrate the interaction model. Most studies now use this procedure. (See, for example, Jain and Mahajan 1979; Ghosh 1984; Black, Westbrook, and Ostlund 1985.)

To calibrate the MCI model using OLS, a logarithmic transformation of equation 5.5 is performed as follows:

$$\ln(P_{ij}/P_{i^*}) = \sum_{l=1}^{L} \alpha_l \ln(A_{lj}/A_{l^*}) + \beta \ln(D_{ij}/D_{i^*}) \qquad (5.6)$$

where $\quad P_{ij} = \left(\prod_{j \epsilon N_i} P_{ij}\right)^{1/n_i}$

$$A_{l^*} = \left(\prod_{j \epsilon N_i} A_{l^*}\right)^{1/n_i}$$

$$D_{i^*} = \left(\prod_{j \epsilon N_i} D_{ij}\right)^{1/n_i}$$

$\quad n_i$ = number of alternatives considered by individuals at i

Because equation 5.6 is linear-in-parameters, it can be estimated by OLS using one of the many standard computer packages for regression analysis. It should be noted, however, that the equation does not have the intercept term commonly used in linear regression models. Many computer packages for calibrating regression models do provide the option of suppressing the intercept term. If the option is unavailable, the alternative transformation proposed by Nakanishi and Cooper (1982) can be used.

Once the parameters of the interaction model have been estimated, the predicted frequency of travel from any zone i to a store j can be calculated by inverse log-centering:

$$P_{ij} = \frac{\exp\left[\sum_{l=1}^{L}\alpha_l \ln(A_{lj}/A_{l^*}) + \beta \ln(D_{ij}/D_{i^*})\right]}{\sum_{k \epsilon N_i}\left\{\exp\left[\sum_{l=1}^{L}\alpha_l(A_{lk}/A_{l^*}) + \beta \ln(D_{ik}/D_{i^*})\right]\right\}} \qquad (5.7)$$

Given information on the characteristics of each store in the area and the distance separating each origin i from the set of stores in the choice set, the probability of an individual at origin i visiting a store j, P_{ij}, can be calculated from equation 5.7. The equation can also be used to predict the impact of changes in store characteristics or the introduction of a new store on store-choice probabilities. The introduction of a new store changes the value of the denominator in equation 5.7, thereby affecting the predicted choice probabilities.

Incorporating Binary Variables in the MCI Model

Calibrating equation 5.6 using OLS requires logarithmic transformations and the calculation of geometric means. Since both geometric means and logarithmic transformations are undefined for zero values, binary (or dummy) variables that are assigned values of 0 or 1 to reflect the presence or absence of attributes cannot be directly included in the MCI model. Binary variables are useful, however, to indicate special features of a store. For example, they may be used to indicate whether a store is located at an intersection or to indicate the presence of specialized services such as credit card services or ATMs. To incorporate binary variables in the MCI model, a number of different transformation procedures have been suggested in the literature. (See, for example, Nakanishi, Cooper, and Kassarjian 1974; Mahajan, Jain, and Ratchford 1978.) One simple procedure is the exponential transformation. In this a binary variable A_{kj} is transformed as follows:

$$A_{lj} = \exp(1) = 2.7183 \quad \text{if } A_{lj} = 1$$
$$A_{lj} = \exp(0) = 1.0 \quad \text{if } A_{lj} = 0 \tag{5.8}$$

The transformed variable can be directly included in the interaction model.

The Multinomial Logit (MNL) Model

An alternative procedure for estimating the interaction model is to use the multinomial logit (MNL) form of the model using disaggregate, individual-level data. In this case, the focus in on discrete choices made by consumers on individual shopping trips rather than on the aggregate proportion of trips made from each subarea. The multinomial logit form of the interaction model can be written as follows:

$$P_{ij} = \frac{\left(\prod_{l=1}^{L} e^{\alpha_{lj}A_{lij}}\right)\left(e^{\beta_{ij}D_{ij}}\right)}{\sum_{k \epsilon N_i}\left[\left(\prod_{l=1}^{L} e^{\alpha_{lik}A_{lik}}\right)\left(e^{\beta_{ik}D_{ik}}\right)\right]} \tag{5.9}$$

The logit model can be calibrated at a disaggregate level using observations on individual shopping trips. Maximum-likelihood procedures are commonly used to estimate disaggregate multinomial logit models. Later in this chapter, we present the study by Weisbrod, Parcells, and Kern (1984) which uses the MNL model to analyze the pattern of trips to shopping centers.

Application of Spatial-Interaction Models

This section illustrates, through a series of three examples, the use of empirical spatial-interaction models in developing a retail sales forecasting and simulation system. The first example concerns predicting the market shares and sales of seven supermarkets in a midwestern town and illustrates the calibration of a simple spatial-interaction model as well as the creation of a simulation system to forecast sales. The focus of the second illustration is much broader in terms of both the size of the study area and the number of alternatives that are considered. The study uses spatial-interaction models to predict the market shares of fifty-eight general hospitals in the state of North Dakota. The final example illustrates the use of the multinomial logit (MNL) formulation of the spatial-interaction model for analyzing the shopping trips to major regional shopping centers in the Boston metropolitan area.

The Competitive Environment of Supermarkets

The market area of supermarkets is strongly influenced by location and geographic accessibility—distance has a strong impact on supermarket patronage decisions. At the same time, patronage decisions are also influenced by store size and the attractiveness of the outlet. To determine the impact of these factors on supermarket patronage and to analyze the competitive environment of supermarkets, a spatial-interaction model was calibrated with data from a midwestern town. The town has a population of about fifty thousand people and has seven major supermarkets operated by three separate chains.

To calibrate the interaction model, the study area was divided into twenty-nine customer zones based on neighborhood characteristics and topographic features. Three hundred households in the study area were randomly selected to collect information on the existing pattern of supermarket patronage. The market share distribution of grocery purchases originating from each zone was calculated from these household interviews. The individual in each household who was responsible for the most grocery purchases was asked to name grocery stores visited at least once during the previous year. The proportion of trips made to each store was then estimated by asking the respondent the relative frequency of visiting each store. Individual responses from each origin were aggregated to measure the value of P_{ij} for each origin-store pair. Similar data were also collected from forty individuals representing twenty different origins. These data, which were not used to estimate the model, provided means of testing the accuracy of forecasts from the model.

The survey respondents were also asked to rate the seven stores in terms of their image, quality of merchandise, price, product availability, and parking facilities. They generally reported that the stores were extremely homogenous except for some variation in the range of products carried. Subsequent investigations revealed that the availability of goods was highly related to the size of the store. Therefore, store size and distance were the two variables used in the spatial-interaction model. It should be noted, however, that the inclusion of only store size and distance in the model does not necessarily imply that other factors are unimportant. Rather, since these are the only two variables on which the stores differ, the market share distribution can be best explained by these variables. The distance from the centroid of each zone to each store was calculated using the city block metric because of the gridlike layout of the road system in the city.

To calibrate the interaction model, the data were first organized in the form of equation 5.7. With only store size and distance as the explanatory variables, the model takes the following form:

$$\ln(P_{ij}/P_{i^\circ}) = \alpha\ln(S_j/S_\circ) + \beta\ln(D_{ij}/D_{i^\circ}) \qquad (5.10)$$

The variables P_{i° and D_{i° were defined for each origin by calculating the geometric mean of the observed share distribution of shopping trips from each origin and the corresponding distances to the stores. The variable $S_\circ$ was defined by calculating the geometric mean of the relative size of each store. To calibrate equation 5.10 using OLS, the data need to be organized such that each i,j combination is a row of observations in a regression framework. Since there are 29 origins and 7 stores, this should have resulted in 203 (29 × 7) rows of observations. Not all seven stores, however, were included in the choice set of residents of all zones. Residents in some zones patronized only a subset of the stores. For this reason, the actual number of observations used in estimating the model is 186.

The OLS estimates of α and β are 1.453 and -2.025, respectively. Both of these are significantly different from zero at the $p = .001$ level, indicating a noteworthy impact of store size and distance on trip patterns. As expected, the distance parameter is negative and the size parameter is positive—both accessibility and size increase the relative frequency with which an outlet is patronized. The share of trips from any zone i to store j can be predicted as follows:

$$P_{ij} = \frac{\exp[1.45\ln(S_j/S_\circ) - 2.02\ln(D_{ij}/D_{i^\circ})]}{\sum_{k\in N_i}\{\exp[1.45\ln(S_k/S_\circ) - 2.02\ln(D_{ik}/D_{i^\circ})]\}} \qquad (5.11)$$

These predicted values can be used to check how well the model fits actual trip patterns. The correlation coefficient between predicted and observed trip frequencies indicates the degree of fit of interaction models. In this case, the correlation is .89, which indicates that the model fits observed data very well, and the model's predictions are significantly better than what would occur by chance. To further test the predictive validity of the model, the calibrated parameters were used to predict the travel patterns for the hold-out sample (the forty individuals whose patronage information was not used in calibrating the original model). The correlation coefficient between the observed and predicted values for the hold-out sample was .86. The high degree of fit with the hold-out observations adds confidence in the predictive validity of the model.

Table 5–2 shows, for each origin, the predicted share of trips to each of the seven stores included in the study. The pattern reflects the relative size and accessibility of each store. As may be expected, the outlet closest to any zone usually accounts for the greatest share of trips originating from it.

Table 5–2
Forecasts of Supermarket Drawing Power
(percent share of trips to each store by zone)

	Store						
Zone	A	B	C	D	E	F	G
1.	10	2	75	5	1	4	3
2.	16	9	65	4	1	3	2
3.	30	42	20	5	2	0	1
4.	10	0	79	3	2	5	1
5.	51	9	31	1	0	3	5
6.	40	45	0	2	1	8	4
7.	27	3	60	4	0	2	4
8.	66	10	6	4	3	3	8
9.	88	5	2	2	3	0	0
10.	65	15	1	6	10	1	2
11.	8	2	0	2	78	6	4
12.	34	2	3	6	6	3	46
13.	78	3	1	5	1	2	10
14.	3	4	3	1	59	27	3
15.	0	1	1	2	61	32	2
16.	9	6	36	21	4	6	18
17.	4	0	21	52	2	3	18
18.	29	4	1	9	5	5	47
19.	22	12	2	9	10	16	29
20.	15	3	4	12	17	29	20
21.	1	0	2	2	30	55	10
22.	5	2	1	2	30	48	13
23.	7	2	32	42	2	6	9
24.	2	0	5	76	1	2	14
25.	11	3	5	46	1	6	28
26.	2	1	3	9	0	12	73
27.	4	0	3	5	10	59	19
28.	6	7	3	0	22	51	11
29.	3	0	1	0	4	91	1

Note: Totals may not equal 100 percent due to rounding.

Store *C*, for example, attracts the largest share of trips originating from zones 1, 2, 4, 7, and 16. The drawing power of this store is especially high for residents in zones 1 and 4. The store attracts at least three-quarters of all trips originating from these zones. This is because the next-closest alternative for these residents (store *A*) is relatively far away. The relative inaccessibility of the competing stores enhances the drawing power of store *C*. The opposite effect can be seen in the case of zone 16. Although store *C* is the closest alternative for these residents, only 36 percent of the trips originating from this zone are made to this store. In this case, store *C*'s drawing power is reduced because stores *D* and *G* are also relatively accessible to this zone. These two stores, therefore, attract a sizable portion of the trips originating from zone 16.

The drawing power of a store also depends on its relative size. Note, for example, the pattern of trips made by residents of zone 29. More than 90 percent of the trips originating from this zone are to store *F*. This store is the nearest store for these residents and also the largest store in the area. The combined effect of high accessibility and large size greatly enhances the competitive position of this store to the residents of this zone. The disadvantage of smaller size, on the other hand, is evident from inspecting the pattern of trips to store *B*, the smallest store in the region. On an average, this outlet attracts the lowest number of shoppers. Its total market share is only 6.62 percent. The store attracts less than 5 percent of trips from 19 of the 29 zones. Indeed, it fails to attract any trips from six zones. Even when it is the store closest to a zone, it does not receive a majority of the trips originating from the zone, as seen with zones 3 and 6.

Inspecting the predicted trip patterns serves a number of useful purposes. First, it provides a simple diagnostic tool for the analyst to check the validity of predictions from the model. The predicted trip patterns can be compared against the actual trip patterns collected from the survey. As shown earlier, the correlation coefficient between these two patterns can be computed to indicate the degree of correspondence. Alternatively, absolute or percent forecast errors can be computed to measure the degree of fit between actual and predicted trip patterns.

The predicted trip patterns are also useful for forecasting sales and revenues of new outlets and simulating the impact of changes in the retail environment on the performance of these stores. Table 5–3 illustrates the basic procedure for arriving at such forecasts. The expected weekly sales of store *C* for two different scenarios are shown in the table. To arrive at these forecasts, the share of trips attracted by store *C* from each origin is first calculated (obtained from the column for store *C* in table 5–2). Next, the population of each zone is estimated. This may represent current population data or forecasts depending on the time horizon of the study. To forecast the sales from each zone, the average weekly per capita grocery expenditure for the study

Table 5–3
Sales Forecast for Store C under Two Scenarios

Zone	Share of Trips from Zone	Population of Zone	Sales from Zone Scenario 1	Sales from Zone Scenario 2
1	75%	1,980	$49,005	$51,945
2	65	1,150	24,667	26,147
3	20	1,025	6,765	6,968
4	79	830	21,638	22,936
5	31	1,570	16,061	17,025
6	0	1,460	0	0
7	60	1,630	32,274	32,274
8	6	2,900	4,950	4,950
9	2	2,810	1,855	1,855
10	1	2,320	766	766
11	0	2,910	0	0
12	3	3,040	3,010	3,010
13	1	3,440	1,135	1,135
14	3	2,190	2,168	2,168
15	1	2,260	746	746
16	36	1,300	15,444	15,444
17	21	1,540	10,672	10,672
18	1	1,660	548	548
19	2	2,320	1,531	1,531
20	4	1,980	2,614	2,614
21	2	2,100	1,386	1,386
22	1	2,020	667	667
23	32	2,450	25,872	25,872
24	5	1,940	3,201	3,297
25	5	1,340	2,211	2,277
26	3	1,472	1,457	1,500
27	3	1,360	1,346	1,427
28	3	1,620	1,604	1,700
29	1	1,310	432	458
Total			234,025	241,318

area must be obtained from secondary sources. Based on the information on per capita sales, population size, and expected market share, store C's expected weekly sales from each zone can be calculated. The estimates for each zone are then summed to forecast the total sales of the store. As shown in table 5–3, in scenario 1, which represents the market as it is, the predicted weekly sales for store C are $234,025. The forecast for scenario 2 takes account of predicted changes in the size of population residing in each zone. Because of the expected completion of a number of housing projects in the near future, some of the zones in the study area are expected to have an influx of new residents. The second sales forecast reflects this expected population change.

Table 5–3 illustrates the basic procedure for arriving at sales forecasts for individual stores based on the spatial-interaction model. This basic procedure can be refined in a number of ways. First, in arriving at the forecast, an average per capita expenditure figure was used to calculate the sales from each zone. Per capita expenditures may, however, differ from one zone to another due to differences in family size and composition. It has been found, for example, that grocery expenditures are lower for single-person families and families in the early stage of the life cycle due to a higher propensity for eating out. Families with young children, on the other hand, tend to spend more on grocery purchases. To refine the sales forecasts, the expected per capita sales for each zone may be adjusted to reflect the population characteristics of the zone.

A further adjustment to the forecast is often necessary to account for cross shopping. Recall that the underlying assumption of the interaction model is that there is no cross-shopping. In practice, however, there is always some amount of cross-shopping. Residents from the study area may do some of their shopping at stores not included in the study. Thus, there is some potential for loss of sales to these stores. In the context of supermarkets, there is always some sales "leakage" to small neighborhood grocery and convenience stores in the study area that are not included in the model. It is common to adjust the forecast by a fixed amount based on the analyst's experience to account for potential sales leakage.

One of the advantages of the spatial-interaction model is the ability not only to forecast sales under existing conditions, but also to simulate the impact of potential changes in the retail environment on outlet performance. One can investigate, for example, the impact on sales of increasing the size of a store or the impact of competitive actions. An illustration of this type of simulation is provided later in the chapter. Interaction models are also useful for projecting the sales of new stores and, based on these projections, for determining optimal sites for new outlets. Site-selection procedures based on the interaction model are discussed in detail in the next chapter.

The Market Share of Hospitals

Interaction models are helpful not only for analyzing the trade areas of stores selling goods and merchandise but also for institutions providing services to a geographically dispersed population. In this context, Folland (1983) provides an interesting application of the interaction model to predict the market shares of hospitals in South Dakota. As Folland notes, "Hospitals, like all businesses, are concerned about their share of the market" (p. 34). Market share information is important to hospital administrators for resource-allocation decisions and for projecting capacity utilization. Hospital market share data are useful for health-planning agencies in projecting admission and demand patterns from different areas. Market share models provide an understanding of the dynamics of the competitive health care market and the relative competitive position of individual hospitals.

To study the spatial pattern of hospital trips, the author estimated a multiattribute spatial-interaction model. To calibrate the model, information on the spatial origin of patients entering 58 general short-term–care voluntary hospitals in North Dakota was obtained from a patient-origin survey conducted in 1977. From the survey, the author calculated each hospital's share of patients originating from each county in the state. This information was used to define the probability of an individual in county i patronizing a hospital in city j, P_{ij}. Ideally, areal units smaller than counties should be used to define the origin zones or subareas. Counties may be too large in geographic area and population size to provide accurate representations of consumer choices. This level of aggregation masks significant differences in patronage patterns within counties. Nevertheless, the study provides important insights into the competitive structure of the hospital industry and the determinants of hospital market shares.

Many previous studies of hospital utilization have relied on distance alone to explain the observed spatial pattern of hospital visits. Distance, however, is only one of the many factors influencing hospital patronage decisions. The author, therefore, defined an interaction model including eight explanatory variables in addition to distance. The variables and their operational definitions are shown in table 5–4. The first two variables in table 5–4—*DIST* and *PRICE*—are measures of the cost associated with visiting a hospital and were thus hypothesized to have a negative impact on market share. All the other variables measure different aspects of the attractiveness of hospitals. The variable *BEDS* measures the number of beds in the hospital and is similar to the size variable used in most retail-store market-share models. In addition to size, hospital admissions depend critically on physician referral patterns. To account for this, the number of physicians associated with the hospital (*PHYS*) was also included as an explanatory variable. The variables *ICU*, *EMR*, and *PSYCH* indicate the kinds of services available in the hospital. The greater the range of services, it was hypothesized, the higher the drawing power of the hospital. Similarly, accreditation of the hospital (*JCAH*) was expected to positively affect the hospital's market share. The four variables *ICU*, *EMR*, *PSYCH*, and *JCAH* were all measured on a binary scale indicating the presence or absence of the attribute.

The final variable in the model, *SALES*, was included to "represent 'collateral' opportunities" (Folland 1983, p. 37). This measured the attractiveness not of the hospital per se, but of the city in which the hospital is located. Operationally, it was defined as the sales tax revenue of the city in which the hospital is located and it served as an index of retail potential of that city. It was hypothesized that hospitals located in larger cities had a competitive

Table 5–4
Independent Variables Used in Hospital Study

Variable	Definition
DIST	Distance between county of origin and hospital
PRICE	Average inpatient revenues adjusted for case mix
BEDS	Number of beds in hospital
JCAH	Hospital accreditation by Joint Commission for accrediting hospitals
PSYCH	Inpatient psychiatry unit in hospital
EMR	Emergency room in hospital
ICU	Intensive care unit in hospital
SALES	Sales tax revenue from city
PHYS	Number of physicians associated with hospital

Source: Sherman T. Foland, "Predicting Hospital Market Shares," *Inquiry* 20 (Spring 1983): 34–44. Used with permission of the Blue Cross and Blue Shield Association. All rights reserved. Reprinted with permission.

advantage over their counterparts in smaller towns. All other factors being equal, rural patients are likely to choose a hospital in a city with which they may be familiar.

Using different subsets of the independent variables, a number of different versions of the interaction model were fit to the observed patient-flow data. Results from two of the models are shown in table 5–5. Model A is a restricted version which included only four explanatory variables: *DIST, BEDS, PHYS,* and *SALES.* Model B, on the other hand, included all the nine variables listed in table 5–4. Both models fit the data very well. Model A with only the four explanatory variables can account for more than 66 percent of the variation in trip patterns. All the explanatory variables in the model had the expected sign and were statistically significant, although the relationship between *PHYS* and market share was relatively weak.

As expected, due to the additional explanatory variables included, model B accounted for more of the variation in trip patterns than model A. The increase in explanatory power was, however, not substantial: from 66.3 percent to 67.6 percent. The parameters associated with three of the five new variables in this model—*PRICE, PSYCH,* and *ICU*—were statistically significant. *PRICE* had a negative impact on patronage. The presence of inpatient psychiatric units (*PSYCH*) had a positive impact and significantly increased market share. The parameter for *ICU* was significant but negative. This implies that the presence of intensive care units reduces the competitive advantage of hospitals. According to the author, this counterintuitive finding may have resulted from unevenness in the data-reporting procedure. The two other parameters in the model, those for *JCAH* and *EMR,* were not significantly different from zero.

Table 5–5
Estimated Coefficients of Two Hospital Interaction Models

Variable	Model A		Model B	
	Coefficients	t-value	Coefficients	t-value
DIST	−1.65	40.9	−1.66	41.7
BEDS	0.40	3.0	0.24	1.7
PHYS	0.19	1.6	0.20	1.6
SALES	0.21	2.1	0.26	2.5
PRICE			−0.51	2.5
JCAH			−0.05	0.4
PSYCH			0.67	4.0
EMR			0.14	1.0
ICU			−0.29	2.3

Source: Sherman T. Foland "Predicting Hospital Market Shares," *Inquiry* 20 (Spring 1983): 34–44. Used with permission of the Blue Cross and Blue Shield Association. All rights reserved. Reprinted with permission.

Note: Model *A* includes variables *DIST, BEDS, PHYS,* and *SALES.* Model *B* includes all nine variables.

It is important to note that the lack of statistical significance of *JCAH* and *EMR* does not necessarily mean that accreditation or the presence of emergency room facilities are unimportant in attracting patients. The statistical results may simply reflect the structure of the data. It is likely that with 80 percent of the hospitals having emergency rooms, the lack of variation led to insignificant parameters. Explanatory variables that have very little variation across alternative destinations, in general, are likely to have low levels of explanatory power. This does not imply that these characteristics are unimportant, but, rather, because of their similarity across alternatives, other attributes are used to choose among alternatives.

Another potential reason for the lack of significant relationships between *JCAH* and *EMR* and market share is multicollinearity in the data. Although details are not provided by the author, it is possible that the various measures of hospital attractiveness are related to each other. Hospitals with large numbers of beds and physicians are also likely to have emergency rooms and to be accredited. As discussed in the previous chapter, collinearity among the explanatory variables can affect the statistical results in regression analysis. Multicollinearity may also be the reason for the merely marginal improvement in explanatory power of model *B* compared to model *A.* Although there are five additional variables in model *B,* the explanatory power does not improve substantially. It is likely that some of the additional variables are correlated with one or more of the variables included originally, such as *BEDS.* The fact that the coefficient for *BEDS* differs substantially between the two models indicates that this variable may be correlated with some of the other independent variables.

There are a number of ways of measuring the predictive performance of interaction models. The simplest measure is the R^2 or F statistic computed from the regression model. The Folland study reports on two other indices of model performance which are also commonly used. To calculate these indices, the total patient flow to each hospital is first predicted using the estimated parameters of the two models. The correlation coefficient between the predicted and actual total-utilization level provides a concise measure of model accuracy. For both models, the correlations were greater than 0.99, indicating a high level of correspondence between predicted and actual utilization levels. The second index is the average absolute percent error in predicting the total utilization of individual hospitals. The error for model A was 20.4 percent. For model B, it was 19.8 percent. The level of error can be compared against similar statistics from other forecasting methods to assess the relative accuracy of the interaction model.

Market Attraction of Shopping Centers

This final example of spatial-interaction modeling demonstrates the use of the multinomial logit (MNL) formulation. Weisbrod, Parcells, and Kern (1984) analyzed 170 shopping trips made to six Boston metropolitan area shopping centers by 80 households during a week in 1977. The MNL model was estimated for this data using the maximum-likelihood (MLE) calibration procedure. Each of the 170 discrete choices made by the households served as a unit of observation in the estimation process.

The variables used by the authors to explain individual shopping choices are listed in table 5–6. The first five variables measure the time and cost of travel and the mode of transportation used by the shoppers. It should be noted that unlike the two earlier models, in this case, travel time is defined separately for two modes of transportation: private automobiles and public transportation. Further, the actual cost of the shopping trip was calculated instead of relying on distance as a surrogate measure. In the interaction model, separate coefficients were estimated for travel time for the two modes of transportation to reflect the differential effect of travel time under the two modes.

The final five variables measure different characteristics of the shopping centers hypothesized to influence shopping choice. These variables measure the total number and mix of the types of stores in the centers. The authors posited that the presence of clothing and shopping goods outlets increases the attractiveness of shopping centers in general. The number of variety stores, on the other hand, reflects the availability of lower-priced merchandise and the attractiveness of the centers to lower-income shoppers. The final variable,

Table 5–6
Explanatory Variables in the Joint Choice of Shopping Destination and Travel Mode

Variables	Units
Variables that affect mode choice	
1. Auto mode constant	= 1 for auto alternatives = 0 for transit alternatives
2. Number of autos owned in household (for auto choice)	Number (for auto alternatives only)
Variables that vary among mode and destination combinations	
3. Auto travel time	Minutes for a one-way trip (including in-vehicle time and walk to destination after parking) (for auto alternatives only)
4. Transit travel time	Minutes for a one-way trip (including in-vehicle time, wait time at origin and transfer points, and walk time at origin and destination) (for transit alternatives only)
5. Out-of-pocket cost per $1,000 of income	Cents for a one-way trip/$1,000 (half of round-trip total cost, including gasoline, parking fee, transit fare) (for auto and transit alternatives)
Variables that describe each destination	
6. Total number of stores	Number at destination
7. Clothing and general merchandise	Proportion of all stores at destination
8. Other shopping goods	Proportion of all stores at destination
9. Variety stores	Proportion of general merchandise stores at destination (for lower-income households only)
10. Planned center	= 1 for planned shopping center = 0 for otherwise

Source: G.E. Weisbrod, R.J. Parcells, and C. Kern, "A Disaggregate Model for Predicting Shopping Area Market Attraction," *Journal of Retailing* 60 (Spring 1984): 65–83.

planned center, is a dummy variable that differentiates planned suburban malls from downtown and strip shopping areas (Weisbrod, Parcells, and Kern 1984, p. 72).

To measure the relative impact of each variable on shopping center choice, the authors used the multinomial logit (MNL) formulation of the interaction model. (See equation 5.9.) The MNL model, too, can be rewritten to be linear-in-parameters and estimated by the least-squares procedure. The authors, however, estimated the model using the maximum-likelihood method. Instead of aggregating the respondents into different origin zones, a disaggregate model was calibrated using the observations on individual shopping trips. Each observation included information on the travel mode and destination chosen for the trip and the characteristics of the chosen and non-chosen alternatives. In addition, information on travel time and cost was also included. The MLE procedure is based on the assumption that, if shopping choice can be described by the MNL model, the probability of observing all the choices in the sample is given by:

$$\phi = \prod_{i=1}^{I} \frac{\prod_{l=1}^{L}\left(e^{\alpha_{lic}A_{lic}}\right)\left(e^{\beta_{ic}D_{ic}}\right)}{\sum_{k \epsilon N_i}\left[\left(\prod_{l=1}^{L} e^{\alpha_{lk}A_{lik}}\right)\left(e^{\beta_{ik}D_{ik}}\right)\right]} \tag{5.12}$$

where I is the total number of trips in the sample, and c denotes a chosen alternative. All other parameters are as defined previously. Expression 5.12 is called the likelihood of the sample. The MLE method estimates the values of the parameters that maximize this likelihood. Computer packages for MLE estimation are available for both mainframe and micro computers. For a more general discussion of MNL models, see McFadden (1974) and Hensher and Johnson (1981).

To explain the observed pattern of trips, the authors initially posited a general model that included all the variables shown in table 5–6. In this full model, the variable *planned center* was associated with a negative sign. This was counter to the original expectation that, all else being equal, planned regional centers would be preferred over strip centers and downtown shopping areas. A possible reason for this counterintuitive result is the correlation between this and other explanatory variables—the multicollinearity problem.

To eliminate the possible impact of multicollinearity, the authors estimated a second model that did not include the *planned center* variable. The results from this model are shown in table 5–7. In the second model, all coefficients except the one for number of autos were significantly different from zero. The total number of stores in the center and the proportion of clothing, shopping, and variety stores all have positive impacts on patronage. On the other hand, as one would expect, greater time and higher cost of travel negatively affect patronage. The magnitudes of these latter impacts depend, however, on the travel mode used. The significant and positive auto-mode parameter reflects the greater propensity for travel when the automobile rather than public transportation is used for travel. Not surprisingly, shoppers are more willing to travel to distant centers when they drive to the centers.

The goodness-of-fit of the model to the observed shopping choices was measured by the ρ statistic. This statistic is similar to the R^2 statistic of regression analysis. The value of ρ typically obtained in empirical analysis, however, is quite low. A value of .4 is considered to reflect a satisfactory fit between predicted and observed shopping patterns.

Once the model was calibrated, the authors used the estimated coefficients to forecast the pattern of patronage to the different centers for a number of scenarios. The forecasts were based on the residential patterns of

Table 5–7
Estimated Coefficients of the Logit Equation for Shopping Center Choice

Variable	Coefficient	t-value
Auto mode constant	2.545	2.76
Number of autos	0.027	0.09
Auto travel time	−0.090	−2.95
Transit travel time	−0.046	−2.03
Travel cost/income	−0.765	−3.24
Number of stores	0.008	7.33
Clothing and general merchandise	15.640	6.90
Other shopping goods	35.560	4.81
Variety stores	1.866	2.66
Ln likelihood at $\beta = 0$ (all alternatives equally likely)		−366.90
Ln likelihood for maximum likelihood value of β		−219.88
ρ^2		.40

Source: G.E. Weisbrod, R.J. Parcells, and C. Kern, "A Disaggregate Model for Predicting Shopping Area Market Attraction," *Journal of Retailing* 60 (Spring 1984): 65–83. Reprinted with permission.

Note: ρ^2 is the goodness-of-fit statistic generally used for models estimated by the maximum-likelihood method. This index, which is analogous to the R^2 in ordinary regression analysis, is defined by the formula:

$$\rho^2 = 1 - \frac{(Ln \text{ likelihood at maximum likelihood values of } \beta)}{(Ln \text{ likelihood at } \beta = 0)}$$

475 census tracts constituting the market area of the six shopping centers. Information on population size, income, and socioeconomic characteristics of each tract was obtained from the census. Information on travel times and costs was obtained from publications of the metropolitan transit authorities in Boston.

Table 5–8 shows the downtown shopping area's (CBD) share of shopping trips originating from the 475 census tracts. The first column of the table shows the share of trips predicted for the current situation, categorized by the type of transportation used and by the income level of the shopper. As can be seen from the table, the shopping pattern differs significantly for the low- and high-income groups. One-fourth of all trips made by low-income shoppers are expected to go to the CBD. For the higher-income group, the corresponding figure is 32.5 percent. Since the different income groups tend to live in distinct geographic areas, the disaggregation of forecasts by income group and transport mode allows the location analyst to pinpoint differences in shopping patterns originating from various residential zones.

The expected shares of trips to the CBD in four other scenarios are also shown in table 5–8. The first three scenarios—free public transportation to

Table 5–8
Forecasts of Auto and Transit Trips to the Boston Central Business District as a Percentage of All Trips to Six Major Shopping Areas

Mode	Base Case	Zero Transit Fare	Zero Downtown Parking Fee	Elimination of Suburban Mall	50% Rise in Gas Price
Low-income families[a]					
Transit	21.6%	23.1%	13.7%	22.0%	22.2%
Auto	3.5	3.4	54.3	6.6	0.8
Total	25.1	26.5	68.0	28.6	23.0
High-income families[b]					
Transit	3.3	4.2	2.0	3.6	4.4
Auto	29.2	28.5	47.8	46.5	22.1
Total	32.5	32.7	49.8	50.1	26.5

Source: G.E. Weisbrod, R.J. Parcells, and C. Kern, "A Disaggregate Model for Predicting Shopping Area Market Attraction," *Journal of Retailing* (Spring 1984): 65–83. Reprinted with permission.

[a]Family income less than $25,000 in 1969 dollars.

[b]Family income of $25,000 or more in 1969 dollars.

the CBD, free parking for CBD shoppers, and elimination of a suburban shopping mall—have often been proposed as possible means of increasing shopping in the CBD. The fourth scenario looks at the impact of a drastic increase in gasoline price on shopping patterns.

Of the four scenarios, only the elimination of downtown parking fees is predicted to have a significant impact on the CBD's share of trips for both income groups. The CBD's share of trips is expected to increase to 68 percent for the low-income group and to nearly 50 percent for high-income families under this scenario. In addition to increasing the overall level of shopping at the CBD, elimination of parking fees also leads to more automobile use for downtown shopping. This is especially so for lower-income shoppers. Under present conditions, about 25 percent of all shopping trips made by the low-income group are to the CBD and public transportation is preferred for more than 85 percent of these trips. Elimination of parking fees would drastically reduce mass transit use to only 20 percent of all trips.

The next scenario investigated by the authors is the provision of free public transportation to the downtown shopping area. While often advocated as a way to increase the vitality of the CBD, this is not projected to have a significant impact on the share of trips to the CBD for either income group. The CBD's share of trips increases only marginally in this scenario. The elimination of the suburban mall, on the other hand, is expected to have a significant impact on the shopping pattern of high-income families—the proportion of trips to the CBD increases to about 50 percent. The low-income group, however, is expected to be relatively unaffected by the elimination of the suburban mall. The final scenario considered the possible impact of a 50 percent increase in gasoline prices on shopping patterns. According to the forecasts, this would not increase shopping at the CBD. As the authors note, this is counter to the suggestion made during the gasoline crisis that higher gasoline prices would lead to greater use of mass transportation and downtown shopping.

The study demonstrates the use of spatial-interaction models to forecast shopping patterns in diverse future scenarios. It also illustrates the use of a disaggregate logit model to calibrate spatial-interaction models. Since each observed shopping trip is an observation in the MNL model, one advantage of this calibration technique is that only a relatively small number of shopping choices need be observed. The result is "a tool of forecasting at modest expense the shopping choices of individuals and the aggregate market shares of competing shopping areas under a wide variety of scenarios" (Weisbrod, Parcells, and Kern 1984, p. 68).

In general, the three case studies illustrate the use of spatial-interaction models and the steps in setting up a retail forecasting system. They demonstrate alternative procedures for calibrating interaction models and procedures for checking the validity of the results. As illustrated, the models can be used to analyze the competitive environment of a wide variety of retail outlets and to forecast the sales and market share of individual outlets under different scenarios. Interaction models provide a versatile and powerful tool for location analysis.

The Spatial Nonstationarity Problem

Spatial-interaction models have been successfully used to assess the forces affecting consumer shopping patterns and to obtain aggregate forecasts of market-share distributions across outlets. These models provide an overall description of the competitive environment and its impact on consumer shopping patterns in a study area. The parameters of the interaction model provide a measure of the relative impact of different store and site characteristics on consumer choice.

Although interaction models are formally specified at the level of individual origins or zones, they are usually calibrated at an aggregate level providing a single set of parameters for the study area. The parameters, therefore, represent the aggregate effect of that variable on shopping patterns in the area. The aggregate parameters may, however, mask significant differences among individuals or groups of individuals in the process by which shopping choices are made. Persons residing in certain residential areas, for example, may be much more sensitive to distance than the rest of the population because of lack of access to transportation. Thus, their "true" distance-decay parameter would be more negative than the average parameter computed for the study area as a whole. The "true" parameter values may, therefore, vary geographically across the study area.

Differences in the spatial organization of alternatives considered by individuals is another reason for the parameters of spatial-interaction models to vary over space. The spatial structure of the choice set considered by an individual affects the individual's choice process. This, in turn, affects the relative importance given to different distance and nondistance factors and the values of the parameters associated with these factors. It has often been found, for example, that the distance-decay parameter tends to be less negative for accessible origins located at the center of a region than for origins located at the periphery (Haynes and Fotheringham 1984). Since the spatial configuration of the choice set usually varies across different parts of the study area, this too results in spatially varying parameters in the spatial-interaction model.

Such spatial variation in parameters of interaction models is called "spatial nonstationarity" (Stetzer 1977). If the true parameters of an interaction model are spatially nonstationary, predictions of the pattern of shopping trips originating from the different zones based on the aggregate parameters can be misleading even when the overall statistical fit is satisfactory. To forecast the pattern of shopping trips, it is important to check for spatial nonstationarity in the model.

In this section, we first briefly review some of the causes of nonstationarity. Procedures for detecting nonstationarity are discussed next. Two approaches for dealing with the nonstationarity problem are then presented.

Causes of Nonstationarity

Although spatial-interaction models are widely used by researchers to predict consumer retail-patronage decisions, the question of spatial nonstationarity has been largely ignored. Researchers have only recently begun to analyze systematically the effect of spatial structure on the parameters of retail-choice models. A number of early studies had, however, noted the existence of the problem. In their study of grocery purchase behavior, Clark and Rushton (1970) found, for example, that a consumer's sensitivity to distance depends critically on the distance to the nearest alternative. The greater the distance to the nearest alternative, the greater the propensity to bypass it. Consequently, the impact of distance on store choice is less when the closest alternative is farther away. Similarly, Bucklin (1971), in a study of hospital-patronage decisions, found the impact of distance to be related to the ratio of distances to alternative facilities. A number of recent experimental studies have also found evidence that spatial variation in consumer's choice sets significantly affects the weight or importance attached to the distance parameter in the interaction model. (See, for example, Meyer and Eagle 1982; Eagle 1984.)

Nonstationarity can also result from systematic variations in socioeconomic characteristics of individuals at each origin. Car owners and higher-income individuals, for example, can travel longer distances and give more importance to nondistance factors in choosing shopping destinations (Dixon and McLaughlin 1970; Goldman 1976). On the other hand, low-income groups (with their poorer access to automobile transportation and lower disposable incomes) are likely to patronize stores located nearby. If residential patterns are segregated by socioeconomic characteristics, spatial nonstationarity is highly likely. One way to overcome the effect of nonstationarity arising due to population heterogeneity is to calibrate the model separately for different population groups (Hubbard 1979). Although this increases the cost of data collection because of larger sample-size requirements, by calibrating the model separately for different population segments, the potential for nonstationarity is reduced.

Detecting Spatial Nonstationarity

Dealing with nonstationarity due to the spatial organization of choice sets is a difficult task. Prior to discussing ways of dealing with the problem, we demonstrate the impact of spatial organization on retail choice using the supermarket data set analyzed earlier. Recall that the data set contained information on shopping trips from twenty-nine origins to seven supermarkets in the study area. The estimates of the coefficients of size and distance (the two variables used in the model) were 1.453 and -2.025, respectively. The model provided a good fit to the observed data for both the calibration and a hold-out sample. The purpose now is to investigate whether the estimated parameters are stable or whether the true parameters vary from one origin to another. If the parameters are indeed nonstationary, the forecasts of trips from individual origins will be prone to error even though the overall sales forecasts are quite accurate.

A simple procedure for detecting whether the parameters are spatially nonstationary is to estimate separate models for each origin. This would result in twenty-nine different interaction models—one for each origin. However, calibrating separate models for each origin requires observations on trip flows to a large number of destinations from each origin. There must be a large number of stores in the study area to permit estimation of separate models. Since the supermarket study area contains only seven stores, it is not possible to estimate a separate model for each origin.

An alternative approach for detecting nonstationarity is to use the "jack-knife" technique. This technique allows for testing the stability of the parameters without requiring large sample sizes (Fenwick 1979). Popularized by Tukey (1958), the jackknife procedure first obtains a global estimate of a parameter using all the available data. A series of new estimates are then obtained by systematically excluding a subsample from the original data and calibrating the model for these reduced subsamples. In the spatial-interaction model, subsamples can be created by excluding the data for each origin in turn and calibrating the MCI model for each of the resulting subsamples. Let $\hat{\beta}_{all}$ be the global estimate of a parameter and $\hat{\beta}_{-i}$ the estimate obtained by excluding from the total sample observations from origin i. The normal jackknife (pseudovalues) for origin i can then be calculated as follows:

$$J(\hat{\beta})_i = m\,\hat{\beta}_{all} - (m - 1)\hat{\beta}_{-i}$$

where m is the number of subsamples.

The jackknife pseudovalues offer evidence of the stability of the parameters and indicate the degree to which intersample differences affect the results. To detect nonstationarity in the supermarket data set, twenty-nine sets of pseudovalues were calculated by excluding from the total sample, in turn, the data for each origin. The pseudovalues for both α and β show considerable place-to-place variation. The pseudovalue of α has a mean value of 1.66 and standard deviation of 2.41; the β value has a mean of -2.02 and a standard deviation of 0.64. The high degree of variation in the pseudovalues leads one to suspect that the parameters are nonstationary. The relative impact of distance and store size on trip patterns differs from one origin to another. The aggregate parameters ($\alpha = 1.453$ and $\beta = -2.025$) represent average values that best describe the overall pattern of shopping trips. While the overall market share predictions based on these average values may be satisfactory, predictions of flows from individual origins may be suspect.

Developing Nonstationary Models

A number of alternative approaches have been suggested for dealing with nonstationarity. Since nonstationarity is related to the spatial characteristics of the destination set considered by each individual, in general, these approaches involve introducing origin- or destination-specific measures of location characteristics in the model. We first discuss an approach that introduces origin-specific parameters in the model. Then, an alternative approach based on destination-specific parameters is presented.

A straightforward test of the impact of spatial structure on the parameter values is to calculate the correlations between the pseudovalues for each origin and different measures of spatial structure defined for each origin. To perform such a test, the pseudovalues of α and β were correlated with four spatial morphological indices defined for each of the twenty-nine origins.

These measures were: (1) distance to the nearest store from each origin, (2) range of distance to all alternatives measured from each origin, (3) mean distance to all stores measured from each origin, and (4) ratio of the distance to the farthest and closest stores from each origin. Each of these measures represents characteristics of the spatial organization of supermarkets as viewed by the residents of each origin.

The pseudovalues of α were not significantly correlated with any of these morphological measures. Thus, although this parameter exhibits considerable place-to-place variation, one cannot reject the hypothesis that this nonstationarity is simply due to chance. Pseudovalues of the β parameter, on the other hand, were correlated significantly with two of the measures: the distance to the nearest store and the ratio of distances to the closest and farthest store in the choice set. The correlation with distance to the nearest store is -0.537 and the correlation with the ratio measure is 0.807. Both correlations are statistically significant at the $p = .005$ level. The implication of this result is that the impact of distance on store choice depends on the spatial organization of the choice sets. The closer the nearest store is to an origin, the greater the impact of distance on the pattern of patronage made by the residents of that origin. Similarly, the true distance-decay parameter is greater for origins where the ratio of the distances to the farthest and the closest stores is high. Since these morphological measures vary from origin to origin, the distance-decay parameter in the choice model is spatially nonstationary.

The high correlation between the origin-specific pseudovalues and the morphological measures indicates the need for specifying an extended model to account for spatial nonstationarity in the distance-decay parameter. The extended model must contain origin-specific morphological measures. In the case just described, since the pseudovalues had the highest correlations with the ratio measure, the original model was extended to include the ratio measure as a separate variable. This was done by the following method: Define R_i as the ratio of distances of the farthest and the closest stores measured from origin i, and β_i as the true distance-decay parameter for origin i. Now assume a linear relationship between these two variables:

$$\beta_i = \omega + \theta R_i$$

Substituting this relationship in the original model leads to the following interaction model:

$$\ln(P_{ij}/P_{i*}) = \alpha \ln(S_j/S_*) + \omega \ln(D_{ij}/D_{i*}) + \theta \ln(D_{ij}/D_{i*})R_i$$

By incorporating the new variable in the model, the impact of distance is essentially decomposed into two categories. The parameter ω measures the systemwide impact of distance on choice, while θ measures origin-specific impacts. Since R_i varies for each origin, the third variable is a measure of origin-specific effects. To check for the impact of this variable on store choice, one performs the t-test under the null hypothesis that the true value of θ is zero. If the null hypothesis is not rejected, the model reduces to equation 5.10.

The new model was calibrated by the OLS procedure. For the supermarket data, all three parameters are statistically significant. The estimates of the three parameters were $\alpha = 1.519$, $\omega = -2.531$, and $\theta = 0.090$. The statistical significance of the θ parameter reflects the systematic impact of spatial structure on spatial choice. The effect of distance on store choice varies significantly according to the ratio of distances to the nearest and farthest stores.

To compare the predictive accuracy of the original and extended models, the models were tested on a hold-out sample. The hold-out sample contained information on twenty origins and was not included in the data used to calibrate the model. The correlation coefficient between the observed and predicted market shares from each origin was .865 for the original model and .890 for the extended specification. The extended model reduced the mean squared and the mean absolute error of prediction by 18.19 and 15.49 percent, respectively. More important, the extended model, since it controlled for spatial structure, significantly reduced some of the extreme prediction errors in the original model. When the original model was used to predict the travel pattern of the hold-out sample, remotely located travel origins were associated with high prediction errors. The predictions of the extended model for these origins were consistently and significantly better. Overall, the predictions of the extended model were more accurate for seventeen of the twenty origins in the hold-out data set. (For more details of the study, see Ghosh 1984.)

The Competing-Destination Model

An alternative approach to dealing with nonstationarity, based on destination-specific attributes, has been suggested by Fotheringham (1983). He argues that the retail-choice process should be viewed as a hierarchical one in which individuals first select a cluster of retail outlets or a part of the study area and then select the individual outlet from that cluster. To determine the probability of an individual outlet being chosen, therefore, one would have to first predict the probability that the area in which the store is located would be chosen and then the probability of selecting that particular store in the area. The product of these two probabilities determines the likelihood that an individual store would be chosen. To model such a hierarchical choice process, Fotheringham presents a *competing-destination* formulation of the interaction model.

In the competing destination model, the accessibility of a retail alternative to all the other potential destinations is first measured. Let this variable be denoted as I_j. The probability of an individual at origin i choosing retail alternative j, P_{ij}, is now written as:

$$P_{ij} = S_j^\alpha D_{ij}^\beta I_j^\gamma \Big/ \sum_{k \in N_i} S_k^\alpha D_{ik}^\beta I_k^\gamma$$

Since the variable I_j measures the relative accessibility of an alternative from all stores in the area, a positive value would indicate that stores located close to each other have an advantage over isolated outlets. This may be the case for goods that require comparison shopping. A negative value of the parameter, on the other hand, may be expected for convenience goods for which there is little variation in price and quality and, thus, little comparison shopping. In this case, clustered outlets are at a disadvantage compared to isolated stores that have a spatial monopoly in a local market area. The actual value of the parameter would, of course, vary from one empirical situation to another. Unfortunately, to our knowledge, no empirical test of this model in a retail setting has yet been reported.

The problem of spatial nonstationarity needs further attention from researchers. We have briefly demonstrated here the nature of the problem and a method for detecting the presence of nonstationarity. Two alternative approaches to dealing with nonstationarity in retail-choice models were also illustrated. Some may argue that individual-store–choice models must be specified to solve the nonstationarity problem. This would, however, considerably increase the burden of data collection and the cost of model calibration. One reason for the popularity of interaction models is the simplicity of data collection and estimation. The two approaches suggested here deal with nonstationarity without requiring additional data collection.

Conclusion

Spatial-interaction models provide insight into the store-choice process and predict quite well the pattern of shopping trips in an area. These models provide considerable assistance to the retail analyst in simulating the impact of changes in market factors on the performance of individual outlets. Central to any interaction model is the data base used in calibrating the model. The data base should be created with care, since the accuracy of the forecasts depends on it. Data on shopping patterns should be collected from a representative sample of consumers and all store characteristics likely to impact on store choice must be included. To determine the relative impact of factors on shopping patterns, the model must then be calibrated using standard statistical procedures.

Many commercial "gravity" forecasting systems tend to undermine the importance of data collection and empirical calibration of the interaction model. In these forecasting systems, only size and distance are used as explanatory variables and the impact of these variables on store choice is approximated by a "normal" formula based on the subjective judgment of the analyst. Since the predictions from this "normal" formula often do not replicate actual sales patterns well, the model is adjusted by introducing for each store a subjective measure of "image." Iterative search procedures are usually used to "balance" the model. The examples presented in this chapter provide a more comprehensive view of the state of the art in the theory and application of interaction models for retail forecasting.

Although existing models provide a valuable tool for retail researchers, considerable opportunities exist for additional research. Existing models can be refined by incorporating additional variables to improve their predictive performance. In addition, there is a need to measure more accurately the variables themselves. For example, measures of relative accessibility derived from the morphological structure of an area would provide a better indicator of the actual effort expended by consumers in visiting different retail alternatives. Similarly, more refined measures of consumer perception of store images need to be incorporated.

Underlying the spatial-interaction model is the hypothesized consumer utility function for evaluating stores. Current models generally use a compensatory type of utility function in which consumers "are hypothesized to trade off the disutility of distance with the benefits of store attributes" (Craig, Ghosh, and McLafferty 1984, p. 29). Noncompensatory models, on the other hand, do not allow trade-off between attributes. The appropriateness of noncompensatory models of choice has been demonstrated by a number of studies on brand choice. In the retailing context, Recker and Schuler (1981) found a noncompensatory model to provide better predictions of store choice than compensatory ones. Further research comparing these two types of models is necessary. Another avenue of further research is to explore the role of direct utility assessment using structured-choice experiments. Instead of relying on observations of past choice, these methods use consumer evaluations of hypothetical store descriptions to calibrate the utility function. (See, for example, Parker and Srinivasan 1976; Burnett 1982; Louviere and Woodworth 1983; Ghosh and Craig 1986.) Properly conducted experimental studies can provide considerable insight into consumer behavior and patronage decisions while allowing the separation of the spatial context of choice from the choices themselves.

References

Berry, B.J.L. (1967). *The Geography of Market Centers and Retail Distribution.* Englewood Cliffs, N.J.: Prentice-Hall.

Black, W.C.; Ostlund, L.E.; and Westbrook, R.A. (1985). "Spatial Demand Models in an Intrabrand Context." *Journal of Marketing* 49: 106–113.

Bucklin, L.P. (1971). "Retail Gravity Models and Consumer Choice: A Theoretical and Empirical Critique." *Economic Geography* 47: 489–497.

Burnett, K.P. (1982). "The Application of Conjoint Measurement to Recent Urban Travel" in R. Golledge and J. Rayner (eds.), *Data Analysis in Multidimensional Scaling.* Columbus: Ohio State University Press.

Clark W.A.V., and Rushton, G. (1970). "Models of Intra-Urban Consumer Behavior and Their Implications for Central Place Theory." *Economic Geography* 46: 486–497.

Craig, C.S.; Ghosh, A.; and McLafferty, S. (1984). "Models of Retail Location Process: A Review." *Journal of Retailing* 60(1): 5–36.

Davies, R.L. (1977). *Marketing Geography: With Special Reference to Retailing.* London: Methuen.

Dixon, D.F., and McLaughlin, D.J. (1970). "Low Income Consumers and the Issue of Exploitation: A Study of Chain Supermarkets." *Social Science Quarterly* 51: 320–328.

Eagle, T.C. (1984). "Parameter Stability in Disaggregate Retail Choice Models: Experimental Evidence." *Journal of Retailing* 60(1): 101–123.

Fenwick, I. (1979). "Techniques in Market Measurement: The Jackknife." *Journal of Marketing Research* 16: 410–414.

Folland, S.T. (1983). "Predicting Hospital Market Shares." *Inquiry* 20: 34–44.

Forbes, J.D. (1968). "Consumer Patronage Behavior" in R.L. King (ed.), *Marketing and the New Science of Planning.* Chicago: American Marketing Association.

Fotheringham, A.S. (1983). "A New Set of Spatial Interaction Models: The Theory of Competing Destinations." *Environment and Planning A* 15: 1121–1132.

Gautschi, D.A. (1981). "Specification of Patronage Models for Retail Center Choice." *Journal of Marketing Research* 18: 162–174.

Ghosh, A. (1984). "Parameter Nonstationarity in Retail Choice Models." *Journal of Business Research* 12: 425–436.

Ghosh, A., and Craig, C.S. (1986). "An Approach to Determining Optimal Locations for New Services." *Journal of Marketing Research* 23: 354–362.

Goldman, A. (1976). "Do Low Income Consumers Have a More Restricted Shopping Scope?" *Journal of Marketing* 40: 46–54.

Haines, G.H.; Simon, L.S.; and Alexis, M. (1972). "Maximum Likelihood Estimation of Central City Food Trading Areas." *Journal of Marketing Research* 9: 154–159.

Hansen, M.H., and Weinberg, C.A. (1979). "Retail Market Share in a Competitive Environment." *Journal of Retailing* 56(1): 37–46.

Haynes, K., and Fotheringham, A.S. (1984). *Gravity and Spatial Interaction Models.* Beverly Hills: Sage.

Hensher, D.A., and Johnson, L.W. (1981). *Applied Discrete Choice Modeling.* New York: John Wiley & Sons.

Hubbard, R. (1979). "Parameter Stability in Cross Sectional Models for Ethnic Shopping Behavior." *Environment and Planning A* 11: 977–992.

Huff, D.L. (1962). "Determination of Intra-Urban Retail Trade Area." *Real Estate Research Program.* University of California at Los Angeles.

Huff, D.L. (1963). "A Probabilistic Analysis of Shopping Center Trade Areas." *Land Economics* 39: 81–90.

Huff, D.L. (1964). "Defining and Estimating a Trade Area." *Journal of Marketing* 28: 34–38.

Huff, D.L., and Blue, L. (1966). "A Programmed Solution for Estimating Retail Sales Potential." Center for Regional Studies, University of Kansas.

Jain, A.K., and Mahajan, V. (1979). "Evaluating the Competitive Environment in Retailing Using Multiplicative Competitive Interactive Models" in J. Sheth (ed.), *Research in Marketing.* Greenwich, Conn.: JAI Press.

Louviere, L., and Woodworth, G. (1983). "Design and Analysis of Simulated Consumer Choice or Allocation Experiments: An Approach Based on Aggregate Data." *Journal of Marketing Research* 20: 350–367.

Luce, R. (1959). *Individual Choice Behavior.* New York: John Wiley & Sons.

Mahajan, V.; Jain, A.K.; and Ratchford, B.T. (1978). "Use of Binary Attributes in the Multiplicative Interactive Choice Model." *Journal of Consumer Research* 5: 210–215.

McFadden, D. (1974). "Conditional Logit Analysis of Qualitative Choice Behavior" in P. Zarembkar (ed.), *Frontiers in Economics.* New York: Academic Press.

Meyer, R.J., and Eagle, T.C. (1982). "Context-Induced Parameter Instability in a Disaggregate Stochastic Model of Store Choice." *Journal of Marketing Research* 19: 62–71.

Nakanishi, M., and Cooper, L.G. (1974). "Parameter Estimates for Multiplicative Competitive Interaction Models—Least Squares Approach." *Journal of Marketing Research* 11: 303–311.

Nakanishi, M., and Cooper, L.G. (1982). "Simplified Estimation Procedures for MCI Models." *Marketing Science* 1: 314–322.

Nakanishi, M.; Cooper, L.G.; and Kassarjian, H.H. (1974). "Voting for a Political Candidate under Conditions of Minimal Information." *Journal of Consumer Research* 1: 36–43.

Parker, B.R., and Srinivasan, V. (1976). "A Consumer Preference Approach to the Planning of Rural Primary Health-Care Facilities." *Operations Research* 24: 991–1029.

Recker, W., and Schuler, H. (1981). "Destination Choice and Processing Spatial Information: Some Empirical Tests with Alternative Constructs." *Economic Geography* 57: 373–383.

Rogers, D.S. (1984). "Modern Methods of Sales Forecasting" in R.L. Davies and D.S. Rogers (eds.), *Store Location and Store Assessment Research.* New York: John Wiley & Sons.

Stanley, T.J., and Sewall, M.A. (1976). "Image Inputs to a Probabilistic Model: Predicting Retail Potential." *Journal of Marketing* 40: 48–53.

Stetzer, F. (1977). "The Application of Nonstationary Spatial Models." Ph.D. Dissertation, Department of Geography, University of Iowa, Iowa City.

Tukey, J.W. (1958). "Bias and Confidence in Not-Quite Large Samples." *Annals of Mathematical Statistics* 29: 614.

Weisbrod, G.E.; Parcells, R.J.; and Kern, C. (1984). "A Disaggregate Model for Predicting Shopping Area Market Attraction." *Journal of Retailing* 60(1): 65–83.

6
Developing
Retail-Outlet
Networks

Opening new stores is one of the most important avenues of growth for retail firms. Locating new outlets, whether in existing markets or in new areas, expands the geographic area served by the firm and increases the potential for sales and profits. Developing a network of outlets also provides a hedge against the uncertainties of the market environment. To create a market presence and achieve economies in advertising, distribution, and labor, retail firms are increasingly establishing networks of outlets to serve consumers in a wide geographic area.

Organizing such networks is a critical task for retail managers. Traditional methods of site selection are not well suited for this purpose since they are limited to analyzing single-store locations. These single-store procedures ignore the impact that an individual store might have on other outlets in the market area operated by the same firm. Establishing a network of two or more outlets, on the other hand, requires systematic evaluation of the impact of each store on the entire network of outlets operated by the firm and consideration of the "system-wide store-location interactions" (Achabal, Gorr, and Mahajan 1982, p. 8).

Because of the importance of the multistore-location decision, a number of approaches to selecting multiple sites and organizing the spatial network of outlets in an area have been proposed in recent years. Most of these methods fall under the rubric of location-allocation models. The term *location allocation* refers to two basic elements of any site-selection procedure. The models determine: (1) the best *locations* for new retail outlets based on stated corporate objectives and (2) the *allocation* of consumers to those outlets based on the expected pattern of consumer travel. These allocations determine the trade area of each outlet and are used to forecast sales and profits. Since the optimal locations depend on consumer shopping patterns, and the shopping patterns depend on store locations, both the optimal locations and the allocations must be determined simultaneously. By considering these two fundamental aspects of siting together, location-allocation models are a powerful tool for analyzing retail-location patterns. The models provide an efficient procedure for systematically evaluating store locations and finding sites that maximize corporate goals such as profits or market share. Location-allocation models can be used to design a network of retail outlets in an unserved market area or to analyze the benefits of adding new stores to existing networks. Location-allocation models are also useful in deciding how to relocate or close existing stores.

Because of these advantages, interest in the application of location-allocation models for designing multiple-facility networks, for both private and public services, has grown rapidly in the past decade. These models have been used in the siting of warehouses, corporate receivable collection systems, day care centers, schools, emergency medical centers, fire stations, and retail outlets. Examples of the use of location-allocation models in retail settings are given by Zeller, Achabal, and Brown (1980), Achabal, Gorr, and Mahajan (1982), Ghosh and McLafferty (1982), Ghosh and Craig (1983), Goodchild (1984), Goodchild and Noronha (1987), and Ghosh and Craig (1986), among others. The ongoing interest in these models reflects their flexibility in dealing with a variety of planning situations and different kinds of retail outlets.

In this chapter, we illustrate the application of retail location models for designing retail networks. The chapter is organized into four major sections. First, we discuss the basic components of location-allocation models. In the next three sections, a number of case studies covering a variety of retail situations are presented. The case studies illustrate how diverse types of performance measures and sales forecasting procedures can be incorporated in location-allocation models. Through these examples, we illustrate the application of location-allocation models for site selection and designing the network of outlets.

Location-Allocation Models

Designing a network of retail outlets is a complex task. Planning such networks requires decisions on the number of outlets to open in the market area, the locations of these outlets, and the characteristics of the outlets. All of these decisions are interrelated and must be made within a single decision-making framework. These decisions must take into account the spatial and socioeconomic characteristics of the market and the overall corporate and marketing goals of the firm. Location-allocation models provide an efficient and powerful technique for developing location strategies for retail firms.

Value of the Models

Location-allocation models address the question: How can a set of retail facilities be located to best serve a dispersed population? For retail applications, the geographic accessibility of stores and spatial coverage of market areas are important concerns in location decisions. As noted in previous chapters, because individuals bear the cost of travel, distance and travel time have important effects on consumer shopping decisions and, ultimately, on the profitability of retail outlets. This, coupled with the high cost of relocating retail outlets, makes the location decision one of the most important and difficult decisions for retail managers. Location-allocation models provide a method for evaluating alternative network configurations and determining the sites that are most accessible to consumers. At the same time, the models take into consideration the manner in which consumers trade off accessibility with other store characteristics. By looking at both distance and nondistance factors simultaneously and taking into consideration the spatial pattern of demand and the locations of other outlets in the area, these models are uniquely suited to plan the organization of retail networks.

A critical component of any location strategy is the decision regarding the number of outlets to open in a market area. Making such a decision poses a unique challenge to the retail analyst. In deciding how many stores to operate, the firm must trade off the likely revenue generated by increasing the number of outlets in an area with the cost of establishing and operating those outlets. In attempting to maximize the population's access to retail outlets, the firm would ideally want to locate a large number of outlets so as to reduce the distance consumers must travel to patronize the outlets. In general, the greater the number of outlets, the less the distance travelled by consumers. (See figure 6–1a.) By adding more outlets and, thus, increasing accessibility to consumers, the firm can attract more customers and increase its market share. At the same time, operating a large number of outlets increases the cost of establishing and maintaining the retail network. (See figure 6–1b.) In choosing the optimal number of stores, the retailer must, therefore, balance the increased revenue from additional outlets against the increased costs of facility construction and operation. The point at which marginal benefits equal marginal costs defines the optimal strategy for the firm.

Yet, in determining the optimal number of stores for a market area, the firm must also consider the question of location. A smaller number of well-located stores may generate higher revenues than a larger number of poorly located outlets. For any given number of stores, then, it is essential to know which locations within a market area afford maximum revenues and profits. Location-allocation models help identify such locations.

The Components of Location-Allocation Models

Location-allocation models consist of five basic components: the objective function, demand points, feasible sites, distance or time matrix, and allocation rule.

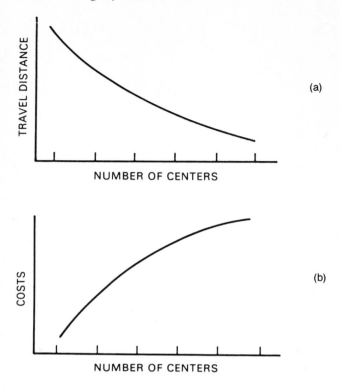

Figure 6–1. Relationships among Number of Centers, Travel Distance, and Costs

Objective Function. The first, the *objective function,* states the objectives to be optimized in selecting store locations. It is the yardstick against which alternative-location plans are compared. In retailing applications, the objective function is usually a measure of accessibility or economic viability of the outlets. Depending on the amount of data available and the type of service to be located, a firm may specify a variety of objective functions ranging from simple measures of market penetration and accessibility to complex profitability measures that incorporate both costs and revenues.

Demand Points. The second component of location-allocation models is information on the geographic distribution of demand for retail goods and services. In general, demand is represented by a set of spatial coordinates referred to as *demand points.* Each of these points represents the center of a zone containing a certain level of demand for the goods and services provided.

Typically, these demand zones are small, compact geographic locales such as census tracts or zip code areas for which population data are readily available. The total demand at each location is estimated from census reports or other secondary sources as discussed in chapter 3.

Feasible Sites. A third component of location-allocation models is information on a set of *feasible sites* for store locations. These are sites that meet certain minimal requirements concerning land, access, and infrastructure for the location of new stores. In selecting the feasible sites, such factors as land availability, zoning restrictions, cost, and ease of access and egress must be taken into consideration. A checklist, similar to that shown in table 3–4, is useful for identifying feasible sites.

Some applications of location-allocation models, referred to as "planar" models, do not require that feasible sites be first identified. These models assume that any point in the area is a feasible site—no location is infeasible. In these applications, optimal locations for new outlets are first identified and then areas near those locations are searched for feasible sites. Such a procedure reduces the need to identify all the feasible sites in the area before performing the analysis. There are two drawbacks to this approach, however. First, there are often no feasible sites at the optimal locations identified by the model. For example, the selected sites may be in areas whose zoning code does not permit commercial development. The identified location plan, therefore, cannot be implemented, thereby reducing the validity of the model. Second, by not first identifying the feasible sites, the impact of real estate cost on outlet profitability cannot be directly considered.

Distance or Time Matrix. The fourth component of location-allocation models is a *distance or time matrix* which shows the distance or travel time from each demand point to each feasible store location. The distance or time matrix is generated by calculating the shortest distance or travel time between each pair of points over the road network. For the distances accurately to reflect actual travel times, factors such as physical and social barriers to travel, the model of transportation used, traffic congestion, and other influences on individual travel must be taken into account. This requires extensive information, not only on the underlying transportation network in the study area, but also on the social and economic characteristics of consumers and their levels of geographic mobility. (See the discussion on calculating travel times and distances in the previous chapter.)

A simpler strategy is to calculate distances mathematically in reference to a spatial coordinate system. Most often, this involves computing straight-line Euclidean distances between demand points and potential store locations. Another option, again using the spatial coordinate system, is to use the city-block metric which measures the distance between two points as the sum of the horizontal and vertical distances between the respective coordinates. This corresponds to the distance measured along a right-angle path between the two points, and it provides a good approximation of the true travel distance in areas with a gridlike street pattern. The main advantage of coordinate distances, as opposed to actual travel distances, is the ease with which they can be calculated. Calculating actual travel times requires detailed information on street or road networks, travel speeds, and mode of transport used, whereas coordinate locations and distances can be easily calculated from a map. These advantages come at the expense of accuracy, however. In areas with irregular or sparse road networks or where consumers differ greatly in mobility and access to transportation, coordinate distances may bear little relationship to true travel distances.

The decision as to which type of distance measure to use is a matter of judgment which depends not only on the resources available for data collection and analysis, but also on the estimated degree of error introduced by using simple coordinate measures. For ease of presentation, henceforth we use the term *distance matrix* to mean either a distance or travel-time matrix. We assume that in any application, the most accurate measures of either distance or, preferably, travel time will be used.

Allocation Rule. The fifth and final component of location-allocation models is the *allocation rule*. The allocation rule specifies the manner in which consumers are expected to choose among the different outlets in the area and simulates the expected pattern of shopping trips. It is used in forecasting the trade areas of the outlets and the sales and market share of each outlet. It is crucial, therefore, that the allocation rule be specified with care. Since the consumer decision process differs from one situation to another, there is no single allocation rule that is appropriate for all situations. One of the advantages of location-allocation models is the ability to change the allocation rule depending on the type of application.

Since the allocation rule represents the manner in which consumers make patronage decisions, knowledge of the consumer choice process is necessary in specifying this component of the location-allocation model. In some situations, for example, consumer choice may be based solely on accessibility. In other cases, consumers may trade off distance and nondistance factors in determining store choice. Similarly, choice may be a deterministic process, in which a single store is always patronized or a number of stores are patronized with different frequencies.

In the previous chapters, different procedures for determining the trade area of retail outlets were described. These are the basis on which allocation rules are specified. In the following sections, we illustrate the application of location-allocation models with a number of case studies covering a variety of retail settings. They demonstrate the use of different allocation rules and performance criteria. In the first example, the *proximal area* principle is used to specify the allocation rule. The assumption, therefore is that consumers patronize the nearest store. Sales forecasting procedures based on proximal areas were discussed in chapter 4. We now demonstrate how proximal areas can be used to identify optimal sites for new outlets. This example also demonstrates the use of a simple accessibility criterion as the objective function for evaluating alternative location plans.

Our second example is a continuation of the supermarket example discussed earlier in chapter 5. That chapter demonstrated the estimation of a spatial-interaction model and the application of such models for sales forecasting and market area assessment. The focus here is on utilizing the results of the spatial-interaction model to determine good sites for opening new outlets. The final section illustrates the use of "covering" models. Covering models are especially useful in service and service-related industries for designing service center networks. In each case, we discuss the underlying assumptions of the method and the type of situations for which they are appropriate.

Models Based on Proximal Areas

To demonstrate the basic approach to using location-allocation models for retail location analysis and to demonstrate the steps necessary in implementing a location-allocation model, we use a simple hypothetical example as our first illustration. Consider a retail firm that wishes to open a single outlet in an area. The service to be provided is completely new, and there are no competing retailers nearby. Thus, the new outlet will be the only one providing that service. The study area for this illustration is shown in figure 6–2. The area contains eight demand points, which are the centroids of their respective demand zones. The centroids are designated by numerals in the figure. Three feasible sites for opening new outlets (sites *A, B,* and *C*) are also shown in the figure. A small number of demand points and feasible sites are used so that relevant computational details can be shown clearly. In any real application, the number of demand points and feasible sites will, of course, be much larger.

A key step in implementing the location-allocation model is to specify the allocation rule. The allocation defines the way consumers choose among alternative outlets. Here, we use a simple allocation rule in which store choice is based solely on distance: Consumers patronize their nearest outlet and each store serves a well-defined proximal market area. The greater the accessibility of the outlet, therefore, the higher the total level of patronage. Given the importance of accessibility, the objective is to maximize consumer access to the

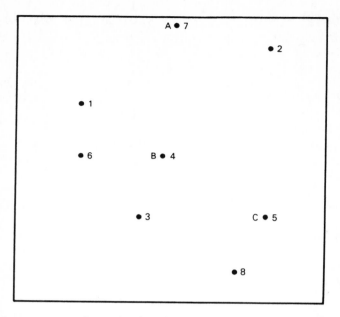

Note: Numbers represent demand points. Letters represent feasible sites.

Figure 6-2. A Hypothetical Study Area

network of outlets. Operationally, the desirability of a location pattern can, therefore, be measured by the average distance consumers need to travel to reach the outlets. This is the objective function.

To find the location pattern that minimizes consumer travel, the distance matrix must first be calculated. This is shown in table 6–1. Each row in the matrix shows the distance between each feasible site and the corresponding demand zone. The last column of the matrix shows the relative demand in each zone. There is considerable spatial variation in demand in the area. The highest level of demand is at zones 5 and 8. Zones 1 and 4, on the other hand, are sparsely populated. Because of this variation in demand, the choice of location is crucial. The problem now is to determine where the new outlet(s) should be located. We first consider the location of a single outlet.

The new outlet can be located at three possible sites: *A, B,* or *C.* To determine the optimal choice, the objective function corresponding to each of these three options must be evaluated. This involves calculating the total distance consumers will have to travel to patronize the outlet, as shown in table 6–2. The distance travelled by consumers from each of the eight zones is shown for the three feasible sites. The first column, for example, is the travel distance to site *A.* If the outlet is located at site *A,* consumers in zone 1 will

Table 6–1
Distance Matrix for Three Possible Sites by Zone

Zone	Distance to Site in Miles			Relative Demand Weight
	A	*B*	*C*	
1	4.2	3.6	7.2	2
2	3.2	5.0	6.0	5
3	7.1	2.2	4.0	4
4	5.0	0.0	3.6	2
5	7.6	3.6	0.0	8
6	5.8	3.0	6.3	5
7	0.0	5.0	7.6	6
8	9.2	4.5	2.2	7

Table 6–2
Weighted Travel Distance to Three Possible Sites by Zone

Zone	Site		
	A	*B*	*C*
1	8.4	7.2	14.4
2	16.0	25.0	30.0
3	24.4	8.8	16.0
4	10.0	0.0	7.2
5	60.8	28.8	0.0
6	29.0	15.0	31.5
7	0.0	30.0	45.6
8	64.4	31.5	15.4
Total weighted distance	213.0	146.3	160.1

have to travel 4.2 miles to patronize that outlet. Since the relative demand for this zone is 2, the weighted distance is 8.4 miles. If the outlet is located at site *B,* on the other hand, the weighted distance increases to 7.2 miles. Site *C* is the least accessible to this zone; the weighted distance is 14.4 miles. The sum of the weighted distances for each zone is the value of the objective function. Since the objective is to maximize accessibility, the site with the minimum total weighted distance is best. Based on this criterion, the outlet should be located at site *B* since the total travel distance is only 146.3 miles compared to 213.0 miles and 160.1 miles for sites *A* and *C,* respectively.

The criteria of weighted distance can also be used to design multiunit networks. Consider, for example, the problem of locating two outlets in the area. There are three ways in which the two outlets can be located: at sites *A* and *B,* at sites *A* and *C,* and at sites *B* and *C.* To calculate the weighted distance corresponding to these three location plans, the proximal area for each outlet must be determined. The proximal areas are as shown in figure 6–3. The figure shows, for each of the three plans, the nearest facility location for each zone. If the outlets are located at sites *A* and *B,* for example, the proximal area for site *A* will contain zones 2 and 7. All other zones will be in the

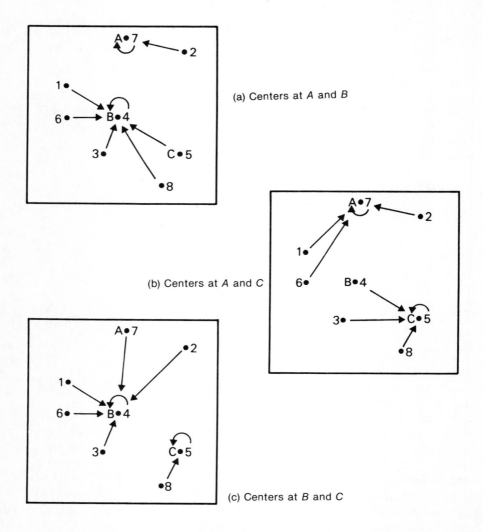

(a) Centers at *A* and *B*

(b) Centers at *A* and *C*

(c) Centers at *B* and *C*

Figure 6–3. Proximal Area for Two Centers

proximal area of site *B*, since they are closer to that site than to site *A*. Moving the facility at site *B* to site *C* increases the proximal area of site *A*. Since zones 1 and 6 are closer to site *A* than site *C*, these zones are now assigned to site *A*'s proximal area. Once the proximal areas for a plan are determined, the travel distance can be calculated easily. The total travel distance is the sum of the weighted distances from each zone to its closest facility. The calculations are shown in table 6–3. As can be seen from the table, total travel distance is lowest when the outlets are located at sites *A* and *C*. This, therefore, is the optimal spatial configuration for locating two outlets.

This simple example illustrates the use of location-allocation models for developing a network of multiple outlets. It demonstrates the basic approach to location analysis and the various data collection and computational steps necessary in implementing location-allocation models. The key elements of this procedure are: (1) specification of the allocation rule to calculate the trade area of outlets, (2) specification of the objective function for evaluating alternative location plans, and (3) creation of a geographic data base containing the distance matrix and the spatial pattern of demand in the area. A fourth element of location-allocation models is an efficient computational system for systematically generating and evaluating alternative location plans. In large problems, with many demand zones and feasible sites, a computer algorithm is necessary to keep track of all calculations and select the optimal network configuration. The examples in the later sections illustrate this element of location-allocation models.

The p-Median Problem

The previous example, albeit simple, is based on a classical location-allocation problem known as the p-*median model*. This model has been widely used for many types of facility-location problems and is one of the most discussed location models. The objective of the p-median problem is to find the locations for a given number (p) of outlets that minimize the average distance consumers must travel to reach their nearest outlet. Thus, the objective function of the model, as in the previous example, is to maximize consumer access to the network of outlets. The p-median problem was first expressed by Alfred Weber, who considered the location of a factory between raw material sites and the market. In choosing a location for the factory, he argued, the objective should be to minimize the total costs of transporting raw materials to the factory and finished products from the factory to the market (Friedrich 1929). Weber proposed simple mechanical and graphic methods for solving this problem. It was not until several decades later that researchers were able to design a mathematical algorithm to the p-median problem.

Weber's problem has a direct analog to retail applications where maxi-

Table 6–3
Travel Distances for Two-Center Locations

	Centers Located at		
Zone	A and B	A and C	B and C
1	7.2	8.4	7.2
2	16.0	16.0	25.0
3	8.8	16.0	8.8
4	0.0	7.2	0.0
5	28.8	0.0	0.0
6	15.0	29.0	15.0
7	0.0	0.0	30.0
8	31.5	15.4	15.4
Total	107.3	92.0	101.4

mizing the accessibility of outlets to customers is a major objective. In the retail case, the criterion for selecting a location plan is to minimize the average distance separating consumers from their nearest outlet. To state the problem mathematically, define w_i as the demand for retail goods in the ith demand zone and (x_i, y_i) as the location on some fixed coordinate system of the centroid of the ith demand zone. The objective function of the p-median problem for locating a single retail store can then be written as:

$$\text{Minimize} \sum_{i=1}^{n} w_i[(x^* - x_i)^2 + (y^* - y_i)^2]^{1/2}$$

The objective is to find the location (x^*, y^*) that minimizes the total distance travelled by potential consumers. This corresponds to minimizing the sum across demand areas of the product of the total demand in each area and the distance to the retail outlet. The problem can be solved efficiently using an iterative method developed, independently, by Kuhn and Kuenne (1962) and Cooper (1963).

The Competition-Ignoring Model

The Weber problem is the foundation for all proximal-area based location-allocation models. Though the Weber problem was first developed to find the location for a single outlet, in retailing applications, it is more realistic to consider a firm locating several stores or adding a store to an existing network. This would be the problem faced by, for example, a retail chain wishing to enter or increase its presence in a market area. In developing such a network, the firm's objective may be to maximize access to outlets and thereby increase the level of service to potential consumers. To deal with such location problems, Goodchild (1984) proposed a variation of the p-median model called the competition-ignoring model (CIM). The objective of the CIM is to find locations for p stores such that the total distance travelled by consumers to the nearest outlet is minimized. In order to evaluate a potential location configuration, the CIM model uses the nearest-center allocation rule—that is, all consumers are assumed to patronize the nearest outlet belonging to the chain.

Mathematically, the CIM model can be defined as follows: Let the location of n demand zones be denoted by their coordinates (x_i, y_i) and the relative demand at each zone by $w_i (i = 1, 2, \ldots, n)$. The set of feasible sites in the area is denoted by F, and E is the set of existing outlets in the area belonging to the same firm. The objective function of the CIM can then be written as follows:

$$\text{Min} \sum_i \sum_{j \in J \cup E} x_{ij} w_i d_{ij}$$

where, $J (J \in F)$ is the set of chosen locations

$$X_{ij} = \begin{cases} 1 \text{ if } d_{ij} < d_{ik} \text{ for all } k \in J \cup E, \ k \neq j \\ 0 \text{ otherwise} \end{cases}$$

$$d_{ij} = [(x_i - x_j)^2 + (y_i - y_j)^2]^{1/2}$$

Note that x_{ij} operationalizes the allocation rule, since it defines the set of demand points served by each outlet. The variable takes the value of one when the outlet at j is closest to zone i. Since it takes the value zero otherwise, only the distance to the closest facility from each zone is included in the objective function. The objective function minimizes the total distance travelled by consumers to the nearest stores belonging to the firm.

To determine the best location pattern, the objective function must be minimized subject to the following constraints:

$$\sum_{j \in J} x_{ij} = p$$

$$x_{ij} \leq x_{ij} \qquad \text{for all } i, j$$

The constraints ensure that only p facilities are located and that consumers are not allocated to a site that has no outlets.

The CIM model can be interpreted as one that maximizes potential demand for the goods or services sold by the stores by maximizing the accessibility of stores to consumers. The basic argument is as follows: Under certain minimal assumptions about the elasticity of demand with distance, distance acts as a surrogate for the demand for retail goods and services. If we assume that demand is a decreasing linear function of distance (see figure 6–4), then, in seeking locations that minimize total travel distance, the CIM also finds the locations that maximize total demand. The ability to choose sites that offer the highest potential sales for the firm is an attractive feature of the CIM model.

An illustration of the use of CIM in retail site selection is provided by Goodchild (1984). In this application, a restaurant owner used the CIM model to design a network of three restaurants in London, Ontario. Two of the stores (sites 1 and 2 in figure 6–5) were already in operation, but the third site was yet to be chosen. The owner had identified the primary target market for the restaurant as individuals in the 15-to-44 age group with household incomes above $25,000 per year. Since the new restaurant was thought to offer a unique service, the owner chose the CIM location strategy that ignores competitors' locations. The objective was to find the site that maximized accessibility to potential customers and thereby maximized its potential demand.

Figure 6–5 shows the optimal site for the third restaurant in relation to the residential pattern of the target market and the location of the existing outlets. Contour lines around the site indicate the loss in accessibility if the firm chooses to locate away from its optimum position. For example, the level of accessibility for a site on the 90 percent contour line is 90 percent of that at the optimum site. This information can be used in evaluating the rela-

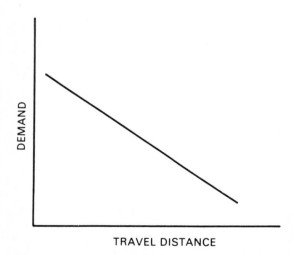

TRAVEL DISTANCE

Figure 6.4. Relationship between Demand and Travel Distance Assumed in *p*-Median Model

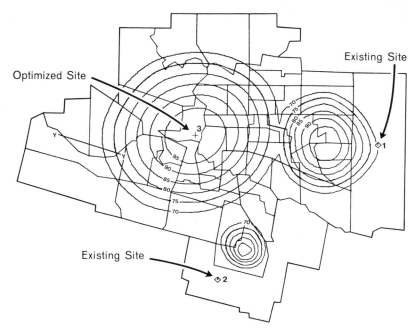

Source: M.F. Goodchild, "ILACS: A Location-Allocation Model for Retail Site Selection," *Journal of Retailing* 60 (Spring 1984):84–100. Reprinted with permission.

Figure 6–5. Optimization of a New Site for a Restaurant Chain Using CIM

optimal site are more desirable for store location. In this particular case, the optimal location had another advantage—it was found to maximize access to the daytime population. Thus, the location was also ideal for serving the lunchtime market, the restaurant's secondary target market. Consequently, the firm began negotiating for an available site in that area.

As its name suggests, the CIM formulation ignores the locations of competing stores in determining optimal sites. The assumption is that consumers first decide on the particular chain they wish to patronize and then travel to the outlet of that chain that is most accessible to them. Consumers, for example, may have a strong preference for a particular type of restaurant and have strong loyalty to that firm. Further, the model also assumes, quite realistically, that the more accessible the network of outlets operated by the firm, the greater the probability that potential consumers will select that chain. A consequence is that the firm's stores may be placed in close proximity to competitors' stores if the latter are located near areas of high demand. CIM, therefore, represents an aggressive corporate strategy that seeks to maximize market penetration without concern for the presence of competing stores. Of course, if all competing firms used a similar approach, the result would be complete clustering of competing stores at prime sites.

The Market-Share Model

For situations where it is important to take into account competitors' locations in the site-selection process, an alternative model called MSM (market-share model) has been proposed by Goodchild (1984). This model assumes that consumers travel to the closest available outlet irrespective of which chain operates the outlet. This may be true, for example, in cases where there is little difference in the competitive offerings or the images of the stores or when store loyalty is low. The objective of MSM is to maximize the total demand within the proximal market areas of the outlets operated by the firm. Following the same notations as earlier, the objective function can be written mathematically as:

$$\text{Max} \sum_i \sum_{j \epsilon J \cup E} x_{ij} w_j$$

$$x_{ij} = \begin{cases} 1 \text{ if } d_{ij} < d_{ik} \text{ for all } k \epsilon J \cup E \cup C \\ 0 \text{ otherwise} \end{cases}$$

where C is the set of competing outlets.

Given the nearest-center–allocation rule and the locations of competitors, the MSM finds the locations that maximize market share for the firm. It searches for gaps in the existing coverage of the market and locates stores in the inadequately served areas distant from the competitors' stores. The model, therefore, represents a more conservative corporate strategy that avoids areas served by competitors and tries to establish the firm's own geographic niche.

The basic principle of this model is illustrated by the series of diagrams shown in figure 6–6. They illustrate how the proximal area of a site is affected by the changes in location. In the diagrams, the solid circles represent locations of competing stores and the open circles the proposed sites for new outlets. Each diagram displays the proximal area for the proposed store at different locations. The proximal areas are determined by the method of Thiessen polygons discussed in chapter 4. The diagrams in the figure show how the size of the proximal area and, therefore, the potential demand change as the location of the new outlet is moved. The objective of the model is to find the location that maximizes the amount of demand contained within the proximal area of the new outlet(s).

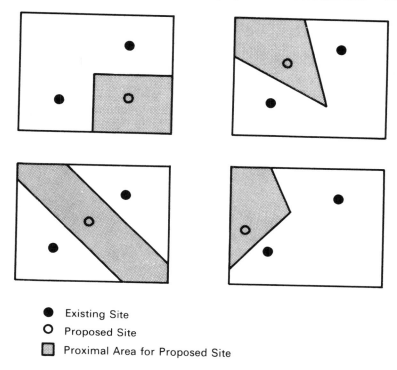

●   Existing Site

○   Proposed Site

▦   Proximal Area for Proposed Site

Figure 6-6. Proximal Areas for Different Locations

Summary

In summary, the distance-based models are useful in determining sites that maximize the population's accessibility to retail services. A major advantage of these models is their simplicity. Because they assume proximal market areas rather than more complex probabilistic allocations, they can be used without gathering detailed information on consumer shopping patterns. The accuracy of the model, of course, depends on the degree to which consumer shopping decisions approximate the nearest-center hypothesis. For low-order retail activities and convenience-oriented stores, where distance is known to have an important effect, these models are quite appropriate. And even for higher-order retail activities, in the absence of detailed information, the models can help identify poorly served areas and pinpoint highly accessible sites. As Goodchild (1984) has argued, given the high degree of uncertainty about competitive actions and reactions as well as future market conditions, there are distinct advantages to using simple models.

Optimal Location Strategy Using Interaction Models

Not all patronage decisions are based solely on accessibility. Consumers often trade off distance and nondistance factors (such as store size) in order to determine store choice. Proximal-area–based allocation rules do not capture such compensatory decision rules because they assume that travel distance is the only factor affecting store choice. In this section, we illustrate how the spatial-interaction model can be used to define allocation rules in location-allocation models. Spatial-interaction models provide an understanding of consumer travel patterns and the determinants of market share in complex retail environments.

This example also illustrates the use of direct performance measures as objective functions in location-allocation models. Instead of relying on travel distance, which provides only an indirect measure of outlet performance, these models evaluate location patterns in terms of expected market share and profit. Another feature is that the optimal number of stores is determined directly from the location model. In the earlier examples, the number of new outlets to be located was specified exogenously. In contrast, the models discussed here determine simultaneously the optimal number of outlets and their locations. As we shall demonstrate, the two decisions are interrelated and should be made jointly.

As a case study, we consider the supermarket example discussed in the previous chapter. Recall that in that example, three competing supermarket chains operated seven outlets in the market area. Three of the outlets were operated by chain *A,* while its competitors (chain *B* and chain *C*) operated two stores each. Now consider the following location problem: To improve its market presence and increase its market share, chain *A* plans to open new outlets in the area. The problem facing the management is to determine a location strategy that will maximize the firm's performance, given the locations of its existing outlets, the location of competitors' outlets, and the spatial pattern of consumer demand. The location strategy must encompass a number of related decisions including the number of stores to locate, the characteristics of these outlets, and their locations.

Choosing a location strategy for new retail outlets requires an understanding of the dynamics of the competitive environment and the determinants of market share. As discussed in the earlier chapters, store location acts in concert with many other factors in influencing consumer patronage decisions. The competitive advantage of any outlet depends on the level of these factors as well as the location of the outlet(s). The first step in implementing a location-allocation procedure, therefore, is to identify the factors that influence consumer choice in the particular situation in which the model is to be applied.

As shown in the previous chapter, consumer choice of supermarkets in the study area is affected jointly by distance and size of outlet. While accessibility is important, consumers shop more frequently at larger stores and are willing to travel farther to patronize larger stores. Thus, in addition to location, the sizes of existing and new stores must be considered in determining the location strategy. This also implies that one of the strategic variables for management consideration is store size. The attractiveness of the network can be enhanced by increasing the size of the outlets.

Although theoretically, store size is a continuous variable, in practice, firms usually consider a limited number of discrete size levels because of constraints on alternative design configurations and the size of land parcels. In this case, the supermarket chain followed two standard sizes, designated here as "large" and "small," for constructing outlets. A large store is more expensive to construct and operate, but it can offer a wider assortment of products and, therefore, attract more customers and generate more revenue. On the other hand, the small store, while being less costly to establish and operate, has less potential for generating revenue. In determining the best strategy, the firm must consider the potential costs and revenues associated with the two available sizes.

Another strategic variable that the firm must consider is the number of outlets to open. In this case, management has not specified the number of new supermarkets to open in the area, but is interested in finding the number that will maximize market share while maintaining profitability for the chain. Overall financial constraints dictate, however, that no more than three new outlets be opened in the market area. Thus, management must decide whether to open one, two, or three new outlets.

Combinations of different levels of these two strategic variables define the strategic options available to the firm for implementing the location strategy. We refer to these strategic options as *macrostrategies*. Each macrostrategy defines a possible combination of strategic variables other than location. For example, in this case a total of nine macrostrategies can be identified. As shown in table 6–4, each of these macrostrategies represents a possible combination of store size and number of outlets. For example, if the firm decided to open only one outlet, it could be either a large or a small one. Thus, there are two macrostrategies associated with opening a single outlet. Similarly, there are three macrostrategies associated with opening two outlets: (1) two large stores, (2) two small stores, and (3) one large store and one small store. Finally, there are four macrostrategies for the three-store option as shown in the table. In general, the number of macrostrategies depends on the number of strategic variables to be considered (other than location) and the number of levels or options for each strategic variable.

The macrostrategies define the overall strategies that the firm may adopt. The performance of each macrostrategy, however, depends on the location of the outlets. A well-chosen location plan will lead to a much better perfor-

Table 6–4
List of Macrostrategies

Macrostrategy	Number of Stores	Store Sizes	Number of Location Options[a]
1	1	Small	21
2	1	Large	21
3	2	Both small	210
4	2	One small, one large	420
5	2	Both large	210
6	3	All small	1,330
7	3	One large, two small	3,990
8	3	One small, two large	3,990
9	3	All large	1,330
	Total number of strategies = 11,522		

[a]Only one store can be located at each feasible site.

mance for a macrostrategy than a poor location configuration. To evaluate each macrostrategy and calculate the expected level of performance, the location options available to the firm must also be identified. The number of location options associated with a macrostrategy depends on the number of feasible sites available to the firm. The larger the set of feasible sites, the greater the number of possible location configurations.

In the present study, 21 feasible sites for opening new outlets had been identified based on land availability, zoning regulations, and site characteristics. (See figure 6–7.) This means that if only one store is to be located, there are 21 alternative sites for it. Thus, there are 21 possible ways of executing macrostrategies 2 and 3, both of which involve locating only a single store. When a macrostrategy involves opening more than one store, the number of alternative location plans increases combinatorially. Thus, there are 210 alternative configurations for opening two equal-sized outlets and there are 1,330 ways in which three equal-sized stores can be located.

When the stores are not of equal size, the number of location options increases even further, since the impact of opening different-sized outlets at the various locations must be taken into consideration. For example, in locating one small and two large stores (macrostrategy 8), it is necessary to consider 3,990 location configurations. The one that maximizes performance under this macrostrategy must be identified in order to evaluate the desirability of the macrostrategy. The performance of each macrostrategy, therefore, depends on the particular location option that is chosen. Thus, decisions regarding the optimal number of stores to be opened, their sizes, and locations are interrelated and must be determined simultaneously.

Given the large number of possible location options, an efficient com-

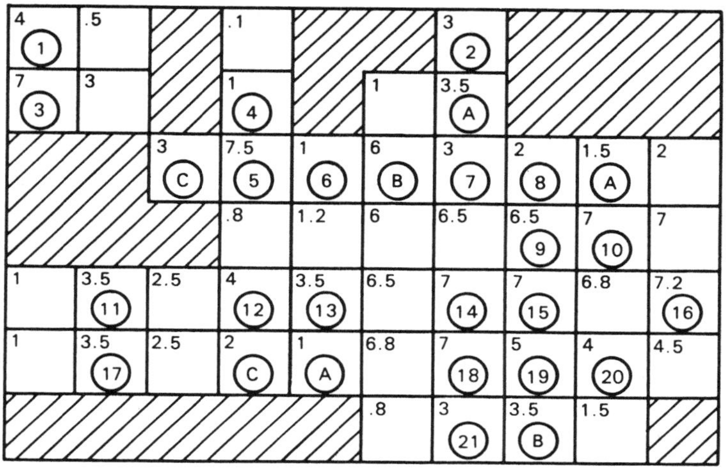

Note: Numbers in upper-left-corner indicate relative zone attractiveness, with higher numbers indicating greater attractiveness. Circles indicate occupied or feasible sites. A's, B's, and C's show existing store locations.

Figure 6-7. Schematic Map of Study Area for Supermarket Location Problem

putational procedure is required for finding the optimal strategy. Several procedures for finding the best location strategy have been suggested in the location-allocation literature. These include mathematical-optimization methods such as integer programming, heuristic algorithms such as the vertex substitution procedure, and complete enumeration and random sampling procedures. Conceptually, the simplest procedure for finding the optimal solution is complete enumeration. As the name suggests, in this approach, each of the possible location options is evaluated to select the one that maximizes performance. Since all possible location options are evaluated, this method will always find the optimal solution. The drawback, however, is that complete enumeration of all location options is feasible only for problems in which the total number of options is small. When the number is large, a random sample of the available options can be enumerated to reduce the computation burden (Achabal, Gorr, and Mahajan 1982). The risk, of course, is that the optimal solution may not be included in the sample and, therefore, will not be found.

In addition to complete enumeration, mathematical-optimization procedures such as integer programming guarantee globally optimal solutions. For most real-world problems, however, mathematical-optimization procedures are difficult to implement because of the large computer resource requirements. Consequently, these methods are rarely used in practice.

The most commonly used technique for solving location-allocation problems is heuristic algorithms. Heuristic algorithms are simple iterative search procedures which find good solutions, but not *necessarily* the optimal one. The advantage of heuristic algorithms is that they are simple to implement and are computationally efficient. Algorithms based on the vertex-substitution procedure proposed by Teitz and Bart (1968) are among the most popular heuristic ones for location problems. One problem with using heuristic algorithms is that global optimality cannot be guaranteed. That is, the algorithm may terminate with a solution that is good but not necessarily the best. Experience has shown, however, that heuristic procedures work very well for solving location problems and they usually find a very near optimal, if not *the* optimal, solution. A description of the vertex-substitution heuristic algorithm is given in appendix 6–1.

Complete Enumeration

To determine the location strategy for the supermarket, the complete enumeration procedure was used to solve the location-allocation problem. This procedure entails evaluation of a large number of location options and requires an efficient algorithm for performing this task. The different steps necessary for enumerating all location plans and calculating their expected performance under each macrostrategy is summarized in the flow diagram in figure 6–8. The first step is to specify the macrostrategy to be tested by initializing the store-size matrix (matrix S) and specifying the number of outlets to be located. For example, figure 6–8 shows the size matrix initialized for macrostrategy 4: one large store and one small store. The indices i and j refer to the locations of the first and second store respectively and a specifies the particular combination of store sizes being considered—a row of S. As we have thus identified the attributes of the location plan, the expected performance of the plan can be calculated in terms of market share, profit, service level, or any other objective the firm may set for itself.

The expected level of performance of course depends on the location of the outlets. Therefore, as shown in figure 6–8, the locations of the outlets are varied systematically to enumerate all possible location options for this macrostrategy. New location options are generated by changing the value of either i or j, the two location indices. This is done by substituting a site in the current solution with another feasible site that has not been evaluated yet. Every time such a change is made, the performance of the new plan is evaluated in terms of the stated objective function. For example, to evaluate options for adding two outlets, one starts by placing the outlets at sites 1 and 2. After this option has been evaluated, the value of j is changed from 2 to 3 and the performance of sites 1 and 3 is evaluated. Next, sites 1 and 4 are evaluated and so on. Since there are 21 feasible sites, after sites 1 and 21 are

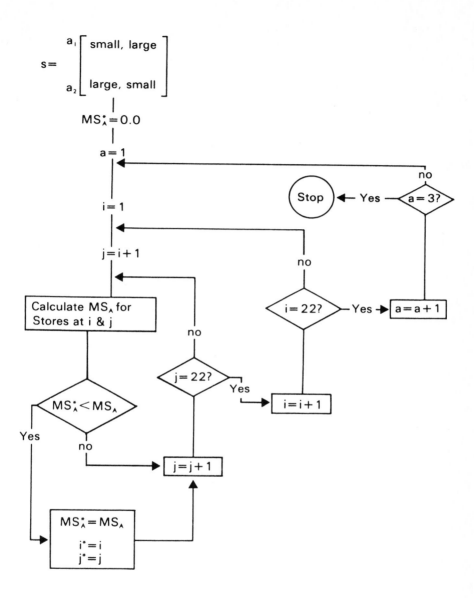

Optimal locations are sites i* and j*

Highest Market Share = MS_A^*

Figure 6-8. Flow Diagram of Steps in Evaluating a Macrostrategy

evaluated, the value of i and j are changed to 2 and 3, respectively, and the evaluation process is restarted with sites 2 and 3. In this way, all the 420 possible location options for this macrostrategy are evaluated.

The procedure described in figure 6–8 is repeated for all the macrostrategies and the best performance under each macrostrategy is noted. The total number of location options evaluated is the sum of the location options for each macrostrategy. In this case, the total number is 11,252. For complete enumeration to be feasible, the sum total of all location strategies must not be too great. In general, complete enumeration would be cumbersome if the number of location options exceeded 100,000.

As seen from the flow diagram, a key component of the procedure for evaluating location strategies is to calculate the expected level of performance of different location options. Although the criteria used for evaluating the plans may differ, the basis is always the expected pattern of patronage of the retail outlets. The patronage pattern determines the potential market share and the expected revenue of the individual outlets. As noted earlier, the patronage pattern is specified in the location-allocation model through the allocation rule. This rule should reflect the manner in which consumers make store-patronage decisions.

In this case, the appropriate allocation rule is the multiplicative competitive interaction (MCI) model since, as seen in chapter 5, the consumer choice process for supermarkets in this market area can be represented by this type of spatial-interaction model. The two explanatory variables included in the model are size and distance since these were found to be strongly correlated with market share. Given store size and distance as the two variables plus the empirically estimated values of the parameters associated with these variables, the market share of a new store can be predicted as follows:

$$\hat{MS} = \sum_{j=1}^{n+p} \sum_{i} a_i \hat{P}_{ij} \qquad (6.1)$$

where

$$\hat{P}_{ij} = \frac{\exp[1.45 \ln(S_j / S^*) - 2.02 \ln(D_{ij} / D^*)]}{\sum_{j=1}^{n+p} [1.45 \ln(S_j / S^*) - 2.02 \ln(D_{ij} / D^*)]} \qquad (6.2)$$

and a_i is an index reflecting population size and retail buying power in zone i, $j = 1, 2, \ldots, n$ are locations of existing stores, and $j = (n + 1), \ldots (n + p)$ are the proposed locations. Since relative accessibility is a major determinant of the probability of patronizing a store, any change in the location plan affects the value of $\hat{P}_{ij}$ and, therefore, the market share of the stores.

Thus, every time the location of an outlet is changed, equation 6.1 must be reevaluated to assess the impact of the location change on market share.

Equation 6.2 provides the basis for estimating the expected level of patronage at individual outlets. Our interest, however, is in calculating the total market share of all firms belonging to the chain and not just that of an individual outlet. For the retail chain, the optimal strategy is one which maximizes the total profitability of all outlets, both existing and new. To calculate the total market share of all the outlets operated by chain *A*, the consumers' propensity for visiting the chain's outlets must be considered. This is done by summing the market shares of all such outlets. The relative desirability of alternative locations is usually quite different when the total market share of the chain is used as a criterion rather than the market share of the new outlets. The new outlets attract their customers not only from competing chains' outlets but also from the chain's existing outlets. Thus, the new outlets will cannibalize to some extent the sales of existing stores belonging to the chain. The problem, therefore, is to find sites for the new stores that offer high market potential, while having minimum impact on the sales of existing stores.

Model Implementation and Results

Implementing the model expressed in equation 6.1 requires data on the level of demand for the firm's products, travel distances, and locations of competing firms. In this case, the study area was divided into 48 demand zones based on neighborhood characteristics, residential patterns, and topography. The relative demand in each zone was estimated from secondary sources, with the estimates shown in figure 6–7. The distances between each of the 48 demand zones and the 21 feasible sites were calculated using the Euclidean metric. Finally, information was obtained on the locations and sizes of competitive outlets and other outlets belonging to the same chain.

Figure 6–9 shows how the total market share of chain *A* varies with location when one small store is added to the existing network. As can be seen from the figure, there is considerable spatial variation in the expected market share level. The optimal location is at site 14. By opening a store at this site, the chain can increase its expected market share to 55.52 percent. The least attractive location, on the other hand, is site 3. Locating a store at this site would increase the market share from the present level of 45.70 to only 46.40 percent. The attractiveness of site 14 results from its being near areas of high demand concentration but not very close to any of chain *A*'s existing stores. Thus, a new outlet at this site helps chain *A* to improve its overall accessibility to the target market and fill a spatial void in its existing network. In comparison, a location such as site 18, while attractive when only the market share of the new store is considered, does not help the chain as a whole. This is because a store at this site would attract many of its customers from chain

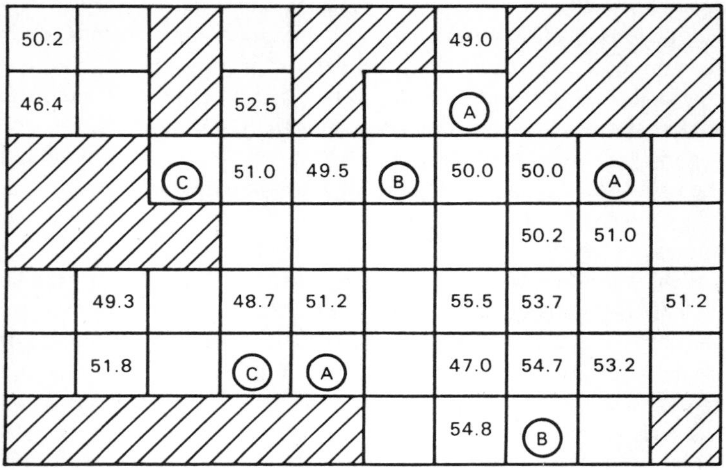

Note: Numbers in upper left-hand–corner indicate relative zone attractiveness, with higher numbers indicating greater attractiveness. Circles indicate occupied or feasible sites. *A*'s, *B*'s, and *C*'s show existing store locations.

Figure 6–9. Variation in Chain *A*'s Market Share with New Store Locations

A's existing outlet nearby and cannibalize the sales of that outlet significantly.

The same general pattern holds for locating more than one new store. Under macrostrategy 3, for example, there are 210 different ways in which two equal-sized stores can be located. The optimal plan out of these 210 possibilities is to locate stores at sites 12 and 19. This combination of sites results in the greatest increase in market share for the chain. With new outlets at these sites, the chain's expected market share increases to 61.45 percent from the present level of 45.70 percent.

Although the market share for the chain increases by more than fifteen percentage points, the market share earned by the two new stores is considerably greater than 15 percent. The new stores attract almost half their customers from chain *A*'s existing stores, as shown in table 6–5. When the two new outlets are opened, the market share of *A*'s three existing stores drops from 45.7 percent to 31.35 percent though the market share for the chain as a whole increases substantially. In total, about 47 percent of the expected patronage of the new stores results from a shift in patronage from the chain's existing stores. It is possible that some other location plan may yield a market share of more than 30.1 percent for the new stores alone; however, such a plan would not yield as much additional market share for the total chain as would the optimal plan.

The optimal location strategy for each of the macrostrategies is shown in

Table 6–5
Shift in Market Share Using Macrostrategy 3

	Market Share	
Stores	Before Opening	After Opening
Chain A's old stores	45.7%	31.35%
Chain A's new stores	—	30.10
Chains B and C	54.3	38.55

Source: A. Ghosh and S. McLafferty, "Locating Stores in Uncertain Environments:
A Scenario Planning Approach," *Journal of Retailing* 58, no. 4 (1982): 5–22.
Reprinted with permission.

table 6–6. The expected market share for the chain varies from about 55 percent for macrostrategy 1 to about 68 percent for macrostrategy 9. Increases in market share from one macrostrategy to another represent the potential revenue gains achieved from either adding new stores or increasing store size. From table 6–6, it is evident that the addition of new stores leads to the largest increase in share. Changes in store size have relatively less effect on market share. Since each macrostrategy represents a different level of corporate investment, marginal improvements in market share must be weighed against their marginal costs. While the addition of each new outlet increases market share substantially, the increase may still not be large enough to justify the investments required to open and operate the new stores.

The optimal location plans for each macrostrategy demonstrate an important feature of multiple-location problems. Note that the optimal location for a single store is present in only one of the three optimal two-store

Table 6–6
Market Share and Optimal Store Locations For
Nine Macrostrategies

Macrostrategy	Market Share	New Stores at Locations
1	55.52%	14
2	56.42	14
3	61.45	12, 19
4	62.18	12, 14
5	62.73	12, 19
6	66.34	12, 18, 15
7	66.89	12, 18, 15
8	67.29	12, 18, 15
9	67.69	12, 18, 15

configurations and does not appear in any one of the optimal three-store configurations. Similarly, the optimal three-store configuration is quite different from that for the two stores. In general, the optimal configuration for *n* stores is not necessarily a subset of the optimal *n* + 1 locations. The implication is that one cannot use the single-store–location model sequentially to arrive at the best strategy for multiple stores. The best single-store location for chain *A* is site 14. If a single-store model is used again assuming that a store is already built at site 14, the choice for the second store is at site 12. The best location configuration for two stores, however, is sites 12 and 19. Locating outlets at sites 12 and 14 would be myopic (Scott 1971) since it would not yield the maximum potential market share for the chain. Thus, even if construction is to be phased over a finite time period, a multiple-location model should be used to determine the optimal configuration of multiple outlets so that the long-run performance of the network is maximized. Selecting locations one at a time may lead ultimately to a spatial pattern that is not consistent "with the overall development of the network" (Achabal, Gorr, and Mahajan 1982, p. 8).

Location-allocation models are useful not only for deciding how to expand existing store networks, but also for designing new networks and for relocation and store-abandonment decisions. If, for example, the chain wishes to relocate one of its existing stores, the approach outlined in the previous section can be used to find the optimal relocation strategy. One can determine, for example, the particular store to be moved and the optimal site for relocation. Table 6–7 shows the impact on market share of relocating each of the chain's existing stores. If the outlet near site 13 is closed, the best site for relocation is 15. This will increase the chain's market share from the present level of 45.7 percent to 48 percent. Moving the store near site 2, on the other hand, decreases the chain's competitive advantage and reduces market share to 43 percent. Given the location of competitive outlets and feasible sites as well as the spatial demand pattern, that site is an attractive location for the chain and should not be vacated. The best relocation strategy is to move the outlet near site 8 to site 15. This will increase expected market share to 50 percent. Thus, a four–percentage-point increase in market share can be achieved without adding to the number of stores. Note that in all three cases, the optimal site for relocation is 15, an attractive location because of its proximity to high-demand zones.

Choosing among Macrostrategies

Two general procedures may be used for evaluating the relative costs and benefits associated with each macrostrategy. First, one can compute the cost of opening and operating outlets of different sizes and compare these costs with the expected revenues associated with different market share levels

Table 6–7
Alternative Relocation Strategies

Store Relocated	Optimal Site for Relocation	Chain A's Market Share after Relocation
Outlet near site 13	15	48%
Outlet near site 2	15	43.0
Outlet near site 8	15	50.0

(Huff 1963; Achabal, Gorr, and Mahajan 1982; Ghosh and Craig 1983). By calculating the costs and revenues for each strategy, the expected level of profit can be determined and the strategy with the highest profit level chosen. The expected level of profit associated with a particular strategy is calculated as:

$$D = \sum_{t=1}^{T} [MS_t C - F_t]$$

where D is profit, MS_t is the market share in real dollars expected from following the macrostrategy, C is the net profit margin per unit of revenue, F is the fixed cost including the cost of real estate (or rent) expressed in real dollars, and T is the time horizon of the decision. The fixed cost, F, depends on the size of the stores as well as the cost of land. Thus, using this method requires information on the costs of different sites and the cost of construction or acquisition if an existing structure at the desired site is to be purchased. In addition, estimates of operating costs for stores of different sizes are also required. For retail chains that already operate several outlets, such information may be readily available. Recall too that MS incorporates information on retail expenditures in the area as shown in equation 6.1.

The levels of profit and return on investment for each of the macrostrategies are shown in table 6–8. For the purpose of these calculations, it was assumed that the fixed cost of a small store is $100,000, that of a large one is $125,000, and the net profit margin on sales is 1.6 percent. The investment required in working capital is $500,000 for a small store and $700,000 for a large one. These figures are used for illustration only and do not reflect the actual costs in this study area. As might be expected, the level of profit increases as more outlets are located. The expected profit for macrostrategy 1 is $715,900 compared to $609,700 for the current strategy. Thus, the cost of adding another outlet to the system is more than compensated by the increase in market share. Similarly, if two small stores are added to the system, profit increases to $740,400. The profit expected from a network with three new small stores is $743,100. Table 6–8 also shows the impact of store size on the

Table 6–8
Expected Profit and Return on Investment for Nine Macrostrategies

Macrostrategy	Profit	ROI
1	$715,900	35.8%
2	709,800	32.3
3	740,400	29.6
4	730,800	27.1
5	727,300	26.4
6	743,100	24.8
7	729,700	22.8
8	713,100	20.9
9	696,500	19.3
Existing network	609,700	40.6

level of profit. The additional revenue generated by large stores is not enough to cover the stores' higher fixed costs. In all cases, the expected profit drops when the size of the store is expanded.

The last column of the table shows the expected returns on the investment in working capital for each macrostrategy. Like all capital-budgeting decisions, the expected return on investments in store networks must at least equal the firm's marginal cost of capital. Thus, if the firm's marginal cost of capital is less than 24.8 percent, adding three new small outlets to the network would be deemed a profitable investment. Note, however, that the ROI decreases as more outlets are added to the network. This is inevitable since the marginal increase in market share due to new outlets decreases as more of them are added. It is essential, therefore, to look also at the incremental or marginal ROI in table 6–9. If we consider macrostrategies 1, 3, and 6 (adding small stores only), the marginal ROI of adding one store is 21.24 percent, while the marginal ROI for adding two and three stores are 4.9 percent and 2.7 percent, respectively. Because of the small marginal ROIs, macrostrategies 3 and 6 may be undesirable from a financial viewpoint. However, given

Table 6–9
Return on Investment for Macrostrategies 1, 3, and 6

Macrostrategy	Profit	Marginal ROI
Existing Network	$609,700	—
1	715,900	21.24%
3	740,400	4.90%
6	743,100	2.7%

the high level of overall profitability, a firm may choose to locate these additional outlets to preempt competition and increase market presence.

Rather than evaluating strategies in terms of profit alone, a second option is to consider some trade-off between profit and market share. A firm may wish to sacrifice short-term profits in order to capture a larger share of the market and forestall future competition. By establishing a greater number of outlets, the firm can also achieve greater scale economies. To determine the most desirable strategy, therefore, management can be asked to rank the alternative strategies or be presented with paired comparisons of alternatives from which an overall ranking can be derived (Mahajan, Sharma, and Srinivas 1985). An alternative procedure for ranking alternatives is to develop a trade-off model depicting management's subjective evaluation of the relative importance of profit and market share in judging location plans. Various approaches for obtaining such trade-off information have been developed in the decision-making literature. (See, for example, MacCrimmon and Wehrung, 1977; MacCrimmon and Siu 1974; Keeney and Raiffa 1976.) In general, these methods involve presenting management with hypothetical location strategies that have different market share and profit characteristics and eliciting management's preference concerning those strategies. These preferences provide the information for calculating a trade-off function that shows the relative importance given to market share and profitability. The trade-off function can then be used to evaluate the overall desirability of different macrostrategies.

Summary

The preceeding section illustrated the use of location-allocation models for developing a network of multiple outlets and assessing overall performance of the network. In doing so, we demonstrated the importance of determining network size, outlet locations, and store characteristics jointly within a single decision-making framework. The importance of assessing the impact of new-store locations on the performance of the total network of stores was also shown. Adding new stores affects the market areas and profitability of existing stores, which in turn impacts the profitability of the chain as a whole. A major drawback of traditional methods of site selection is that by looking at locations one at a time, they ignore the impact of one location on the performance of other outlets operated by the same firm.

The supermarket case study illustrated the use of a complex spatial-interaction formulation to specify the allocation rule in the location-allocation model. The interaction model considered the impact of both accessibility and store size on shopping probabilities. This serves to highlight the fact that location-allocation models are not limited to deterministic allocation rules, but can easily incorporate a variety of complex allocation rules to evaluate the impact of location and store characteristics on performance. A major difference between allocation rules based on spatial-interaction models and those based on proximal areas is that interaction models assume that the total demand for the retail good in the area is fixed. The interaction model determines how the total demand will be allocated among the different outlets in the area. These types of models, therefore, are especially useful for supermarkets, drug stores, and other nonimpulse-type shopping good stores for which the total demand level may be assumed to be fixed. Location and accessibility are still important, however, since they affect the share of the total demand accruing to individual outlets.

Covering Models for Retail-Facility Location

In addition to the MCI and proximal-area–based models, a third type of location-allocation model of interest in retailing is the *covering model*. Covering models are especially useful in service and service-related industries for designing service-center networks. Location is always important for retail services where accessibility is a major determinant of patronage of individual outlets as well as the total level of utilization of the service. An important objective in designing such service networks is to determine the optimal level of service to be provided. By locating more outlets, a firm increases accessibility and, hence, the level of service it can provide to a target population. However, at the same time, the greater number of outlets increases the cost of providing the service and may adversely impact profits. Conversely, locating too few outlets may result in an inadequate level of service and low levels of utilization. By inadequately meeting the needs of the target population, the firm may not realize the full potential.

In this section, we discuss the application of covering-location–allocation models which allow a direct assessment of the level of service provided by a network of outlets over a region or trade area. While covering-location–allocation models were developed and have been mostly used for locating emergency services such as fire stations and ambulances (see, for example, ReVelle et al. 1977; Eaton, Church, and ReVelle 1977), the techniques can be applied to evaluate any network of outlets where the objective involves the trade-off between the potential for utilization and the cost of providing the service (Craig and Ghosh 1984).

The objective of covering models, as the name itself implies, is to identify locations that provide potential users with *coverage* within a specified distance or time constraint. Such coverage is important in situations where access plays a critical role in utilization of service. For many convenience stores, for example, the bulk of the volume is generated by consumers living within one or two miles of the store. Similarly, it is reported that 85 percent of the revenue of a typical fast-food restaurant comes from people residing within a three-mile radius of the outlet (Zeller, Achabal, and Brown 1980). Such diverse businesses as movie houses and ice cream parlors also attract a majority of their customers from within the immediate neighborhood. Customers of these outlets may obtain substitute products or services, or completely forgo consumption, if the outlets are not accessible to them. A measure of the level of service provided by these types of outlets, therefore, is the proportion of total population that is located within the immediate neighborhood of the outlets. Thus, in designing a network of outlets, the objective should be to find locations that maximize the number of people within a specified maximum distance or travel time constraint. This is the objective of covering models.

Covering models are also useful for locating a wide range of service activities, such as repair centers for appliances, branch banks and ATMs, fast-food restaurants, emergency medical centers, and franchised income tax and legal services, to name only a few. The important characteristic of covering models is that, like the CIM model discussed earlier, these models are applicable in noncompetitive situations or in situations where the location of competitive outlets does not directly affect the consumer's choice of outlet. For example, once a consumer has opened an account with a particular bank, the location of competitive branches or ATMs does not affect that consumer's choice of a bank. Consumers will simply choose a convenient outlet of the bank with which they have accounts. However, the decision to open an account with the bank in the first place may have been affected by the location and level of service provided by the bank and access to its ATM network (Rao and Tibrewala 1985). In designing a network of ATMs to serve customers, therefore, a bank may use a covering model that maximizes consumer accessibility to the network.

While a number of different types of covering-location–allocation models have been discussed in the literature, two that are most applicable to retail situations are the (1) *set-covering model* and (2) the *maximal-covering location (MCL)* model. Both are discussed in this section. We first present brief descriptions of the models and demonstrate their application in designing a network of service outlets. Then, a number of extensions to the basic covering model are discussed.

Set-Covering Model

The assumption underlying all covering models is that accessibility to a service network within some critical travel distance or time is an essential determinant of service utilization. It is assumed that consumers residing beyond the specified maximum distance or travel time from an outlet are not adequately served by the outlet and are unlikely to utilize the services offered by the center. In designing a network of service centers, therefore, a relevant objective is to maximize the proportion of the population within the specified distance from service facilities and, thereby, maximize the level of service provided.

Uses of the Model. An important question in creating a service network is the number of centers required to adequately serve all consumers within the stated distance criterion. The smaller the distance or time criterion, the greater the number of centers required to provide adequate service to all customers and, thus, the greater the total investments. A critical issue, therefore, is the trade-off between the level of service to be provided and the volume of investment required to achieve this service level. Using set-covering models, the location analyst can perform a cost–benefit analysis in a systematic manner and also find optimal locations for the service centers.

The objective of the set-covering model is to determine the number of outlets required and their locations such that all consumers have access to the service within the specified travel time or distance. The model ensures that the distance or travel time separating customers from their nearest outlet is less than the specified constraint (Toregas and ReVelle 1972). If the accessibility standard is three miles, for example, the model determines the minimum number of centers required and their locations to guarantee that no potential consumers are more than three miles from their nearest outlet. In general, the smaller the specified distance constraint, the greater the number of centers needed to achieve complete coverage of the population.

Mathematically, the set-covering model may be stated as follows: Given a set of demand points I and a set of potential facility locations J, an $I \times J$ matrix of shortest distances or travel times between each demand point and each potential location, and a critical accessibility constraint S:

$$\text{Min} \sum_{j \in J} x_j$$

Subject to:
$$\sum_{j \in N_i} x_j > 1 \text{ for all } i \in I$$

$$N_i = (j \in J \mid d_{ij} \leq S) \text{ for all } i \in I$$

$$x_j = \begin{cases} 1 \text{ if facility at } j \\ 0 \text{ otherwise} \end{cases}$$

where i and j are individual elements of the sets I and J, respectively, and d_{ij} is the distance between i and j.

The critical operational variable of the set-covering model is the set N_i, which is defined for each of the demand points. This represents the set of outlets that are within the constraint of S distance or time units from the location of demand point i. Thus, it defines the set of facility locations that can provide adequate service to that demand point. If the closest outlet from demand point i is beyond the maximum distance constraint, N_i is a null set implying that the demand point cannot be adequately served by the network. The solution to the set-covering model, however, ensures that the chosen network covers all demand points within the specified distance. This condition is imposed by the constraint in the model. The objective function of the model is to minimize the sum of x_j (the number of facilities opened), while covering all demand points within the specified maximum distance. In determining the number of outlets, the model simultaneously determines the best locations for the outlets. Thus, as in the models discussed earlier, the set-covering model explicitly relates decisions concerning the optimal number of centers and their locations. The minimum number of centers that is specified is valid only if the corresponding location plan is followed.

An important aspect of set-covering models is the maximum distance or time constraint (value of S) for determining adequate and inadequate coverage of the population. The solution to a particular problem depends critically on the specified accessibility criterion. If the accessibility constraint is very strict—that is, consumers must be very near to an outlet to be covered—the minimum number of outlets required to provide complete coverage will be large. With a larger distance constraint, on the other hand, the number of outlets required may be quite small. By solving the problem over a range of accessibility constraints, a trade-off curve can be constructed showing the number of outlets needed to provide complete coverage for various possible accessibility levels. Because the cost of the service network depends on the number of outlets located, the trade-off curve can be used in evaluating the costs of developing networks with different target service levels. The marginal benefits of adding service centers can be weighed against the cost of providing new centers and an informed decision can be made as to the appropriate number of facilities.

An Illustration. The following section illustrates the use of the set-covering model in evaluating and planning a new service network. A large organization is planning to operate a network of service centers for repair and maintenance of microcomputers within a heavily populated mixed suburban/urban area of the Northeast. These service centers are to be targeted toward small business owners, who are to "carry in" their microcomputers for repair. Prior to this, the company has offered only on-site repair services. Due to the comparatively high cost of on-site service, the company feels that these carry-in centers will be a better way to provide repair services for personal computers.

The basic geographic information system for solving the location problem is a geocoded data base consisting of the spatial coordinates of 64 demand points representing all towns and cities in the area (figure 6–10). Each of these demand locations is considered to be a feasible site for locating new outlets. Because of the grid pattern of the roads in the study area, road distances are calculated from spatial coordinates using the Manhattan or city-block metric. It should be noted that the study area in this case covers a large geographic region compared to previous examples. Instead of searching for optimal sites within a town, the focus here is on finding the towns in which service centers should be located. Once these towns are identified, management can look for specific sites to locate the centers.

The potential demand for the service is estimated in three stages. First, the number of small businesses in each demand zone is estimated from secondary sources. Second, a sample of small business owners in the market area is surveyed to estimate the level of microcomputer usage. Finally, the likelihood of businesses using the carry-in repair centers is ascertained from a survey of these small business owners. The survey shows that a critical determinant of the use of carry-in repair centers is accessibility to the outlets. The probability that a small business owner will use the service center is negatively related to the distance to the center. Questions are also asked to determine how far small business owners are willing to travel to utilize a service center. It is found that the expected rate of utilization falls sharply when distance exceeds five or six miles. A distance of six miles is therefore used as the constraint for population coverage. It is assumed that a business more than six miles from its closest service center will not use the service.

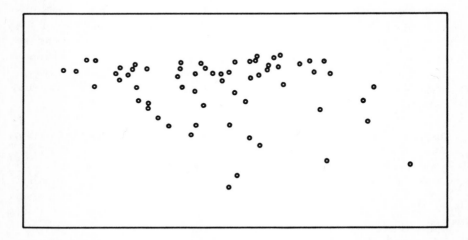

Note: Circles are the location of demand nodes and are also feasible sites.

Figure 6–10. Study Area for Service Center Location Problem

Figure 6–11 shows the minimum number of outlets necessary to provide total coverage in the area over a 4-to-12–mile range of critical accessibility values. These critical values are defined as the minimum distance separating a demand point from its nearest outlet. When the critical distance is 6 miles, for example, a minimum of 17 outlets is required to provide total coverage within this distance. As the critical distance increases, fewer outlets are necessary to ensure coverage. Only 8 outlets are required when the critical distance is 10 miles. For a critical distance of 4 miles, on the other hand, a total of 28 outlets are necessary to ensure total coverage. The stricter the accessibility standard (the lower the value of S), the higher is the level of service. More outlets are needed, however, to provide this higher level of service. Trade-off curves such as the one in figure 6–11 develop the relationship between the level of service and the cost of service provision and are useful in deciding on the actual level of service to provide.

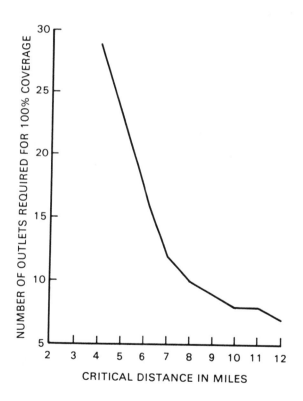

Figure 6–11. Relationship between Critical Distance and Number of Outlets

As might be expected, the shape of the trade-off curve for the number of centers versus critical distance is downward-sloping in a concave fashion. When the critical distance is small, a small increase in the distance constraint results in a sharp decrease in the number of outlets required to cover the demand points. With further relaxation of the accessibility criterion, however, the reduction in the number of outlets required is smaller. When the critical distance is large, a further increase in this distance may produce little or no decline in the number of outlets required. This type of relationship between critical distance and the number of outlets has been found to hold in a variety of applications of set-covering models (see, for example, Eaton, Church, and ReVelle 1977), and it portrays the general trade-off between investment and level of service. Decisions regarding the level of service to provide must be sensitive to consumer travel patterns for the service under consideration, while taking into account the availability of funds for facility construction and operation.

Maximal-Covering Problem

In many retail settings, the goal of providing universal service may not be feasible because of the cost of providing the service. It is often necessary to trade off the cost of locating additional outlets with the potential revenue generated from increased coverage. In the previous case, for example, 17 outlets are required to cover all potential demand within 6 miles, but 5 well-located outlets can cover 75 percent of the demand within the same travel constraint. Clearly, the incremental benefit of providing coverage to the final 25 percent of the population may be too small to justify the cost of 12 additional outlets. Moreover, funds saved by constructing fewer outlets can be used to improve other aspects of the service network, such as the number of personnel and length of opening hours. These in turn help to increase utilization. The decision maker, therefore, may relinquish the goal of total coverage and instead attempt to maximize the amount of potential demand covered within a given maximum distance by a fixed number of service centers.

This question can be analyzed by using a maximal-covering location (MCL) model. Instead of determining the minimum number of outlets required to cover the entire target population within an accessibility constraint, the MCL problem considers a specified number of outlets to be opened. The objective is to determine the locations that will maximize the proportion of demand covered by the specified number of outlets (Church and ReVelle 1974). As in the set-covering problem, a potential customer is considered to be covered only if there is an outlet within the maximum time or distance constraint.

Mathematically, the MCL problem is represented by the following optimization problem:

$$\text{Max} \sum_{i \in I} a_i Y_i$$

Subject to: $\displaystyle\sum_{j \in N_i} x_j \geq y_i \quad$ for all $i \in I$

$$\sum_{j \in J} x_j = p$$

$$x_{ij} = \begin{cases} 1 \text{ if facility at } j \\ 0 \text{ otherwise} \end{cases}$$

$$y_{ij} = 0 \text{ or } 1$$

where a_i is a measure of the relative demand at node i, p is the number of facilities to be located, and all other terms are as defined previously for the set-covering model. The set N_i again plays a crucial role. Recall that this defines the outlets eligible to provide coverage to the demand area—the set of outlets within the specified distance or time constraint from the node. Figure 6–12 clarifies how the N_i variables are defined. The demand points in this hypothetical study area are to be served by three centers (sites A, B, and C). The demand zones covered by each of these centers are shown in the figure and some of the demand points are numbered for reference. Consider demand points 1, 2, and 3. Each of these demand points is covered by a single service facility. Demand point 1 is covered by center A, 2 by center B, and 3 by

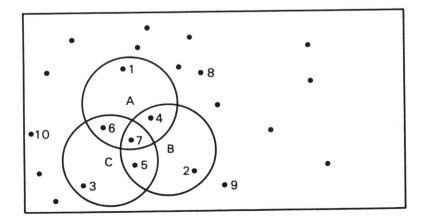

Figure 6-12. Definition of N_i Variable in MCL Problem

center C. The N_is corresponding to these three sites will, therefore, each contain a single element. The sets N_1, N_2, and N_3 will contain the locations A, B, and C, respectively. Demand points 4, 5, and 6 are each covered by two service centers. Thus, N_4, N_5, and N_6 each have two elements: A and B, B and C, and A and C, respectively. Similarly, N_7 will contain the elements A, B, and C, since site 7 is covered by all three centers. Sites 8, 9, and 10, on the other hand, are uncovered sites. From these sites, the distances to the centers exceed the specified constraint. Therefore, N_8, N_9, and N_{10} will be empty (null sets). In the solution to the set-covering problem, none of these sets are allowed to be empty since the constraint in that problem is that all demand points must be covered. The MCL problem, however, does not require universal coverage; therefore, some of the N_is may be empty in the final solution.

The value of the objective function in MCL model depends on the values of the a_i and y_i. Note that by the first constraint, the value of any y_i is determined by the corresponding N_i. This constraint dictates that y_i is equal to 1 only if N_i is nonempty. It is 0 otherwise. Thus, uncovered demand nodes do not contribute toward the objective function since the corresponding y_i variable is assigned a value of 0. The second constraint limits the number of outlets to a specified number, p. The objective function, therefore, maximizes the amount of demand (i.e., the number of potential customers) covered by the p facilities within the accessibility criterion S.

One use of MCL models is to investigate the relationship between the number of outlets and the proportion of demand covered by those outlets within a given distance. As the number of outlets increases, the proportion of demand covered increases, as shown in figure 6–13. The two lines are based on the 64-node network described previously. The trade-off between number of outlets and proportion of demand covered is shown for two accessibility standards—five and six miles. Both trade-off curves exhibit strong diminishing marginal returns to additional outlets. For a critical distance of 5 miles, 8 outlets can provide coverage to about 80 percent of the demand, but an additional 15 outlets are required to cover the remaining 20 percent of the demand within the distance constraint. Similarly, when the distance constraint is 6 miles, 8 outlets cover more than 85 percent of the demand, but a total of 17 outlets are required to cover 100 percent of the demand.

The relationship between the number of outlets and proportion of demand covered is a reflection of the spatial distribution of demand. When, as is true in many market areas, there is a concentration of demand in a few small areas, a relatively large proportion of the demand can be covered by the first few outlets by locating them in areas of high demand density. Thus, for example, 31 percent of the demand can be covered by a single unit when the critical distance is six miles. Adding four more outlets to the network increases coverage to nearly 76 percent of total demand. The locations of these

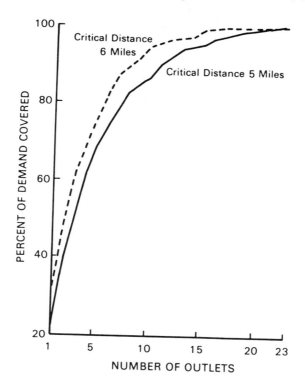

Figure 6-13. Trade-Off between Coverage and Number of Outlets

five centers are shown in figure 6–14. As is evident from the figure, all of these sites are centrally located and are in areas of high demand density. Once these areas of high demand concentration have been adequately served, increased coverage can only come from locating outlets in areas that are relatively remote and contain little demand. The marginal increase in coverage thus decreases significantly as the number of outlets increases. The incremental benefit from these additional outlets may not justify their costs.

The basic structures of both the set-covering and the MCL models can be extended in a number of ways to suit the requirements of particular applications. The basic covering models are concerned only with whether a demand node is covered or not. If the demand node is covered within the specified accessibility criteria, the actual travel time or distance separating the demand node from its nearest outlet is not considered. Thus, if the accessibility criteria is specified as a distance of six miles, a consumer who is six miles from

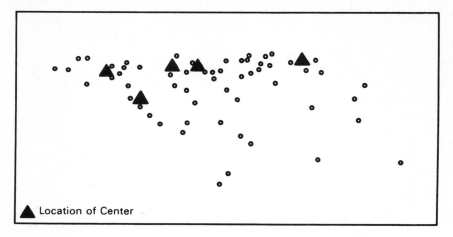

Figure 6–14. Optimal Location Pattern for Five-Center Network Using MCL Model

an outlet is given the same importance weight as one who is only one mile away from the nearest outlet. The levels of service to the two consumers are assumed to be the same. In the set-covering and MCL models, it is assumed that the expected level of utilization is constant as long as the distance from the nearest outlet is less than the critical constraint as shown in figure 6–15(a). Beyond this limit, however, the rate of utilization is assumed to drop to zero. So, if the constraint is six miles, a consumer six miles from the nearest facility is assumed to use it, whereas a consumer slightly farther away is not. The expected level of use remains constant within the distance constraint and then falls abruptly to zero.

In many cases, the relationship between accessibility and the expected rate of utilization is more complex than that assumed in the set-covering and MCL models. Even within the critical distance, consumers closer to service outlets may be more likely to use the service than those farther away. In such cases, the relationship between accessibility and expected utilization may be of the form shown in figure 6–15(b). There, within the critical distance limit, utilization decreases in a stepwise manner with distance. But beyond this limit, utilization is expected to drop to zero.

Weighted-Covering Model

It is not difficult to modify the basic covering model to incorporate a stepwise relationship between utilization and accessibility. To do so, the covered demand points must be weighted by the travel time to their nearest facility in calculating the objective function. Demand areas with a lower travel time

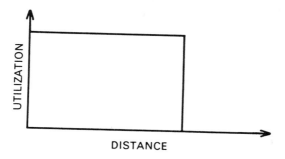

(a) As assumed in set-covering and MCL models

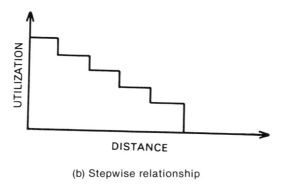

(b) Stepwise relationship

Figure 6–15. Relationship between Utilization and Distance

are assigned a greater weight, since their total level of use is expected to be high. The objective then is to maximize the expected level of utilization. In calculating expected utilization, a number of distance and travel-time classes can be considered and the demand covered within each accessibility class can be weighted according to the expected level of utilization. The actual number of classes to be included in a model and the relative importance weight given to each class must, of course, be decided on the basis of consumer surveys or managerial judgment. Once these have been chosen, the location strategy for maximizing the expected level of utilization can be found by solving a modified version of the maximal-covering problem called the weighted-covering model (Church and Roberts 1983; Ghosh and Craig 1986).

Mathematically the weighted-covering model may be stated as follows:

$$\text{Max} \sum_{i \in I} \sum_{l=1}^{L} a_i S_{il} Y_{il}$$

Subject to: $\quad \displaystyle\sum_{j \in N_{il}} x_j \leq Y_{il}$

$$\sum_{l=1}^{L} Y_{il} = 1$$

$$\sum_{j \in J} x_j = p$$

$$N_{il} = \{ j \in J \mid d_{ij} \text{ is in } l\text{th access class} \}$$

where, a_i is the relative demand at i and S_{il} is the probability that a potential user at i will use a center that is in the lth accessibility class. These variables thus express the relationship between accessibility and likelihood of utilization. Like the MCL model, the weighted-covering model is concerned with consumer accessibility to the network of service centers. In this case, however, a weighting system is incorporated in the objective function to express the goal of maximizing service use.

The first constraint in the model defines for each demand point the set of outlets that can provide coverage within each accessibility class. Note, however, that (in contrast to the MCL problem) in this case, a number of N_i variables are defined for each demand origin — one for each accessibility class. Thus, N_{il} defines the set of outlets within the lth accessibility class of demand node i. As in the MCL problem, the coverage vector for each demand node (the N_{il}) defines the Y_{il} variables used in the objective function. Y_{il} takes on a value of 1 if node i is within the lth accessibility class from an outlet. Thus, if N_{il} is a null set, Y_{il} is equal to 0.

The next constraint ensures that the coverage of a demand node is defined in only one way — that is, only one of the L coverage variables associated with a node is assigned a value of 1. Consider, for example, a node within the first accessibility class of one outlet and the second accessibility class of another. Although the node is covered by both facilities, only one of the coverage variables should be assigned a value of 1, since, otherwise, the expected level of utilization originating from that node will be counted twice in the objective function. In this case, Y_{il} will equal 1 and $Y_{i2}, \ldots, Y_{iL}$ will be 0 because coverage within the first accessibility class contributes more to the objective function. The final constraint in the model restricts the number of centers to a specified number p.

To illustrate the application of the weighted-covering model, the computer-repair–center problem discussed earlier is reanalyzed using a weighted-covering formulation. To apply the model, an explicit relationship between various levels of accessibility to services and the expected rate of utilization must first be developed. Consumer surveys are essential for collecting such information. Surveys of consumer travel patterns in other regions where similar services are offered, for example, would provide some indication of the relationship between accessibility and service usage. For a new type of service, however, such information is not available, so potential users of the service must be asked to estimate this relationship.

As an example, consider the relationship between accessibility and utilization shown in figure 6–16. The figure shows the expected rate of utilization for four accessibility classes: less than 1½ miles, between 1½ and 3 miles, between 3 and 4½ miles, and between 4½ and 6 miles. Consumers who are farther than six miles from their nearest center are not expected to use the service. Note that even when the travel distance is less than 1½ miles, only 58 percent of the potential customers are likely to use the service. Thus, not all consumers are expected to use the service even when it is accessible. As the distance to the service center increases, the probability of usage drops even further. The most significant drop occurs when the distance increases to more than three miles. There is little impact on utilization, however, if the distance increases from 3 miles to 6 miles.

The trade-off curve in figure 6–16 provides information necessary for defining the weights attached to different accessibility classes in the objective function of the weighted-covering model—the S_{il} variables. The other information required is the same as that needed for the MCL model: the level of

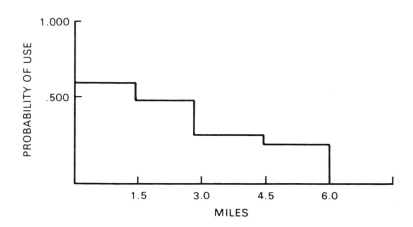

Figure 6–16. Empirical Relationship between Distance and Utilization of Computer-Repair Service

demand at each node, the distances between each demand node and each feasible site, and the value of *p* (the number of centers to be located). The data set utilized for this illustration was constructed in the same manner as the previous data set shown in figure 6–10. This region, however, includes 164 demand nodes. There is considerable spatial variation in the demand (number of small business owners) in the area, making the choice of location a crucial decision in the success of the service-center network. Of the 164 nodes, 124 were designated as feasible sites for opening new centers based on the availability of land and infrastructure.

To determine the optimal location strategy, the weighted-covering model was solved for different values of *p* using a heuristic vertex-substitution algorithm. Table 6–10 shows the level of coverage, expected level of utilization, and profitability of networks with 1 to 8 outlets. As one would expect, the level of coverage (proportion of total demand covered within 6 miles) increases with additional centers, but the rate of increase decreases as more centers are added. There is a particularly sharp drop in incremental coverage for networks which have more than 6 outlets. The seventh center increases coverage by only 2.3 percent and the eighth increases it by a mere 1.3 percent. With 8 centers, 95.2 percent of total demand is covered within 6 miles. While not shown in the table, a total of 18 centers are needed to cover all the demand within 6 miles. Thus, 10 additional outlets are needed to serve the last 5 percent of the potential population.

The third column of table 6–10 shows the number of repair contracts expected to be served by each network. This is the expected level of utilization as expressed in the objective function of the weighted-covering model. To calculate the total utilization, the expected sales of microcomputers in each demand zone was first measured. This is the potential demand for repair service, but not all computer owners are expected to use the service centers.

Table 6–10
Results of Weighted-Covering Model

Number of Centers	Proportion of Small Businesses Covered	Number of Service Contracts	Profit	Marginal Profit
1	29.7%	1,887	$643,500	—
2	49.6	3,247	1,023,500	$380,000
3	65.2	4,381	1,290,500	267,000
4	75.4	4,997	1,298,500	8,000
5	84.7	5,612	1,306,000	7,500
6	91.6	6,085	1,242,500	– 63,500
7	93.9	6,227	1,013,500	– 229,000
8	95.2	6,296	748,000	– 265,500

The likelihood of use depends on accessibility, as shown in figure 6–16. Based on this relationship, the expected number of service contracts can be calculated for each zone. The total level of utilization is obtained by summing this number over all the 164 zones.

Once the expected number of contracts is calculated, the expected revenue for each network can be predicted based on the fee to be charged for each service contract. The cost of operating and maintaining the network can also be determined from engineering estimates of expected breakdowns, repair times, cost of parts, and need for labor and working capital. Based on these estimates, the profits expected from each network can be calculated. This is shown in the fourth column of table 6–10. To calculate profit, it is assumed that annual service fee is $600, average variable cost is $100 per contract, and each center's total annual labor and operating costs are $300,000. These figures are for illustrative purposes only and do not reflect the actual cost of operating a repair center.

The profits associated with each network can be used to decide on the optimal network size. All the networks are highly profitable. The marginal profits are, however, negative for networks with more than five centers. Thus, while the six-center network is expected to earn close to $1.25 million, the return on the incremental funds required to expand the network from five to six centers is negative. The sixth center increases the number of expected contracts by 473. The incremental revenue from these additional contracts is not enough to offset the additional cost of expanding the network. Thus, based on the criterion of marginal profits, the optimal size of the network is five centers.

The five-center network is expected to serve about 5,600 contracts annually and generate profits of about $1.3 million. These estimates, however, are contingent on following the optimal location strategy and opening the centers at the sites selected by the optimization model. The optimal sites for the five-center network are shown in figure 6–17. The figure also shows the service area boundary of each service center and the accessibility of demand nodes to the repair centers. Information on the service area of each center is useful for planning sales-promotion and advertising strategies.

Summary

Covering models are useful for designing networks of outlets for service and service-related industries. In this section, we have illustrated the use of three different types of covering models: the set-covering, maximal-covering, and weighted-covering models. (Table 6–11 summarizes them along with the proximal-area– and spatial-interaction–based models discussed earlier.) The basic approaches presented here can be extended in a number of ways. For example, all our examples involve the creation of a completely new network.

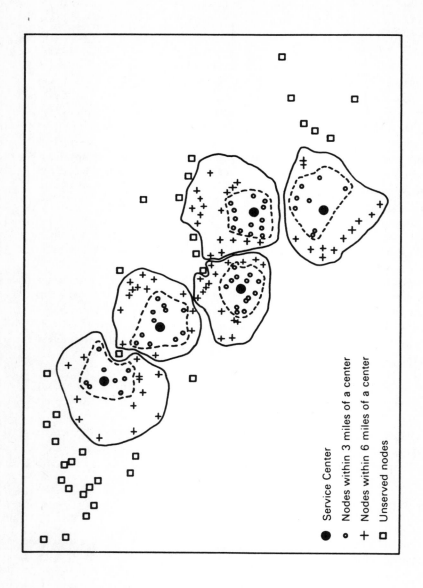

Figure 6-17. Market Areas and Locations of Service Areas

Service Center

● Service Center

∘ Nodes within 3 miles of a center

+ Nodes within 6 miles of a center

□ Unserved nodes

Table 6–11
Synopsis of Location-Allocation Models

Proximal-area–based models

Competition-ignoring model (CIM)
Objective function: Minimize total travel distance
Allocation rule: Travel to nearest center.
Comments: Assumes negative linear relationship between distance and utilization. Ignores competitive locations.

Market-share model (MSM)

Objective function: Maximize demand within proximal ares of outlets belonging to firm.
Allocation rule: Travel to nearest outlet.
Comments: Consider location of competitive outlets. Locates in interstitial sites between proximal areas of existing outlets.

Spatial-interaction–based models

Objective function: Maximize expected market share or profit.
Allocation rule: Based on spatial-interaction model.
Comments: Considers trade-off between distance and nondistance factors. Allocates fixed demand among outlets based on spatial-interaction model.

Covering models

Set-covering model

Objective function: Locates minimum number of outlets to serve all demand within specified accessibility criterion.
Allocation rule: Consumers patronize nearest outlet.
Comments: Optimal location pattern assures universal accessibility.

Maximal-covering model

Objective function: Maximize proportion of demand within accessibility criterion.
Allocation rule: Consumers patronize nearest outlet.
Comments: Determines trade-off between service level and investment in outlets.

Weighted-covering model
Objective function: Maximize utilization.
Allocation rule: Travel to nearest outlet.
Comments: Assumes stepwise relationship between accessibility and utilization.

Covering models can also be used for adding outlets to an existing network or relocating existing centers. This is done by "forcing" centers into the solution at sites where existing stores are located. The model then finds the best locations for the remaining outlets given the location of the fixed sites. Another way of extending the model is to consider both distance and nondistance factors in determining the likelihood of utilization. For example, factors such as hours of operation, price, and service quality can be incorporated in the objective function of the basic covering model. In this way, one can determine both the optimal locations and the optimal service design simultaneously. An example of such an application is given in Ghosh and Craig (1986).

Conclusion

The increasing availability of machine-readable geographic data bases and computer software for analyzing them is changing the methods of retail location analysis. Using the power of the computer, location-allocation models provide an efficient tool for analyzing and planning a network of retail outlets. In this chapter, we discussed the diverse types of location-allocation models and their application in a variety of situations. Location-allocation models are comprehensive planning tools which encompass, within a single decision-making framework, questions about the number, location, and design of outlets as well as forecasts of sales and profitability. In covering these issues, the models take into consideration the spatial variation in demand in the market area, the patterns of consumer travel, and the location of existing outlets. Since these are all important components of location strategy, the models provide a valuable aid for retail managers.

Although retailers need not always choose the optimal plan, it provides an important yardstick against which alternative location strategies can be judged. One can assess the difference in performance between alternative and optimal strategies to see how well a strategy measures up in terms of market share, accessibility, or profits. A strategy whose performance is close to optimal is generally a good choice since it approaches the "best" that can be achieved. On the other hand, if the proposed strategy performs much worse than the optimal one, then it is worth reevaluating the proposal and searching for a better plan.

This chapter has highlighted the diversity of location-allocation models and the range of possible applications. Each model relies on a different spatial-allocation rule which describes how consumers choose among spatial alternatives. Each model also has different strengths and weaknesses related to ease of data collection, analysis, and implementation. As a result, each is appropriate in different situations and for different types of retail and service activities.

References

Achabal, D.; Gorr, W.L.; and Mahajan, V. (1982). "MULTILOC: A Multiple Store Location Model." *Journal of Retailing* 58(2): 5–25.
Church, R.L., and ReVelle, C. (1974). "The Maximal Covering Location Problem," *Papers, Regional Science Association* 30: 101–118.

Church, R.L., and Roberts, K.L. (1983). "Generalized Coverage Models and Public Facility Location." *Papers, Regional Science Association* 53: 117–135.

Cooper, L. (1963). "Location-Allocation Problems." *Operations Research* 11: 331–343.

Craig, C.S., and Ghosh, A. (1984). "Covering Approaches to Retail Facility Location" in *AMA Educators' Proceedings*. Chicago: American Marketing Association.

Eaton, D.; Church, R.L.; and ReVelle, C. (1977). "Locational Analysis: A New Tool for Health Planners." Methodological Working Document 53. Sector Analysis Division, Agency for International Development, Washington D.C.

Friedrich, C.J. (1929). *Alfred Weber's Theory of the Location of Industries.* Chicago: University of Chicago Press.

Ghosh, A., and Craig, C.S.. (1983). "Formulating Retail Location Strategy in a Changing Environment." *Journal of Marketing* 47: 56–68.

Ghosh, A., and Craig, C.S. (1986). "An Approach to Determining Optimal Locations for New Services." *Journal of Marketing Research* 23: 354–362.

Ghosh, A., and McLafferty, S. (1982). "Locating Stores in Uncertain Environments: A Scenario Planning Approach." *Journal of Retailing* 58(4): 5–22.

Goodchild, M.F. (1984). "ILACS: A Location-Allocation Model for Retail Site Selection." *Journal of Retailing* 60(1): 84–100.

Goodchild, M.F., and Noronha, V.T. (1987). "Location Allocation and Impulsive Shopping: The Case of Gasoline Retailing" in A. Ghosh and G. Rushton (eds.), *Spatial Analysis and Location-Allocation Models.* New York: Van Nostrand Reinhold.

Huff, D.L. (1963). "A Probabilistic Analysis of Shopping Center Trade Areas." *Land Economics* 39: 81–90.

Keeney, R.L., and Raiffa, H. (1976). *Decisions with Multiple Objectives: Preferences and Value Tradeoffs.* New York: John Wiley & Sons.

Kuhn, H.W., and Kuenne, R.E. (1962). "An Efficient Algorithm for the Commercial Solution of the Generalized Weber Problem in Spatial Economics." *Journal of Regional Science* 4: 21–33.

MacCrimmon, K.R., and Siu, J.K. (1974). "Measuring Trade-Offs." *Decision Sciences* 5: 680–704.

MacCrimmon, K.R., and Wehrung, D.A. (1977). "Trade Off Analysis: The Indifference and the Preferred Proportions Approach" in D.E. Bell, R.L. Keeney, and H. Raiffa (eds.), *Conflicting Objectives in Decisions.* New York: John Wiley & Sons.

Mahajan, V.; Sharma, S.; and Srinivas, D. (1985). "An Application of Portfolio Analysis for Identifying Attractive Retail Locations." *Journal of Retailing* 61(4): 19–34.

Rao, A.G., and Tibrewala, V. (1985). "Consumer Choice of Banks and the Network Effect." Paper presented at the Fall TIMS/ORSA Conference, Atlanta.

ReVelle, C.; Bigman, D.; Schilling, D.; Cohon, J.; and Church, R. (1977). "Facility Location: A Review of Context-Free and EMS Models." *Health Services Research* 12: 129–146.

Scott, A.J. (1971). *Combinatorial Programming, Spatial Analysis and Planning.* London: Methuen.

Teitz, M.B., and Bart, P. (1968). "Heuristic Methods for Estimating the Generalized Vertex Median of a Weighted Graph." *Operations Research* 16: 953–961.

Toregas, C., and ReVelle, C. (1972). "Location under Time or Distance Constraints." *Papers, Regional Science Association* 28: 133–142.

Zeller, R.E.; Achabal, D.; and Brown, L.A. (1980). "Market Penetration and Locational Conflict in Channel Systems." *Decision Sciences* 11: 58–80.

Appendix 6A
The
Vertex-Substitution
Algorithm

The vertex-substitution algorithm is one of the most widely used procedures for solving location-allocation problems. It is a simple heuristic, consisting of successive substitutions of locations not in the current set of centers for those in the current set. The interchanges continue until no interchange can be found that improves the value of the objective function. Although the vertex-substitution method does not evaluate all possible location patterns, in general it finds a solution whose performance is close to, if *not* equal to, that of the optimal pattern. The method's great accuracy—coupled with its speed and simplicity—makes it highly effective in solving a wide variety of facility-location problems.

To describe the various steps in the vertex-substitution method, consider an example involving N feasible sites for store locations, out of which p sites will be chosen. Under these circumstances, there are a total of $\binom{N}{p}$ possible combinations of store locations that could be evaluated. The total numbers of location patterns increases combinatorially with N and p and is therefore often quite large. For example, when $N = 1000$ and $p = 4$, there are a total of 995 billion location patterns to consider.

Using the method of successive interchanges noted above, the vertex-substitution algorithm evaluates only a subset of all possible location configurations. It employs four steps:

1. Start with any arbitrary combination of p locations. This is known as the "starting solution" and designated here as the set of locations, S^*. Compute the value of the objective function for this location pattern and designate that value as Z^*.

2. Substitute the first location not in S^* from the list of all possible locations (feasible sites) for each node in S^*. After each substitution, compute the value of the objective function. Assuming that the goal is to *minimize* the objective function, we denote the minimum of these values as Z_{min} and set of locations that gives that minimum value as S'_{min}.

3. If $Z'_{min} < Z^*$, then set $S^* = S'_{min}$ and $Z^* = Z'_{min}$. Then return to

step 2. If $Z'_{min} \geq Z^*$; return to step 2 and perform substitution with the next available site from the list of all possible sites.

4. Continue until no further substitutions can be made that improve the value of the objective function. The optimal location pattern, then, consists of the locations in set S^* and the performance level of the optimal pattern is Z^*.

An Example

As an example of the use of the vertex-substitution method, consider the network shown in table 6A–1. The network consists of six demand points connected by a road system, with demand levels as shown in the table. Assume that a firm wishes to locate two stores in the area ($p = 2$) and that each of the six demand points is a feasible site for a store. The firm's objective in choosing locations is to minimize the total distance the population must travel in reaching its nearest store—the p-median objective function.

In order to find the best locations for two stores on the network, we use the vertex-substitution method as shown in table 6A–2. At the outset, it is necessary to specify a starting solution consisting of two locations—in this case, we begin arbitrarily with locations 1 and 2 in the starting solution. With stores located at these sites, the total travel distance is 26. Store 1 serves towns 1, 4, and 5 for a travel distance of 19, and store 2 serves towns 2, 3, and 6 for a travel distance of 7. Thus $S^* = (1, 2)$ and $Z^* = 26$. Now substitute node 3, the first node not in S^*, for each of the two nodes in S^* (nodes 1 and 2). The substitution for node 1 gives a total travel distance of 20. Since the minimum of these two values, 20, is an improvement over the current "best" figure (Z^*) of 26, we switch node 3 for node 2 and the current optimum set is $S^* = (1, 3)$.

Table 6A–1
Distance Matrix for Sample Problem

Place	1	2	3	4	5	6	Place	Population
			Distance to Store					
1	0	2	5	5	2	3	1	3
2	2	0	3	6	3	1	2	1
3	5	3	0	4	4	2	3	2
4	5	6	4	0	3	6	4	3
5	2	3	4	3	0	4	5	2
6	3	1	2	6	4	0	6	1

Now substitute the next node not in S^* (node 4) for each node in S^* and repeat the process. The substitution of node 4 for node 3 gives a travel distance of 17, which is less than the current minimum value, so make the substitution.

The procedure continues with substitutions of nodes 5 and 6 for each node in S^*. However, neither substitution generates a value of the objective function less than 17. Therefore, the current optimum solution remains the set $S^* = (1, 4)$. At this point, we return to the beginning of the list of locations and again try all single substitutions of nodes not in S^* for nodes in S^*. Since no substitutions improve the value of the objective function, the procedure ends and the optimal solution is designated as sites 1 and 4, which give a total travel distance of 17.

Table 6A–2
Iterations of the Vertex-Substitution Algorithm for Sample Problem

1. Starting solution:

$$S^* = (1, 2)$$
$$Z^* = 26$$

2. Substitute node 3 for each node in the set

$$S_1' = (3, 2) \qquad Z_1' = 25$$
$$S_2' = (1, 3) \qquad Z_2' = 20 \qquad\qquad Z'_{min} = 20$$

   Since $Z'_{min} < 26$, make the switch.

$$S^* = (1, 3) \qquad Z^* = 20$$

3. Substitute node 4 for each node in the set

$$S_1' = (4, 3) \qquad Z_1' = 26$$
$$S_2' = (1, 4) \qquad Z_2' = 17 \qquad\qquad Z'_{min} = 17$$

   Since $Z'_{min} < Z^*$, make the switch.

$$S^* = (1, 4) \qquad Z^* = 17$$

4. Substitute node 5 for each node in the set

$$S_1' = (5, 4) \qquad Z_1' = 21$$
$$S_2' = (1, 5) \qquad Z_2' = 22 \qquad\qquad Z'_{min} = 21$$

   Since $Z'_{min} \geq Z^*$, do not make the switch.

5. Substitute node 6 for each node in the set

$$S_1' = (6, 4) \qquad Z_1' = 20$$
$$S_2' = (1, 6) \qquad Z_2' = 24 \qquad\qquad Z'_{min} = 20$$

   Since $Z'_{min} \geq Z^*$, do not make the switch.

6. Repeat process of substitution with node 2 and all other nodes not in Z^*. Since no substitution gives a value of the objective function less than 17, the optimal solution remains $S^* = (1, 4)$ and $Z^* = 17$. STOP.

Advantages

The main advantages of the vertex-substitution method over other heuristic procedures for solving location-allocation problems are its accuracy and speed. In a comparison of the vertex method with an exact algorithm, Rosing et al. (1979) demonstrated that the vertex substitution method found the optimal solution in all but two out of 450 trials. At the same time, the computer times required for the vertex-substitution method were less than 1/100 of those for the exact method. Thus, they concluded, the vertex-substitution method combines a high degree of accuracy with an extremely fast speed of execution. This makes it a valuable tool in solving a wide range of location-allocation problems.

Because of its speed, the vertex-substitution method can be applied to very large problems for which the time and cost of finding an exact solution are prohibitive. The method has been used effectively on problems comprising several thousand demand nodes and several hundred feasible sites. It would be nearly impossible to use an exact solution method in these cases.

Computer programs for the vertex-substitution method are currently available for mainframe computers. (See Rushton, Goodchild, and Ostresh 1973; Hillsman 1980). It is likely that microcomputer versions will be made available commercially in the near future.

References

Hillsman, E. (1980). *Heuristic Solution to Location-Allocation Problems: A User's Guide to ALLOC IV, V and VI.* Monograph 7. Iowa City, Iowa: Department of Geography, University of Iowa.

Rosing, K., Hillsman, E., and Rosing-Vogelar, H. (1979). "A Note on Comparing Optimal and Heuristic Solutions to the P-Median Problem." *Geographical Analysis* 11:86–89.

Rushton, G.; Goodchild, M.; and Ostresh, L., eds. (1973). *Computer Programs for Location-Allocation Problems.* Monograph 6. Iowa City, Iowa: Department of Geography, University of Iowa.

7
Location Strategies in Uncertain Environments

The previous chapter illustrated the use of location-allocation models for planning retail location strategies. The various case studies presented in that chapter focused on well-defined location problems in which the environment could be characterized with certainty. In those applications, the spatial distribution of consumers and the locations of existing stores did not change over time. Similarly, the locations and sizes of competitors' stores remained constant and were not allowed to vary in response to changing conditions. But retail environments are not static. They change as a result of shifts in consumer behavior, demand patterns, and economic conditions, as well as changes in the nature and scope of competition. Indeed, the pace of environmental change has accelerated significantly in the past few years and has created high levels of uncertainty in the retail environment.

To retain their competitive position, retail institutions—like other business organizations—must respond effectively to environmental change and deal with the uncertainties inherent in the environment. This demands, among other things, "a more sophisticated location analysis capability than has hitherto been employed by most retail firms" (Rogers 1984, p. 28). In designing strategies that are viable in the long run, it is important that in addition to looking at the present marketing environment, future changes in that environment also be considered.

There are many possible types of change in the retail environment. First, the competitive environment in which the firm operates can change as a result of competitors' actions in attempting to achieve their own preferred objectives. In the short run, competitors' changes in pricing policy, service level, and merchandise mix have important effects on the profitability of stores at various locations. Over the long run, competitors' addition of new stores and relocation or abandonment of existing stores can radically alter the competitive environment and affect the performance of stores whose locations were chosen without knowledge of such changes. The entry of new competitors into a market, for example, can significantly undermine the performance of existing outlets. The point is that strategic changes by any one firm may lead to reactive changes by competitors attempting to protect their own performance. Thus, in choosing the optimal locations for new outlets, it is important to take into consideration the possible impact of future competitive actions.

Second, in addition to changes caused by competitor reactions, firms must also cope with changes in economic conditions, consumer preferences, life-styles, and demography. Shifts in the spatial distribution of demand caused by population growth or decline and changes in consumer income and expenditure patterns create considerable uncertainty for retailers. Such well-documented trends as suburbanization and gentrification, for example, imply a continuous shifting and redistribution in retail market areas, which in turn affect the profitability of retail outlets. Although it is not possible to predict demographic changes with complete accuracy, successful location-planning procedures should take into consideration as best possible the changing spatial pattern of consumer demand.

Assessing the performance of alternative location plans is difficult when competitive reactions are uncertain and the nature and patterns of consumer demand are in flux. What are needed are precise forecasts of the future, which, of course, are always lacking. Changes in residential patterns and competitive locations are difficult to forecast accurately. It is also difficult to anticipate how competitors may react to a chosen strategy once it is implemented. One way to deal with such uncertainty is through the use of scenario planning and alternative future scenarios. Scenario planning provides a systematic procedure for investigating the impact of uncertainty on strategic plans and assessing the firm's expected performance under a variety of future conditions. Because of its focus on key environmental uncertainties and their impact on performance, the use of scenarios has been a growing part of strategic planning in recent years (Dutta and King 1980; Porter 1984). A number of applications of scenario planning to retail location decisions have been recently reported (Ghosh and McLafferty 1982; Ghosh and Craig 1983; Achabal, Mahajan, and Schilling 1984). The purpose of this chapter is to describe various scenario-planning techniques for dealing with uncertainty in retail location decisions. The chapter is divided into two major sections. In the first, we discuss the concept of *compromise strategies* and demonstrate various techniques for determining them. The second section discusses the principles and uses of *game theory* in anticipating competitive reactions and determining location strategies with such reactions in mind.

Scenario Planning with Compromise Strategies

In an environment in which the future cannot be predicted with accuracy, scenarios describe possible alternative states of the future. A scenario, according to Porter, is "an internally consistent view of what the future might turn out to be" (1984, p. 446). These scenarios are then used in strategic planning to analyze the performance of assorted plans under a variety of possible future conditions. The goal is to find strategies that perform well under all or most of the scenarios and thus provide a hedge against future uncertainty.

In order to create scenarios, it is first necessary to identify the critical elements in the environment that give rise to uncertainty. There may be considerable uncertainty, for example, in the future pattern of demand in a city undergoing rapid changes in population. New zoning laws or plans for the construction of housing units at different locations also create uncertainty about future demand patterns. Another source of uncertainty for retailers is the activity of competitors in the areas of pricing, store location and relocation, and merchandise strategy. Given the high level of uncertainty in retailing and the diverse factors that give rise to it, it is dangerous to rely on a single forecast of the future. Under these circumstances, scenario planning, which uses many alternative forecasts, provides a better description of how the future may evolve.

After identifying the elements that give rise to uncertainty, the next step in scenario planning is to create alternative scenarios by considering the possible states these elements may attain. The scenarios should represent accurate and carefully defined conceptions of possible states of the future based on the analyst's judgment plus any available information. Consider, for example, a city in which three large residential complexes may be constructed in the near future. The projects are still in the planning stage and there is considerable uncertainty regarding which projects will ultimately be approved for construction. Since this construction will result in significant changes in residential location patterns, the future demand for retail activities depends in part on which projects are ultimately completed. The performance of retail outlets at different locations cannot, therefore, be predicted with accuracy until the uncertainty surrounding the projects is resolved.

To consider the impact of the residential projects on retail location decisions, one can construct scenarios to describe the different ways the future may evolve. If, for example, it is known that only one of the three projects will ultimately be built, one can specify three distinct scenarios, each corresponding to the approval and construction of a different residential complex. The scenarios describe the spatial pattern of demand that will result if a particular project is completed. Similarly, if two projects are expected to be completed, three scenarios can be used to designate the different pairs of projects. Again, the different scenarios provide alternative forecasts of the spatial pattern of future demand. If the decision on the number of projects to be completed is itself uncertain, a total of seven scenarios will be needed to anticipate all the different possibilities, as shown in table 7–1.

Constructing scenarios helps the analyst to anticipate future events and

Table 7–1
Illustration of Scenarios

Scenario	Description
1	Project *A* completed
2	Project *B* completed
3	Project *C* completed
4	Projects *A* and *B* completed
5	Projects *A* and *C* completed
6	Projects *B* and *C* completed
7	Projects *A, B,* and *C* completed

systematically assess the impact of these events on the retail environment. The scenarios portray a broad view of the future and provide an alternative to relying on single forecasts in situations where the future cannot be predicted with accuracy. Since the long-term performance of different location strategies depends on how the future actually evolves, it is important that the impact of uncertainty on location decisions be evaluated in a systematic manner.

Once all possible scenarios have been identified, the next step in scenario planning is to evaluate systematically the impact of each scenario on the strategic decisions of the firm. One must ask such questions as: How will the performance of any proposed strategy or strategies be affected by changes in the environment? What is the optimal strategy in each of the different scenarios? Are there strategies that perform well under a variety of scenarios? By comparing the performance of different strategies in each scenario, the analyst can judge the "robustness" of different strategies and assess the likely impact of uncertainty on performance. Such information is necessary in selecting the long-term strategy that the firm should implement.

How should the firm choose the most desirable long-term plan when there are a number of possible scenarios of the future? Clearly, if there exists a strategy that has the highest level of performance in all scenarios, it should be chosen. It is rarely the case, however, that the same strategy is the best choice for all scenarios. Usually, different strategies are optimal for different scenarios, since strategies that perform well in one scenario may not perform well in others. A common approach in this situation is to choose the strategy that performs best in the "most probable" scenario. Planning procedures that ignore uncertainty and rely on single forecasts of the future implicitly assume that the most probable scenario will indeed materialize. The strategy that performs best in this scenario is, therefore, selected for implementation. This approach assumes that the most probable scenario will indeed come true. It thus ignores the uncertainty that was the initial focus of the exercise.

Relying on the most probable scenario is risky because it commits the firm's resources to only one view of the future. When there are no strong a priori reasons to believe that one scenario is more likely to occur than another, firms must hedge their bets and consider the impact of all scenarios in making their strategic plan. The key is to identify strategies that perform well in not just one, but in all or most, of the scenarios. Such compromise strategies (Cohon 1978) provide a hedge against uncertainty by assuring an acceptable level of performance irrespective of the future outcome.

Finding the Compromise Strategy

A simple, often-suggested procedure for finding a compromise strategy is to use the expected-value criterion. In this method, the probability of each scenario occurring is first estimated, and then the performance level of each strategy in each scenario is weighted by the corresponding probability. The weighted performance level across all the scenarios is used as a yardstick to measure the desirability of a strategy. The strategy with the highest expected performance is most desirable in relation to all the possible scenarios.

Although easy to implement, the method has certain drawbacks. An important one is the difficulty of estimating the probability of each scenario occurring. Often, the information necessary to make such estimates is simply unavailable. Even if information is available, the probabilities themselves may be quite uncertain. The expected value of a strategy, therefore, cannot be estimated accurately. In this situation, considerable judgment and analysis are required in choosing the most desirable strategy. A systematic assessment of each strategy in all the scenarios is required.

Since there are usually a large number of alternative strategies to be considered in location problems, an assessment of each strategy in all scenarios is a difficult task. However, it can be shown that this assessment can be limited to only those strategies that are *noninferior*. A strategy is noninferior if it is feasible and no other feasible strategy improves performance in one scenario without decreasing the performance in some other scenario.[1] An *inferior* strategy, on the other hand, is one for which at least one other strategy has the same, if not better, performance in all the scenarios. For this reason, an inferior strategy should never be considered for implementation. Thus, the search for a compromise strategy can be limited to the set of noninferior strategies.

To illustrate the concept of noninferior strategies, table 7–2 presents hypothetical data on the performance (the expected market share) of seven location strategies in two scenarios. Since the two scenarios represent different future conditions, the performance of each strategy differs under the two scenarios. The expected market share from the first strategy, for example, is high under scenario A, but would be much poorer if the future evolved

Table 7–2
Illustration of Noninferior Strategies

| | Market Share in | |
Strategy	Scenario A	Scenario B
1	60	40
2	40	60
3	20	20
4	50	40
5	40	50
6	50	50
7	45	55

according to scenario *B*. The performance of the second strategy, on the other hand, varies inversely to that for strategy 1—the second strategy performs well in scenario *B* but poorly in scenario *A*.

In contrast, strategy 3 does poorly in both scenarios. Irrespective of the future, strategy 3 would be a poor choice as a compromise solution. This strategy is an example of an inferior or dominated strategy since there are other strategies that perform better than it under both scenarios. Although strategies 4 and 5 perform better than strategy 3, they, too, are dominated. Strategy 4 is dominated by strategy 1, for example, since the expected performance of strategy 1 is better than or at least equal to that of strategy 4 in both scenarios.

Strategies 6 and 7, on the other hand, are noninferior, since no strategy can perform better than them in one scenario without sacrificing performance in the other. Strategy 6 is inferior to strategy 1 in scenario *A,* but performs better than strategy 1 in scenario *B*. Similarly, strategy 7 performs better than strategy 1 in scenario *B,* but poorer in scenario *A*. Thus, of the seven strategies shown in table 7–2, strategies 1, 2, 6, and 7 are noninferior, while strategies 3, 4, and 5 are inferior.

The collection of noninferior strategies is often referred to as the noninferior set. In any problem with multiple scenarios, the set of noninferior strategies plays an important role, since the compromise strategy must be selected from this set. To put it another way, irrespective of which scenario ultimately comes true, it is never desirable to choose an inferior or dominated strategy. The reason for this can be easily seen from figure 7–1's graphic representation of the information in table 7–2.

The two axes of the graph in figure 7–1 are the expected levels of performance in the two scenarios. The seven strategies are represented as points on this graph. The noninferior strategies (1, 2, 6, and 7) define the boundary of the region in the graph containing all the possible strategies. The dom-

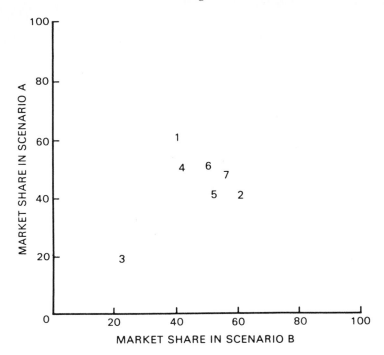

Figure 7-1. Graphic Representation of Noninferior Strategies

inated strategies are located within this boundary because their level of expected performance is inferior to the noninferior strategies'. For each of the dominated strategies, we can find at least one other strategy that performs better in one scenario without sacrificing performance in another.

To determine the set of noninferior strategies in figure 7–1, we can apply the rule that a solution is dominated if there is another solution positioned to the northeast of that point (Cohon 1978). Consider, for example, the position of strategy 4 in the graph. This is an inferior solution since both points 1 and 6 lie to the northeast of it. As long as both axes represent performances to be maximized, a point to the northeast provides a higher level of performance in one scenario without sacrificing it in the other. Applying the northeast rule, it can be easily ascertained that points 3 and 5 are dominated too. The northeast rule is a simple way to determine the set of noninferior strategies when there are two scenarios. While the principle still holds even when there are more than two scenarios, the pictorial representation of strategies is, of course, somewhat different.

Figure 7–2 shows an example of the performances of four strategies in three scenarios. To ascertain if a strategy is dominated, it is necessary to

PERFORMANCE IN SCENARIO

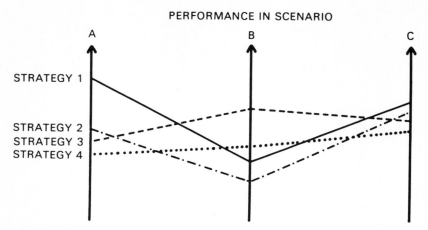

Figure 7-2. Performance of Strategies in Three Scenarios

determine whether another strategy performs better than it in one scenario without sacrificing performance in another. Strategy 2, in this case, is dominated by strategy 1, while strategy 4 is dominated by strategy 3. Strategies 1 and 3, on the other hand, are noninferior since the former has the best expected performance in scenarios *A* and *C,* while strategy 3 is the best in scenario *B.* A choice between these two strategies cannot be made without knowing which of the scenarios will actually occur.

The Weighting Method. An important task in finding a compromise strategy is to identify the set of noninferior strategies. A number of different methods have been suggested in the literature for finding this set. (See, for example, Keeney and Raiffa 1976; Cohon 1978.) Of these, the *weighting method* is particularly well suited for location problems. Prior to describing the application of the weighting method, it is useful to introduce certain notations and terminologies. As discussed earlier, the preliminary step in using scenario planning is to enumerate possible future scenarios. Let the number of such scenarios be $S(s = 1, 2, \ldots S)$. The performance of a strategy k in any scenario s is denoted by Z_{ks}. Let $x_1, x_2, \ldots x_n$ be the decision variables in the optimization problem. (In location problems these are the set of sites under consideration.) Finally, let F be the set of feasible strategies. Now, for any scenario $s,$ the optimal strategy can be found by solving the problem

$$\underset{k}{\text{Max}}\,\bar{Z}_s = \{Z_{ks}(x_1, X_2, \ldots x_n)\}$$

$$k\epsilon F \qquad\qquad (7.1)$$

It is readily seen that the solution to equation 7.1 is a noninferior strategy, since it provides the best performance in scenario *s*, and no other strategy can improve on its performance for this scenario. By solving equation 7.1 for each of the different scenarios, the set of strategies that is optimal in at least one scenario can be generated. The size of this set equals the number of scenarios under consideration. Since each of these strategies has the best performance in at least one scenario, they are all noninferior.

Although a number of noninferior strategies can be generated this way, one cannot be certain that all such strategies will be, since some noninferior strategies may not achieve the highest performance in any scenario. For example, in table 7–2 strategies 6 and 7 are noninferior but do not achieve the best level of performance in either scenario and would not be identified by this procedure. The weighting method generalizes the above approach to determine the entire set of noninferior strategies.

The scenario-planning problem can be formulated as a multiobjective programming problem as follows:

$$\text{Max } Z = \{Z_1(x_1, \ldots x_n); \ldots Z_s(x_1, \ldots x_n); \ldots Z_S(x_1, \ldots x_n)\}$$
$$\{x_1, x_2, \ldots x_n\} \in F \tag{7.2}$$

In most cases, however, there is no unique solution to the problem since it is rare that there is a single strategy that is the best under all scenarios. If the likelihood of each scenario occurring was known, the objective function of the problem could be modified and written as:

$$\text{Max } Z = \sum_{s=1}^{S} w_s \{Z_{ks}(x_1, \ldots x_n)\} \tag{7.3}$$

where w_s is the probability of a scenario occurring. For any given set of probabilities, the optimal solution to equation 7.3 can be found by standard location-allocation procedures. Note that equation 7.1 is a special case of equation 7.3, where w_s is 1.0 and all other w's are equal to zero. It can be shown mathematically (see Cohon 1978, p. 104) that the solution to equation 7.3 for any set of nonnegative weights (w's) is a noninferior solution. While the true likelihood of different scenarios is unknown, Cohon's result can be used to generate the entire set of noninferior solutions by solving equation 7.3 with different sets of weights. Because the solution to each of these problems is noninferior, solving equation 7.3 repeatedly with different values of w would generate the set of noninferior strategies.

Implementation of the Weighting Method. To illustrate the application of the weighting method for generating the set of noninferior strategies, we

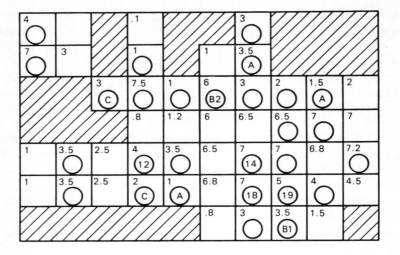

Figure 7-3. Location of Optimal Sites

consider the supermarket location problem discussed in the previous chapter. In that example, a location-allocation model was used to choose the optimal locations for new supermarket outlets. The model, however, did not take into account uncertainty in the retail environment—neither the spatial pattern of demand nor the location of competitors' stores were allowed to change during the planning horizon. In this static scenario, the optimal locations for chain's two new outlets were sites 12 and 19 (figure 7–3). Now we consider the impact of uncertainty on this decision. Assume that the management of chain *A* has received information that one of its competitors, chain *B*, is planning to close one of its two stores in the city. The particular outlet to be closed is not known. Where should chain *A* locate its stores given this uncertainty? Are the sites chosen previously still desirable or would some other combination of sites be better?

The uncertainty in this particular problem stems from the lack of knowledge about which of the competitor's outlets will be closed. If one could predict with confidence the store that chain *B* would ultimately close, there would be no uncertainty and the location-analysis procedures outlined previously could be applied after adjusting the data to reflect the closing of the competitive outlet. But with the closing decision uncertain, the retailer must plan with regard to all possible futures and search for locations that perform well under a variety of conditions. To take into account uncertainty, scenarios corresponding to the different possible futures must be constructed and the implications of the scenarios for the location decision of the firm must be evaluated. In this case, two scenarios can be constructed corresponding to the closing of outlets *B1* and *B2*, respectively. The scenario corresponding to the closing of outlets *B1* is designated as scenario 1, while scenario 2 refers to the closing of outlet *B2*. As a first step to assessing the impact of the scenarios on chain *A*'s location plan, one must determine for each scenario the optimal locations for two new outlets. In rare instances, the optimal location plans in both scenarios are the same, which indicates that the uncertainty regarding store closure has no impact on chain *A*'s strategic choice. In this situation, the optimal plan can be implemented with confidence, since it provides the best performance under all the future scenarios.

As is often the case when there are multiple scenarios, in this problem, the optimal strategy differs under each scenario. In scenario 1 (the competitor closes outlet *B1*), the optimal strategy for chain *A* is to open its two outlets at sites 12 and 19. On the other hand, if outlet *B2* is closed, the chain should open its stores at sites 12 and 14. Since each scenario reflects a different spatial distribution of competitive outlets, the firm's optimal location strategy is different in the two scenarios. The closing of the competitive outlet has a major impact on chain *A*'s long-term location policy. Given the uncertainty about the competitor's decision, which of these two plans should chain *A* choose? Or are there compromise strategies that should be considered instead?

In order to determine a long-term plan, the weighting method was used to generate the set of noninferior strategies for chain *A*. With two scenarios (*B1* closing or *B2* closing), equation 7.3 can be written as:

$$\text{Max } Z = w_1 Z_1 + w_2 Z_2$$

$$w_1 + w_2 = 1$$

$$w_1, w_2 \geq 0 \tag{7.4}$$

where Z_1 is the market share of the stores belonging to chain *A* when store *B1* closes (scenario 1) and Z_2 is the market share of the chain if *B2* closes (scenario 2), and w_1 and w_2 are the probabilities of occurrence of scenarios 1 and 2, respectively.

To solve equation 7.4, a modified version of the vertex-substitution algorithm was used. Recall that the vertex-substitution heuristic systematically evaluates different possible location patterns and chooses the one that maximizes the firm's performance. To calculate the performance of a location pattern, it is first necessary to compute the performance of the location pattern under each scenario separately. Then, these performance values are multiplied by the weights corresponding to that scenario and summed to give a value of *Z*. This procedure is repeated for various alternative location patterns to find the one that maximally increases the expected market share.

Table 7–3
Optimal Strategy for Different Combinations of w_1 and w_2 Values

Value of w_1	Sites
$0 < w_1 \leq .3$	12, 19
$.3 < w_1 \leq .65$	12, 18
$.65 < w_1 \leq 1.0$	12, 14

Source: A. Ghosh and S. McLafferty, "Locating Stores in Uncertain Environments: A Scenario Planning Approach," *Journal of Retailing* 58, no. 4 (1982): 5–24. Reprinted with permission.

To generate the set of noninferior strategies for chain A, 21 different combinations of w_1 and w_2 values were used. The value of w_1 was increased from 0 to 1 at intervals of 0.05 and the value of w_2 was decreased correspondingly. Table 7–3 presents the three noninferior strategies identified by the process. As seen from the table, each strategy is optimal for a certain range of weights. When w_1 (the probability of B1 closing) is less than 0.3, it is best for the chain to locate the two outlets at sites 12 and 19. On the other hand, when the probability of B1 closing is high ($w_1 > 0.65$), the best locations are sites 12 and 14. When the probability of each scenario occurring is about equal ($.30 < w_1 \leq .65$), the best strategy is to locate stores at sites 12 and 18.

Since these three strategies dominate all other possible strategies, the final choice of a location plan must come from this set of three. Thus, although there are a large number of possible ways in which the two stores can be located, the number of strategies that need to be considered in choosing the final plan is only three. This is the major advantage of generating noninferior strategies—even when a large number of feasible strategies exist, the size of the noninferior set is usually small, thereby greatly reducing the complexity of the problem. In this case, with twenty-one feasible sites and two outlets, there are 210 possible location strategies for the chain to consider. Of these, however, only the three strategies shown in table 7–3 are noninferior. The final location choice can be limited to these three strategies.

Although the optimal location plan varies according to the probability of each scenario occurring, it is interesting that site 12 appears in all three noninferior strategies. By locating a store at site 12, chain A can gain a foothold in the western sector of the city and compete directly with one of chain C's outlets. Since the market in this part of the city is not affected by the closure of either B1 or B2, site 12 is a profitable site under both scenarios. The optimal site of the second outlet for chain A, however, depends on the scenario. If B1 closes, the best choice for the second outlet is site 14, whereas if B2 closes, the best choice shifts to 19. Closing store B2 leaves B1 as the only outlet competing with chain *A* in the eastern half of the city. To confront this competition directly, chain *A* should locate its outlet adjacent to *B1*. If *B1* closes, on the other hand, chain *A*'s optimal location is site 14. The shift from site 19 to 14 increases the chain's market share from the areas near the center of the city. Since *B1* would be closed, the northward move by chain *A* does not significantly affect its market share in the south. The remaining non-inferior strategy is a compromise strategy that performs well when neither scenario is much more likely to occur than the other. It places the second site in between sites 14 and 19 and provides a hedge against the uncertainty of the future.

Options Planning

The fact that site 12 appears in all three noninferior strategies offers chain *A* a fortuitous long-term plan: Start construction at site 12 and postpone the decision on the second store until it is known with certainty which outlet chain *B* will close. Clearly, site 12 is a particularly robust location which should be selected irrespective of the future scenario. Scheduling construction of a store at site 12 first and waiting for the future to unfold may be a viable strategy as long as the cost of postponing the opening of the second outlet is not significant. Only constructing at site 12 for now thus provides the chain with some flexibility in dealing with future uncertainty.

Although in this example, site 12 is common to all three noninferior strategies, it is not necessarily the case that the different noninferior strategies have common sites. Since such common sites provide flexibility in selecting the ultimate location plan, Schilling (1982) suggests using an "options planning" procedure to identify such strategic sites. He suggests that the optimal location plan for each scenario should be determined with the constraint that the plans have one or more sites in common. Thus, if the plan involves opening three new stores in an area and there are two future-demand scenarios, the best location pattern under each scenario is determined with the constraint that there be at least one common site in both plans. Schilling argues that typically all facilities are not built simultaneously, but construction is spread over a time period. Thus, at any point in time, the decision maker is required to select only a limited number of sites. The store at the common site can be constructed first so as to retain future flexibility with minimum detriment to the long-term performance of the total network. Then, when the future is known with more certainty, the network can be expanded by locating stores at the other optimal sites. An application of the *options-planning procedure* for determining optimal retail networks is provided by Achabal, Mahajan, and Schilling (1984).

The rationale for the options-planning procedure is that the facilities at the common sites maintain flexibility for adapting the network to the future configuration of demand without much detriment to overall long-term performance. Building outlets at common sites allows the firm to delay the choice among different scenarios until more information for better predictions is available. Despite these advantages, the "delay" strategy can be dangerous since it gives competitors time to preempt desirable sites. The firm may, therefore, lose the strategic advantage of early entry into the market. The advantages of reducing the risk of the decision by postponement must be traded off with the potential loss from competitive preemption of sites.

Goal Programming

A more formal method for choosing among the noninferior strategies is *goal programming*. Goal programming is useful when there are a large number of noninferior strategies and it is, therefore, difficult to select the compromise strategy by inspection. Goal-programming methods allow the simultaneous consideration of different goals or objectives in selecting a strategy (Charnes and Cooper 1961). Decision makers can assign weights to the realization of each goal and select the strategy that minimizes the deviation from these goals as the optimal one. In other words, the optimal strategy is the one that is nearest to the ideal of attaining the maximum level of performance on each goal.

To use goal programming in selecting the best strategy in scenario planning, we consider each scenario as a separate goal. Thus, in this example, the two scenarios can be represented as two goals and the performance of the best strategy in each scenario used as the ideal point. Viewing this ideal point as a target, goal programming finds the noninferior strategy that deviates least from it. To select the optimal strategy by goal programming, it is necessary to specify the criteria for measuring deviations from the ideal point. Two commonly used measures of deviation are:

$$\gamma_k = \sum_{s=1}^{S} |Z_s^* - Z_{ks}| \qquad (7.5)$$

$$\gamma_k' = \sum_{s=1}^{S} (Z_s^* - Z_{ks})^2 \qquad (7.6)$$

where γ_k and γ_k' are measures of the overall performance on noninferior strategy k, and Z_s^* is the target performance level for scenario s. Since these measures indicate the extent of deviations from an ideal state, lower values of these measures are preferred to higher ones. The difference between equations 7.5 and 7.6 is that, compared to the former, the latter penalizes larger deviations disproportionately more than smaller ones. The choice between the two measures depends on the decision maker's attitude toward risk and the relationship between performance and profitability. As defined previously, w_s measures the weight assigned to a goal and reflects the relative importance of achieving each target level as well as an assessment of the likelihood of each scenario. Thus, a larger weight may be assigned to a scenario that is more likely to occur so that there is a greater penalty for deviating from the corresponding target performance level.

To illustrate the use of goal programming, consider the information shown in table 7–4. The table shows the performance of ten noninferior strategies in six possible scenarios. To decide on a compromise strategy, a goal-programming procedure was used to select the one that minimizes total deviation from the ideal point. The maximum performance level achieved in each scenario—the italicized values in the table—were used to define the ideal point. The total absolute and the total squared deviation from the ideal point for each strategy is shown in the table. In calculating these deviations, equal weights were attached to each of the target levels, since each scenario was assumed to be equally probable.

According to both measures of deviation, strategy G emerges as the best choice. While this strategy does not achieve the highest level of performance for any scenario, it is very near to this level for all scenarios as indicated by the low values of γ and γ'. Strategy G, therefore, is a good compromise strategy that provides a hedge against uncertainty. Because strategy G ranks best for both measures of deviation, it rates unequivocally as the best location choice. This situation, however, is an exception rather than the rule. Often, the two measures of deviation lead to different results and a choice must be made between two strategies. Even in this example, strategy F is ranked third according to the absolute-deviation criteria (γ) but only fifth according to the squared-deviation criteria. The latter measure, by weighting large deviations more than small ones, penalizes strategy F's poor performance in scenario 5. When such discrepancies occur, the differential impact of low and high deviations must be considered in choosing the optimal plan.

Once the set of noninferior strategies has been identified, goal programming is a convenient technique for choosing among a large number of noninferior strategies. The procedure helps in determining compromise solutions that perform well under a variety of scenarios. It consists of a series of simple calculations which can often be done by hand, yet, it is flexible in that the sensitivity of the solution to different subjective estimates regarding future scenarios can be incorporated (Ghosh and McLafferty 1982).

Game Theory and Strategic Planning in Competitive Environments

In addition to population shifts and changes in the location of competitive outlets, another potential source of uncertainty in retail environments is the

Table 7–4
Example of Goal-Programming Procedure

Noninferior Solution	Market Share in Scenario						γ_j	Rank γ_j	γ'_j	Rank γ'_j
	1	2	3	4	5	6				
A	64.2	56.1	61.2	52.1	61.0	62.3	30.5	6	286.4	6
B	58.1	64.1	60.0	59.6	60.6	48.3	36.5	7	361.7	7
C	49.1	56.4	58.8	50.5	68.2	54.4	50.0	10	620.0	10
D	59.0	58.2	48.6	63.0	59.0	52.2	47.4	9	484.7	9
E	61.0	63.1	62.6	62.1	66.1	61.6	10.9	2	45.2	2
F	67.2	62.0	60.4	62.1	56.2	60.4	19.1	3	157.7	5
G	66.2	63.7	61.2	59.9	65.2	60.5	10.7	1	25.0	1
H	60.6	59.2	62.5	62.8	60.4	59.1	22.8	4	138.7	3
I	54.2	57.1	58.6	52.2	67.3	55.6	42.4	8	396.3	8
J	58.8	62.1	60.6	58.6	61.2	61.8	24.3	5	147.2	4

Source: A. Ghosh and S. McLafferty, "Locating Stores in Uncertain Environments: A Scenario Planning Approach," *Journal of Retailing* 58, no. 4 (1982): 5–24. Reprinted with permission.

possibility of competitive reactions to a firm's location decision. In a competitive environment, the actions of one firm may lead to reactive changes by competitors as they attempt to protect or improve their own performance. By initiating its own location plan, the firm may induce changes in the retail competitive environment that ultimately affect its own performance since the actions of individual firms in a competitive environment are interdependent. This interdependency gives rise to uncertainty, since the possibility of competitive reaction must be taken into consideration in making any location decision.

Choosing a location strategy in interdependent competitive environments is a complex task. In implementing a long-term plan, the firm must not only evaluate the performance of the strategy in the present environment, but must anticipate how the environment will change because of competitive reactions and evaluate the impact of this new environment on its chosen strategy. The principles of mathematical game theory provide some guidelines for dealing with interdependent location decisions. Game theory provides a useful framework in which to view site selection decisions in competitive environments. (See, for example, Stevens 1961; Isard and Smith 1968; Ghosh and Craig 1983, 1984.) For a review of applications of game theory to other marketing decisions, such as pricing, advertising, and distribution channel management, see Moorthy (1985).

The principles of game theory are based on the assumption that firms are "rational" and that they try to maximize their performance in terms of market share or profits (Moorthy 1985). Additionally, it is also implied that firms view their competitors as rational decision makers. In competitive markets, retailers' location decisions can be modeled as a "noncooperative game" between them. In an interdependent environment, the long-term performance of any location decision made by a firm depends on the particular reactive strategy chosen by its competitor. Consider, for example, the simple scenario shown in figure 7–4.

The figure shows five uniformly spaced locations in a linear market. These sites are the location of consumer origins, each of which has an equal level of demand. The five locations are also the set of feasible sites for locating new outlets. Further, for simplicity, assume that the outlets under consideration are very similar and consumers are expected to patronize their nearest store. If an origin is equally distant from two outlets, the demand at that origin is split equally between them. A retail firm is planning to locate two

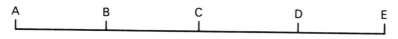

Figure 7–4. A Simple Linear Market

outlets in this market. It expects, however, that its competitor will also enter the market with two outlets of its own. Where should the first firm locate?

Suppose the first firm located its two outlets at sites *A* and *B*. The long-term market share of these outlets will depend on where the competitor locates its two outlets. If the competitor locates at sites *C* and *D,* for example, the first firm will get a market share of 40 percent, since only consumers from sites *A* and *B* will patronize its outlets. All other consumers will patronize the outlets at *C* and *D,* since they will be closer to these outlets than the ones at *A* and *B.* The result would be the same if the competitor locates at sites *C* and *E*—the first firm's expected market share is still 40 percent. If the competitor locates at sites *D* and *E,* on the other hand, the first firm's market share increases to 50 percent. In this scenario, in addition to getting all the consumers from *A* and *B,* it can expect to get half of the demand at *C.* But which one of the three possible pairs of sites would the second chain choose if the first chain chose sites *A* and *B*? If the competitor acts rationally, it would choose either sites *C* and *D* or sites *C* and *E.* Either of these pairs of sites will maximize its performance, given the location of the first firm's outlets. The market share the first chain can expect to get by locating at sites *A* and *B,* therefore, is only 40 percent. This is a guaranteed level of market share that the firm is assured of getting irrespective of the nature of competitive reaction.

The first chain, of course, should try to find a pair of sites that assures it the best market share irrespective of the competitor's reaction. If it locates its outlets at sites *A* and *D,* the best competitive reaction consists of sites *B* and *E* or sites *C* and *E.* (See table 7–5.) In either case, the first chain's market share is 50 percent. Since this is greater than the 40 percent market share it can expect from locating at sites *A* and *B,* this strategy is preferable to locating at sites *A* and *B.* Following this argument, it can be seen from table 7–5 that the firm's best strategy is to locate the outlets at sites *B* and *D* since this strategy guarantees a market share of 60 percent irrespective of how the competitor reacts. Thus, of the ten possible strategies for the first chain shown in the table, sites *B* and *D* are optimal when competitive reaction is expected.

The first chain's strategy of locating at *B* and *D* is an example of a *minimax strategy.* The minimax strategy is the one that maximizes the minimum level of performance the firm is guaranteed to receive. Thus, the minimax strategy is a risk-averse one which assumes that the competitor will react to the firm's strategy by selecting the strategy that maximizes its own performance. Given this expectation, the minimax strategy best protects the firm from the uncertainty of competitive reaction. To determine the minimax strategy in any problem, a payoff matrix like the one shown in table 7–5 must first be constructed. The payoff matrix shows the performance level for each firm for all possible competitive reactions.

The guaranteed level of return from each strategy can be found by com-

Table 7–5
Illustration of Minimax Strategy

First Chain's Location	Competitor Reaction 1		Competitor Reaction 2		Competitor Reaction 3		First Chain's Guaranteed Share
	Competitor Locates at	First Chain's Market Share	Competitor Locates at	First Chain's Market Share	Competitor Locates at	First Chain's Market Share	
A and B	C and D	40%	C and E	40%	D and E	50%	40%
A and C	B and D	40	B and E	50	D and E	50	40
A and D	B and C	60	B and E	50	C and E	50	50
A and E	B and C	50	B and D	40	C and D	50	40
B and C	A and D	40	A and E	50	D and E	60	40
B and D	A and C	60	A and E	60	C and E	60	60
B and E	A and C	50	A and D	50	C and D	60	50
C and D	A and B	60	A and E	50	B and E	40	40
C and E	A and B	60	A and D	50	B and D	40	40
D and E	A and B	40	A and C	40	B and C	40	40

paring the level of returns for the firm across each row in the table. For example, the minimum market share the first firm is guaranteed to receive from opening outlets at sites A and B (row 1) is 40 percent. This is the market share the chain can expect if the competitor locates at C and D or at C and E. Since it is expected that the competitor will try to optimize its own performance, this minimum market share of 40 percent provides a measure of the desirability for the first firm of locating at sites A and B. Measured on this criterion, it is better for the firm to locate at sites A and D. The minimum market share expected from this plan is 50 percent. This decision rule can be generalized further to choose the most desirable strategy for the firm—choose the strategy that provides the maximum minimum-performance level. According to this criteria, the most desirable strategy in table 7–5 is to locate the two stores at B and D. Irrespective of how the competitor reacts, the firm is assured a market share of 60 percent. This is the maximum of the minimum-performance levels—the minimax strategy. No other strategy can guarantee this level of market share.

The minimax principle, because of its focus on the guaranteed return from a strategy in an uncertain environment, provides a useful tool for evaluating the desirability of alternative location strategies in situations where competitive reactions are expected. Examples of the use of the minimax framework are provided by Ghosh and Craig (1983). One difficulty in using this framework, however, is the time and effort required to construct the payoff matrix when there are a large number of alternative plans to be considered. An efficient computerized algorithm is required to find the minimax strategy without having to evaluate all possible strategies. Ghosh and Craig (1984) have proposed a procedure that considerably reduces the computational burden in finding minimax strategies. They describe an application in which a firm considered more than 200 possible location configurations for two new outlets. For each of these plans, an equally large number of competitive reactions was considered. The minimax strategy for the firm was found in less than two minutes of computer time.

Conclusion

Uncertainty is inherent in many planning situations. Rarely can the future pattern of demand and supply be predicted with complete accuracy. In this chapter, we have presented a framework for dealing with uncertainty in location decisions. The framework is based on the technique of scenario planning, which provides a broad perspective for the decision maker by allowing the firm "to move away from dangerous, single point forecasts of the future in instances where the future cannot be predicted" (Porter 1984, p. 447). Scenario-planning procedures look at a spectrum of possible outcomes depending on different states of the future. Since location decisions represent long-term future investments that can be changed only at considerable cost, it is important that the impact of these future uncertainties be evaluated in a systematic manner. Moreover, the process of defining possible future scenarios, since it focuses the decision maker's attention on the future, is in itself a valuable experience.

The normative principles of game theory are useful for dealing with the uncertainty of competitive reactions. The location decisions of competitors have a profound impact on a firm's chosen strategy. The minimax principle, with its focus on maximizing the minimum level of performance, allows the analyst to select the strategy that minimizes the risks of uncertainty. Given the accelerated pace of change in retail environments, we believe scenario planning and game theory techniques should be a part of all retail location decisions. Although, at first glance, the additional computational burdens may seem formidable, as we have seen, the principles can be easily translated into efficient computer algorithms. Thus, the impact of uncertainty on location plans can be assessed in considerable detail with little incremental effort. This results in greater confidence in the outcome of the planning process.

Note

1. The terms *noninferior, efficient, Pareto optimal* and *nondominated* are all used synonymously in the literature.

References

Achabal, D.D.; Mahajan, V.; and Schilling, D.A. (1984). "SLOP: A Strategic Multiple Store Location Model for a Dynamic Environment." University of Santa Clara: Retail Management Institute.

Charnes, A., and Cooper, W. (1961). *Management Models and Industrial Applications of Linear Programming.* New York: John Wiley & Sons.

Cohon, J.L. (1978). *Multiobjective Programming and Planning.* New York: Academic Press.

Dutta, B.K., and King. W.R. (1980). "Metagame Analysis of Competitive Strategy." *Strategic Management Journal* 1:4–14.

Ghosh, A., and Craig, C.S. (1983). "Formulating Retail Location Strategy in a Changing Environment." *Journal of Marketing* 47: 56–68.

Ghosh, A., and Craig, C.S. (1984). "A Location Allocation Model for Facility Planning in Competitive Environments." *Geographical Analysis* 16: 39–56.

Ghosh, A., and McLafferty, S. (1982). "Locating Stores in Uncertain Environments: A Scenario Planning Approach." *Journal of Retailing* 58(4): 5–22.

Isard, W., and Smith, T.E. (1967). "Location Games: With Application to Classic Location Problems." *Papers, Regional Science Association* 19: 45–80.

Keeney, R.L., and Raiffa, H. (1976). *Decisions with Multiple Objectives: Preferences and Value Tradeoffs.* New York: John Wiley.

Moorthy, K.S. (1985). "Using Game Theory to Model Competition." *Journal of Marketing* 22: 262–282.

Porter, M. (1984). *Competitive Analysis.* New York: Free Press.

Rogers, D.S. (1984). "Trends in Retailing and Consumer Behavior" in R.L. Davies and D.S. Rogers (eds.), *Store Location and Store Assessment Research.* New York: John Wiley & Sons.

Schilling, D.A. (1982). "Strategic Facility Planning: The Analysis of Options." *Decision Sciences* 13(1): 1–14.

Stevens, B.H. (1961). "An Application of Game Theory to Problems in Locational Strategy." *Papers, Regional Science Association* 7: 143–157.

8
Conclusion

This book has provided a comprehensive view of retail location strategy. Location, we have argued, is a critical element of corporate strategies for retail and service firms and an essential determinant of their long-term success. It affects not only the size and composition of the market for a firm's products and services, but also the firm's competitive position within the industry. Planning a location strategy requires careful analysis and in-depth investigation, as well as a clear conception of the types of goods and services to be provided and their position within the retail marketplace. This, we have suggested, is the first step in location planning. It consists of defining the firm's value platform and is an essential precursor to analyzing various location strategies.

Once the firm has defined its value platform, it needs to perform various types of analyses to determine an appropriate and effective location strategy. These include assessing the growth potential of assorted regions and metropolitan areas, evaluating the market areas and profitability of potential sites, determining the optimal location or set of locations within a given market, and anticipating competitive responses. For each of these tasks, we have discussed the full range of methods available at the present time and the procedures for implementing them. Since no one method is appropriate in all situations, the discussion has focused on the strengths and limitations of each method and its appropriateness in various contexts. In addition, case studies have been provided to illustrate the use of the models and their application to actual location problems.

The organization of the book reflects the view that location planning is a *process* involving the use of a diverse set of models and methods of analysis as well as interaction with corporate planners. Information provided by the models serves as a basis for informed decision making and corporate planning. The results at any one stage of the modeling effort may suggest new types of analyses that need to be conducted or other types of data that should be investigated. Having examined the results of various models, the firm may either adopt a clearly superior location strategy or it may conclude that no one strategy performs satisfactorily and therefore abandon the search for new locations while focusing efforts on improving the performance of existing outlets. Thus, not only are there a range of possible modeling strategies, but also a wide range of possible decision outcomes.

Models are not a panacea, however. They cannot substitute for intelligent decision making, nor can they incorporate the full complexity of real-world problems. Using location models most effectively requires the insights and judgments of persons directly involved in retail location strategy and corporate planning. Their in-depth understanding of the location environment and competitive conditions in a particular market provides the rich, detailed information that is often lacking from spatial models. Moreover, managerial judgment is also needed in interpreting the results of location models and translating them into corporate strategy.

The importance of including decision maker's inputs in the location-planning process suggests the need for creating interactive *decision support systems* for retail location analysis. Decision support systems are computer-based systems allowing flexible interaction between decision makers and various location modeling strategies. They include detailed demographic and consumer purchase data, procedures for performing a variety of location models, and facilities for the display and analysis of model results. The systems are used interactively. For example, the decision maker might call upon a spatial-interaction model to predict the market share at a specific site and then use a location-allocation model to determine the site that gives the highest market share. Comparing the two market share predictions indicates the loss in share that may result from choosing a nonoptimal site. After seeing these results, the decision maker may wish to examine market shares at other potential sites. The process we have just described requires that the decision maker have access to a variety of location-modeling tools and facilities for the display and mapping of results. The system must be fully interactive, so that initial analyses can be conducted, results examined, and new analyses requested within a short period of time.

A decision support system for retail location analysis must include at least four basic elements. The first is a data base containing information on the population size, purchasing power, and demographic, social and economic characteristics of various market areas and subareas within a market; data on consumer shopping patterns obtained either through the analysis of past shopping behavior or through structured choice experiments; and information on competitive stores. Second, the system should incorporate a range of modeling procedures such as regression, spatial-interaction, and location-allocation models. Third, there should be capability for the display and mapping of model results, such as maps of store locations, trade areas, and geographic variability in model parameters. Fourth, a decision support system must have a human interface component which queries decision makers on the type of questions to be investigated and types of results to be displayed, and allows them to integrate their subjective judgments and knowledge about local areas with the model parameters.

Using such a decision support system, the analyst can assess the expected performance of different location strategies in terms of their market share and sales potential, market area size, and competitive position, and then display the results in a concise and meaningful way. After performing the analyses, the decision maker can compare the results with alternate strategies by changing the locations of the stores or their characteristics and performing the analyses again. This type of flexibility makes it possible to use a large variety of modeling strategies and assess a range of location plans according to a diversity of performance criteria.

Decision support systems are designed to take advantage of the flexibility, computational power, and graphics-display capability of modern microcomputers. These systems have been successfully implemented in such contexts as new-product introduction and sales-force allocation decisions. We view their application to retail location decisions as an important avenue for future development and research. While clearly research should focus on refining and extending particular location models, as has been discussed throughout this book, the possibility of linking geographic information systems, location models, and decision maker's judgments into an integrated analysis system is an exciting agenda for the future.

Index

Page numbers in italics indicate figures; page numbers followed by t indicate tabular material.

About the Authors

Avijit Ghosh is associate professor of marketing at New York University's Graduate School of Business Administration, where he teaches courses on marketing strategy and retail management. He received his bachelor's degree from the University of Calcutta, master's degrees from the Xavier Institute and the University of Iowa, and his Ph.D. from the University of Iowa. His research interests are in the areas of locational analysis, market forecasting, and the application of quantitative models to marketing management. His recent publications, which have appeared in a wide variety of journals, are in the areas of retail location models and the interface between location theory and location allocation models. He is the editor of the *Journal of Retailing* and the co-editor with Professor Gerard Rushton of *Spatial Analysis and Location Allocation Models,* published by Van Nostrand Reinhold.

Sara L. McLafferty is assistant professor of geography at Columbia University, where she teaches courses on location of services, economic geography and quantitative methods. She received her bachelor's degree from Barnard College and her M.A. and Ph.D. degrees from the University of Iowa. Her research interests are in the areas of service facility location, location theory, and the impact of changes in demographic, political, and economic factors on service delivery systems. She has published in a wide variety of social science and marketing journals. She is a member of the Association of American Geographers and the Health Services Research Association.